i

#13 Harry Nelly

ARMY WEST POINT
BLACK KNIGHTS

#14 Joseph Beacham

ARMY WEST POINT
BLACK KNIGHTS

#15 Charles Daly

ARMY WEST POINT
BLACK KNIGHTS

#16 Geoffrey Keyes

ARMY WEST POINT
BLACK KNIGHTS

#17 Hugh Mitchell

ARMY WEST POINT
BLACK KNIGHTS

#18 John McEwan

ARMY WEST POINT
BLACK KNIGHTS

#19 Biff Jones

ARMY WEST POINT
BLACK KNIGHTS

#20 Ralph Sasse

ARMY WEST POINT
BLACK KNIGHTS

#21 Gar Davidson

ARMY WEST POINT
BLACK KNIGHTS

#22 William Wood

ARMY WEST POINT
BLACK KNIGHTS

#23 "Red" Blaik

ARMY WEST POINT
BLACK KNIGHTS

#24 Dale Hall

ARMY WEST POINT
BLACK KNIGHTS

#25 Paul Dietzel

#26 Thomas Cahill

#27 Homer Smith

#28 Lou Saban

#29 Ed Cavanaugh

#30 Jim Young

#31 Bob Sutton

#32 Todd Berry

#33 John Mumford

#34 Bobby Ross

#35 Stan Brock

#36 Rich Ellerson

#37 Jeff Monken

Great Coaches
In
Army Football

From the beginning of Football all the way to Jeff Monken's 2017 team.

You'll like all the stories about the great football coaches beginning first with the Academy's founding in 1820 just under 200 years ago. After introducing West Point, the book takes us through a great ride from the beginning of American football to the beginning of the Army football program in 1890. From here, we look at each and every one of the thirty-seven great Army coaches through the great Red Blaik era in the mid-20th century to today with a revitalized Army Football Team under coach Jeff Monken.

You will learn that like no other football team, the coaches of the USMA have created an environment where the US Army Cadets are trained to be fierce and passionate competitors. You can bet that fFrom the stadium to the classroom to the research lab, the US Army Black Knights are trained to always play to win.

You will learn about first coach Dennis Michie's first official football game in 1890 even before American football had been completely defined. Michie was not only the head coach of the first team in 1890, he was the team captain. Today the Stadium's name is in his honor.

From here, the book moves you one Army coach at time through the immortals—Charles Daly, Biff Jones, Ralph Sasse, and Earl "Red" Blaik. And then, on the way to today, we stop for other fine coaches such as Bob Sutton and Jim Young. Army has had many great seasons with great coaches as well as a ton of great players.

The history of Army coaches as told here is just fascinating as is the entire Army football program. This book captures the many great coaching seasons and the contributions of each of the 37 head coaches and some of the standout players they helped to create such as Army's three Heisman winners—the immortal Felix "Doc" Blanchard, Pete Dawkins, and of course Glenn Davis.

This book is for your reading pleasure but it also can be a great reference tool for when you want to see how well a job a particular coach did in any of the 127 years of the Army football program. If you are an Army Football fan. you will not want to put this book down.

Brian Kelly

Published by: ....LETS GO PUBLISH!
Editor in Chief ....Brian P. Kelly
Email: ....info@letsgopublish.com
Web site .... www.letsgopublish.com

Library of Congress Copyright Information Pending
Book Cover Design by **Brian W. Kelly**
Editor—Brian P. Kelly

ISBN Information: The International Standard Book Number (ISBN) is a unique machine-readable identification number, which marks any book unmistakably. The ISBN is the clear standard in the book industry. 159 countries and territories are officially ISBN members. The Official ISBN for this book is

978-1-947402-07-2

The price for this work is:..........   **$ 13.95 USD**

10	9	8	7	6	5	4	3	2	1

Army Football seasons by Year/Coach.

Army Coach	Year	Wins	Losses	Ties
Dennis Michie & he was captain	1890	0	1	0
Henry Williams (4-1-1)	1891	4	1	1
Dennis Michie (3-1-1)	1892	3	1	1
Laurie Bliss (4-5)	1893	4	5	0
Harmon Graves (3-2)	1894	3	2	0
Harmon Graves (5-2)	1895	5	2	0
George Dyer (3-2-1)	1896	3	2	1
Herman Koehler (6-1-1)	1897	6	1	1
Herman Koehler (3-2-1)	1898	3	2	1
Herman Koehler (4-5)	1899	4	5	0
Herman Koehler (7-3-1)	1900	7	3	1
Leon Kromer (5-1-2)	1901	5	1	2
Dennis Nolan (6-1-1)	1902	6	1	1
Edward King (6-2-1)	1903	6	2	1
Robert Boyers (7-2)	1904	7	2	0
Robert Boyers (4-4-1)	1905	4	4	1
Ernest Graves (2-5-1), Henry Smither (1-0)	1906	3	5	1
Henry Smither (6-2-1)	1907	6	2	1
Harry Nelly (6-1-2)	1908	6	1	2
Harry Nelly (3-2)	1909	3	2	0
Harry Nelly (6-2)	1910	6	2	0
Joseph Beacham (6-1-1)	1911	6	1	1
Ernest Graves (5-3)	1912	5	3	0
Charles Daly (8-1)	1913	8	1	0
Charles Daly (9-0)	1914	9	0	0
Charles Daly (5-3-1)	1915	5	3	1
Charles Daly (9-0)	1916	9	0	0
Geoffrey Keyes (7-1)	1917	7	1	0
Hugh Mitchell (1-0-0)	1918	1	0	0
Charles Daly (6-3)	1919	6	3	0
Charles Daly (7-2-0)	1920	7	2	0
Charles Daly (6-4-0)	1921	6	4	0
Charles Daly (8-0-2)	1922	8	0	2

John McEwan (6-2-1)	1923	6	2	1
John McEwan (5-1-2)	1924	5	1	2
John McEwan (7-2)	1925	7	2	0
Biff Jones (7-1-1)	1926	7	1	1
Biff Jones (9-1)	1927	9	1	0
Biff Jones (8-2)	1928	8	2	0
Biff Jones (6-4-1)	1929	6	4	1
Ralph Sasse (9-1-1)	1930	9	1	1
Ralph Sasse (8-2-1)	1931	8	2	1
Ralph Sasse (8-2-0)	1932	8	2	0
Gar Davidson (9-1)	1933	9	1	0
Gar Davidson (7-3)	1934	7	3	0
Gar Davidson (6-2-1)	1935	6	2	1
Gar Davidson (6-3)	1936	6	3	0
Gar Davidson (7-2)	1937	7	2	0
William Wood (8-2)	1938	8	2	0
William Wood (3-4-2)	1939	3	4	2
William Wood (1-7-1)	1940	1	7	1
Red Blaik (5-3-1)	1941	5	3	1
Red Blaik (6-3)	1942	6	3	0
Red Blaik (7-2-1)	1943	7	2	1
Red Blaik (9-0)	1944	9	0	0
Red Blaik (9-0)	1945	9	0	0
Red Blaik (9-0-1)	1946	9	0	1
Red Blaik (5-2-2)	1947	5	2	2
Red Blaik (8-0-1)	1948	8	0	1
Red Blaik (9-0)	1949	9	0	0
Red Blaik (8-1)	1950	8	1	0
Red Blaik (2-7)	1951	2	7	0
Red Blaik (4-4-1)	1952	4	4	1
Red Blaik (7-1-1)	1953	7	1	1
Red Blaik (7-2)	1954	7	2	0
Red Blaik (6-3)	1955	6	3	0
Red Blaik (5-3-1)	1956	5	3	1
Red Blaik (7-2)	1957	7	2	0
Red Blaik (8-0-1)	1958	8	0	1
Dale Hall (4-4-1)	1959	4	4	1
Dale Hall (6-3-1)	1960	6	3	1
Dale Hall (6-4)	1961	6	4	0
Paul Dietzel (6-4)	1962	6	4	0

Paul Dietzel (7-3)	1963	7	3	0
Paul Dietzel (4-6)	1964	4	6	0
Paul Dietzel (4-5-1)	1965	4	5	1
Thomas Cahill (8-2)	1966	8	2	0
Thomas Cahill (8-2)	1967	8	2	0
Thomas Cahill (7-3)	1968	7	3	0
Thomas Cahill (4-5-1)	1969	4	5	1
Thomas Cahill (1-9-1)	1970	1	9	1
Thomas Cahill (6-4)	1971	6	4	0
Thomas Cahill (6-4)	1972	6	4	0
Thomas Cahill (0-10)	1973	0	10	0
Homer Smith (3-8)	1974	3	8	0
Homer Smith (2-9)	1975	2	9	0
Homer Smith (5-6)	1976	5	6	0
Homer Smith (7-4)	1977	7	4	0
Homer Smith (4-6-1)	1978	4	6	1
Lou Saban (2-8-1)	1979	2	8	1
Ed Cavanaugh (3-7-1)	1980	3	7	1
Ed Cavanaugh (3-7-1)	1981	3	7	1
Ed Cavanaugh (4-7)	1982	4	7	0
Jim Young (2-9)	1983	2	9	0
Jim Young (8-3-1)	1984	8	3	1
Jim Young (9-3)	1985	9	3	0
Jim Young (6-5)	1986	6	5	0
Jim Young (5-6)	1987	5	6	0
Jim Young (9-3)	1988	9	3	0
Jim Young (6-5)	1989	6	5	0
Jim Young (6-5)	1990	6	5	0
Bob Sutton (4-7)	1991	4	7	0
Bob Sutton (5-6)	1992	5	6	0
Bob Sutton (6-5)	1993	6	5	0
Bob Sutton (4-7)	1994	4	7	0
Bob Sutton (5-5-1)	1995	5	5	1
Bob Sutton (10-2)	1996	10	2	0
Bob Sutton (4-7)	1997	4	7	0
Bob Sutton (3-8)	1998	3	8	0
Bob Sutton (3-8)	1999	3	8	0
Todd Berry (1-10)	2000	1	10	0
Todd Berry (3-8)	2001	3	8	0
Todd Berry (1-11)	2002	1	11	0

John Mumford (0-7), Todd Berry (0-6)	2003	0	13	0
Bobby Ross (2-9)	2004	2	9	0
Bobby Ross (4-7)	2005	4	7	0
Bobby Ross (3-9)	2006	3	9	0
Stan Brock (3-9)	2007	3	9	0
Stan Brock (3-9)	2008	3	9	0
Rich Ellerson (5-7)	2009	5	7	0
Rich Ellerson (7-6)	2010	7	6	0
Rich Ellerson (3-9)	2011	3	9	0
Rich Ellerson (2-10)	2012	2	10	0
Rich Ellerson (3-9)	2013	3	9	0
Jeff Monken (4-8)	2014	4	8	0
Jeff Monken (2-10)	2015	2	10	0
Jeff Monken (8-5)	2016	8	5	0
Jeff Monken (8-5)	2017	0	0	0

Army almost always played as an independent Team. However, from 1998 to 2004, the team competed in a fledgling conference known as Conference USA, the Black Knights went back to Independent Status in 2005.

Total Games 1,222
Seasons 127
Total Wins 663
Total Losses 508
Total Ties 51   *** Prior to Overtime Rules**
Stats from   1890 Through August 2017

Acknowledgments:

I appreciate all the help that I received in putting this book together, along with the 123 other books from the past.

My printed acknowledgments were once so large that book readers needed to navigate too many pages to get to page one of the text. To permit me more flexibility, I put my acknowledgment list online at www.letsgopublish.com. The list of acknowledgments continues to grow. Believe it or not, it once cost about a dollar more to print each book.

Thank you all on the big list in the sky and God bless you all for your help.

Please check out www.letsgopublish.com to read the latest version of my heartfelt acknowledgments updated for this book. Thank you all!

In this book, I received some extra special help from many avid football friends including Dennis Grimes, Gerry Rodski, Wily Ky Eyely, Angel Brent Evans, Angel Irene McKeown Kelly, Angel Edward Joseph Kelly Sr., Angel Edward Joseph Kelly Jr., Ann Flannery, Angel James Flannery Sr., Mary Daniels, Bill Daniels, Robert Garry Daniels, Angel Sarah Janice Daniels, Angel Punkie Daniels, Joe Kelly and Diane Kelly.

References

I learned how to write creatively in Grade School at St. Boniface. I even enjoyed reading some of my own stuff as a toddler.

At Meyers High School and King's College and Wilkes-University, I learned how to research, write bibliographies and footnote every non-original thought I might have had. I learned to hate ibid, and op. cit., and I hated assuring that I had all citations written down in the proper sequence. Having to pay attention to details took my desire to write creatively and diminished it with busy work.

I know it is necessary for the world to stop plagiarism so authors and publishers can get paid properly, but for an honest writer, it sure is annoying. I wrote many proposals while with IBM and whenever I needed to cite something, I cited it in place, because my readers, IT Managers, could care less about tracing the vagaries of citations and their varied formats.

I always hated to use stilted footnotes, or produce a lengthy, perfectly formatted bibliography. I bet most bibliographies are flawed because even the experts on such drivel do not like the tedium.

I wrote 120 books before this book and several hundred articles published by many magazines and newspapers and I only cite when an idea is not mine or when I am quoting, and again, I choose to cite in place, and the reader does not have to trace strange numbers through strange footnotes and back to bibliography elements that may not be readily accessible or available. Academicians knowing all the rules of citation are not my audience. In this book, if you are a lover of Army West Point football, you are my intended group of readers

Yet, I would be kidding you, if in a book about the Great Coaches in Army Football, I tried to bluff my way into trying to make you think that I knew everything before I began to write anything in this book. I spent as much time researching as writing. I might even call myself an expert of sorts now about the Army West Point Black Knights. This team literally is America's team. Everybody in America has at one time watched and enjoyed Army football, especially when Army is having winning seasons, and more especially when Army is beating Navy.

Without any pain on your part you can read this book from cover to cover to enjoy the stories about the many Great Coaches in Army Football.

It took me about two months to write this book. If I were to have made sure that a thought of mine was not a thought somebody else ever had, this book never would have been completed or the citations pages would more than likely exceed the prose. Everybody takes credit for everything in sports writing—at least that's what I have found.

I used Army Cadet and Black Night Season summaries and recaps from whatever source I could to get the scores of all the games. I verified facts when possible. There are many web sites that have great information and facts. Ironically most internet stories are the same exact stories. Who's got the original? While I was writing the book, I wrote down a bunch of Internet references and at one time, I listed them right here en masse in this article. They were the least read pages. No more. Unless I am citing a reference in a section of the book, you will not see the URL.

I have no favorite source for information to put in my books. However, I continually hunt for articles written by students to amplify the text I present.

While I was writing this book, because I was not sure that my citations within the text would be enough, and I was not producing a bibliography, I copied URLs into some of the book text in those cases in which I had read articles or had downloaded material and had brought articles or pieces of articles into this book. Hopefully, this will satisfy any request for additional citations. If there is anything which needs a specific citation, I would be pleased to change the text. Just contact me. Your stuff is your stuff.

Many of the facts in this book are also put forth in the Army Football Media Guide, freely available on the Internet. Our thanks for the use of this material for the accurate production of this book.

There is a great site about Army football where you can explore great pictures and great stories about the greatest. It is called "For what they gave on Saturday Afternoon."-- https://forwhattheygave.com
Here is one of the whole links describing the beginning of Army football: https://forwhattheygave.com/2013/08/17/1890-1908-army-navy-football/ Enjoy

Preface:

This book is all about the great coaches in Army football over the years. Whether the team was playing as the Cadets, the Black Knights on the Hudson, or Army West Point, it never seemed to matter to the fans or the players. We have the football history right as we begin this book about Army's great coaches.

Since 1899, in the tenth year of Army football. Army's mascot has officially been a mule because of the animal's historical importance in military operations. For many years, Army's teams were known as the "Cadets." The academy's football team was nicknamed "The Black Knights of the Hudson" due to the black color of its uniforms. In 1999, Army adopted "Black Knights" as its official nickname in all sports. Based on the purpose, they may also use "Cadets" in certain circumstances.

The U.S. sports media like to use "Army" as a synonym for the Academy, while in 2015, the Academy itself declared their name to be "Army West Point." How this all sorts out over time, we'll all see. For this book, we use all the names.

Along the way to today, we study the founding of West Point Academy; then the preliminaries before Army football officially began, and then we delve right into the storied Army Football Program--its struggles; its greatness; and its long-lasting impact on American life. This takes us to the football careers of many great college football coaches and players from the Army team as it engaged tough competition over the years.

As a Pennsylvanian, I admit I wrote a similar book about Penn State Football but only after I had fulfilled the family Irish wish and had written about Notre Dame Football. But, I still recall as a kid with our Admiral Black and White TV, my dad calling us to order for the annual Army-Navy-Game, which was always enjoyable.

I picked Army as my next book because the Cadets have a long and bold tradition of playing great football. With many immortal coaches such as the great Red Blaik, and immortal players, especially the three Heisman winners, Doc Blanchard (1945), Glenn Davis (1946), and Pete Dawkins (1958). Army has four National Championships, 1914, 1944, 1945, 1946 and eight undefeated seasons. I have an honorable discharge from the Army and I am proud to write this book about such a storied institution and a great football program.

Supporters who love Army Football as played by Army West Point will read this book and get an immediate burst of emotions such as warmth and love for their favorite team. You will love this book because it has it all – every great season and every great game and all thirty-seven coaches. Go Army West Point!

This book walks you through the whole Army football journey. We examine coaches, and successes from the early teams to today. This period began in 1890 with the first Army Navy Game. Like all new teams, you can imagine the struggle of playing on a college football team when getting the right equipment was one of the biggest issues.

The 37 great Army coaches are listed within the football seasons in which they coached--from season 1 in 1890 to season 127. In other words, the seasons are examined chronologically and the coaches and certain games are highlighted within the seasons in which the games were played. I sure hope you enjoy this unique approach.

Before Red Blaik put in an eighteen-year stint starting in 1941, few of Army's 24 coaches to that point took the team for more than a couple years. Yet, they still produced some powerful teams with powerful players. Of the 37 coaches in the Black Knights history, most had winning seasons as Army's overall record has 150 more wins than losses. That's a lot of winning for any football program.

Army is a long-time football power

One hundred twenty-eight years is a long time to be playing football. Army has a history of being recognized as one of the finest teams in the nation. For many years, the teams were ready to win a national championship at the drop of the next hat. Though it has been over seventy years since the last championship, Army is still tough and nobody can deny that. With a new coach who brought in a great team in 2016, would it not be great for Army, the major defenders of our Nation to bring home another football championship soon

Your author would like you to know that when football season closes in the second week of January each year, there is now a great football item—this book—that is available all 52 weeks of the year and in fact all 365 days each year. It does not rely on the stadium gates being open for you to get a great dose of Army Football. Just begin reading right here.

It is now available for you to add to your Army Football experience. and your book collection. Once you get this book, it is yours forever unless, of course you give it away to one of the many who will be in awe, and who will accept it gladly. For those who love to use gadgets to read, this book is also available on Kindle.

We open the book with the first story set shortly after the beginning of college football as a sport in America. It then moves on to the first official game with the first official coach and all the way to Coach Jeff Monken's great 2016 record. It tells a story about all the football seasons and the great coaches with many great players and great moments from the first coached game in 1890 to today.

You are going to love this book because it is the perfect read for anybody who loves Army West Point's storied football program and wants to know more about the most revered athletes to have competed in one of the finest football programs of all time.

Few sports books are a must-read but Brian Kelly's <u>Great Coaches in Army Football</u> will quickly appear at the top of Americas most enjoyable must-read books about sports. Enjoy!

Who is Brian W. Kelly?

Brian W. Kelly is one of the leading authors in America with this, his 125th published book. Brian is an outspoken and eloquent expert on a variety of topics and he has also written several hundred articles on topics of interest to Americans.

Most of his early works involved high technology. Later, Brian wrote a number of patriotic books and most recently he has been writing human interest books such as <u>The Wine Diet</u> and <u>Thank you, IBM</u>. His books are always well received.

Brian's books are highlighted at <u>www.letsgopublish.com</u>. Quantities from 20 to 1000 can be made available from <u>www.letsgopublish.com.</u> You may see most of Brian's works by taking the following link <u>www.amazon.com/author/brianwkelly</u>.

The Best!

Sincerely,

Brian W. Kelly, Author
Brian P. Kelly, Editor in Chief
I am Brian Kelly's eldest son.

Table of Contents

About the Author

Brian Kelly retired as an Assistant Professor in the Business Information Technology (BIT) Program at Marywood University, where he also served as the IBM i and Midrange Systems Technical Advisor to the IT Faculty. Kelly designed, developed, and taught many college and professional courses. He continues as a contributing technical editor to a number of technical industry magazines, including "The Four Hundred" and "Four Hundred Guru," published by IT Jungle.

Kelly is a former IBM Senior Systems Engineer. His specialty was problem solving for customers as well as implementing advanced operating systems and software on his client's machines. Brian was a certified Army Instructor before retiring. He is the author of 125 books and hundreds of magazine articles. He has been a frequent speaker at technical conferences throughout the United States.

Brian was a candidate for the US Congress from Pennsylvania in 2010 and he ran for Mayor in his home town in 2015. He loves Army Football and can't wait to see the Black Nights top last year's fine record. God bless the Army West Point Cadets!!

Chapter 1 Introduction to Army West Point Football

Army's 128th Year in 2017!

Coach Monken With the Army Team Ready for the Game

The Army West Point Black Knights football team represents the United States Military Academy in college football. Army is currently a Division I Football Bowl Subdivision (FBS) member of the NCAA. The Black Knights currently play their home games in West Point, New York at Michie Stadium, with a capacity of 38,000. Army is currently coached by Jeff Monken, who is in his 4th season as head coach. Army is a four-time national champion, winning the title in 1914, 1944, 1945, and 1946. You'll hear that a lot in this book. Army has also has a total of eight undefeated seasons.

With the exception of seven seasons (1998–2004) where the team was a member of Conference USA, the Army team has competed as an independent. That means that, like Notre Dame, they have no affiliation with any conference. Currently, Army is one of four schools in the FBS that does not belong to any conference; the other three being BYU, Notre Dame, and UMass. However, all four of these schools belong to conferences for all other sports. Army is primarily a member of the Patriot League, BYU is a member of the West Coast Conference, Notre Dame belongs to the Atlantic Coast Conference, and UMass belongs to the Atlantic 10 Conference.

The Army West Point Black Knights have fielded a team every season since the inaugural 1890 season. That's a lot of football games. To be exact, it's 1,222 games in its 127 seasons, and the Black Knights have a fine all-time record of 663 wins, 508 losses, and 51 ties. That's a lot of great Army football folks.

Officially the Army West Point Cadets recognize a long and great football history that dates back to 1890. If you are from Navy or Air Force or some other rival school, you have to be kind. Such rivals know that Army was born great and then got greater when the immortal Earl "Red" Blaik coached from 1941 – 1958, Before Blaik, out of fifty-one prior years, Army had just four losing seasons. None of the four were worse than one more loss than win.

As noted, Red Blaik did not make Army a great team. They were already great. But, Blaik made the team even greater finishing with seventeen great winning seasons and just one losing season in 1951. He compiled a career college football record of 166–48–14. His Army football teams won three consecutive national championships in 1944, 1945 and 1946, and he was always near the top when not at the top. As good a Blaik was, as noted Army had always been good even before he came to coach. The Cadets had a great record of 293—107—28 pre-Blaik

After Blaik, the Army squad was never quite as crisp but it was not until about 1970 when for an unexplained reason, the team was expected to lose more than win. From Blaik to 1969, the team record was not so bad but not as good percentage wise. The record for this period was 64-41-4. Something happened to the team after 1970.

Nobody can explain it well. From 1970 through 2016, Army had just ten winning seasons with an overall record of 195-332-7.

In 1996 Coach Bob Sutton broke out of the mold and coached the Cadets to a fantastic 10-2 record. It was tough going after Sutton was fired for unexplained reasons. He is held in high regard by most and with the trouble Army has had over the recent years in winning, there have been many calls for his return.

I do not mean to suggest that Bob Sutton did not have his critics because Army alums, like most, are a fickle bunch. But Sutton did two things that none of the three permanent coaches following him has been able to do: He beat Navy on a regular basis, going 6-3 with five straight wins over the Midshipmen. And he gave Army a chance almost every single game of his career regardless of the opponent. That is a lot to say. From Sutton on, life really got tough for Army

So, now with just one winning season in between Sutton and four-year coach Jeff Monken's 8-5 winning season in 2016, we all hope for big things from Army. My analysis is Army is moving forward. The Army West Point Black Knights are ready to win again and losing is no longer an option.

Some are joking after the fantastic 2016 Army victory over Navy that the new Army goal is to out-Navy, Navy. For the moment, that mission has been accomplished.

It's been long coming with just one winning season and one bowl run from 1997 to 2015, and a huge losing streak to Navy along the way, 2016 was the season that the Jeff Monken coaching era needed to kick in. It needed to come when there was a sign that Army football could potentially be decent, and it came up with something even worthy of deep praise. Is Army back? Let's say "yes," to that.

As an independent all of its years, the schedule had been set up to be relatively favorable – with a slew of lightweights and two FCSers mixed in along with some real tough games such as Notre Dame, Air Force, and low-end Power Fivers Duke and Wake Forest.

In his prior years with Army, the ground game always worked under Monken. The 2014 Army team finished fifth in the nation in rushing, and the 2015 team was 12th – both teams, however overall were awful and they posted awful records.

In 2016, something different was in the air. The players had been in place awhile and they did not just average 340 yards per game and finish second in the country, but they actually took over games and went on long, sustained marches. They began to win. There is something contagious about the glorious feeling of winning football games.

It took Monken a few years to find the right pieces on defense and to build up the depth. It all came together. The linebacking corps was inspired and performed stellar. The pass rush was better than it's been in for long, long time, and the young talent in the secondary got beyond their experience and rose up for the nation's sixth-best pass defense. Not too shabby!

Oh yeah, did I mention that Army was invited and went to a bowl game, and they won it.

And the Black Knights came up with an alumni-pleasing big victory over Navy in 2016.

For a program that's been known for trying hard and gaining little more than "try-hard misery" for years and years and years, this season was very important. This coach and this group of football players needed to prove that it is possible to keep winning football games at Army. They did exactly that in 2016.

The rushing team is back again and that is good news for Army and Army fans. Everyone who gained a meaningful rushing yard is back in 2017 behind a fine line that returns four starters. The quarterback situation is deep, experienced and talented, and the receiving corps has some experience but with a leading rushing unit, pressure won't be on the receivers. Their bar is set at just catching an occasional pass, which they ought to do quite handily.

Not everything is perfect as the defense has to replace irreplaceable linebackers Jeremy Timpf and Andrew King, but 11 of the top 14 tacklers return with – and this was what was missing in the past – enough depth to rotate in and keep everyone fresh. If the pass rush is almost as strong, and the young defensive backs that were so good early on can shine again, at the very least, there won't be a massive drop-off. Army is ready for a repeat and even a better performance than 2016. It is a great thought.

2016 cannot go down as a *one-of* or as they like to say in today's parlance, a one-off. Monken is too good for that. The team is too good for that. There are too many strong pieces in place, and – Ohio State game aside – a schedule that most Power Fivers would groove into a nine-win campaign. The message to fans is "Go ahead and get excited for what Army football is becoming."

And of course, it goes without saying that if Army really wants to become the new Navy (at least in terms of its record), that takes just one thing – Go ahead army and beat Navy! Yeah!

This book that you are reading celebrates The United States Military Academy USMA; its founding; its struggles; its greatness; and its long-lasting impact on freedom and American life. People like me, who love Army, will love this book. Army haters, such as those from the Naval Academy will want their own copy just for additional ammo. Yet, it won't help them! Hah!

We begin the rest of the Army football story in Chapter 2 with the founding of USMA West Point over 214 years ago and we continue in subsequent chapters, right into the founding of the full Army West Point football program in 1890 after the Cadets had been begging the argument by exercising playing American football on the campus in an intramural fashion.

The first nighttime football game was played in Mansfield, Pennsylvania on September 28, 1892 between Mansfield State Normal and Wyoming Seminary and ended at halftime in a 0–0 tie. The Army-Navy game of 1893 saw the first documented use of a football helmet by a player in a game. Joseph M. Reeves had a crude leather helmet made by a shoemaker in Annapolis and wore it in the game after being warned by his doctor that he risked death if he continued to play football after suffering an earlier kick to the head.

Football is a great contagion. Rather than not play, Reeves figured out a way to protect his head. Over the years, more injury-preventive devices were created and used by players and teams. Improvements are made every day.

In defining the format of the book, we chose to use a timetable that is based on a historical chronology. Within this framework, we discuss the great moments in Army football history, and there are many great moments. No book can claim to be able to capture them all, as it would be a never-ending story, but we sure do try.

The U. S. Military Academy has produced 3 Heisman Trophy winners

We have already discussed Army's new rise to national football prominence with a great showing in 2016. While the United States Military Academy has slipped from its one-time lofty status as one of college football's top programs, there's no denying the successful past of Army football that produced national championship football teams and players that were recognized as college football's best.

Throughout the college football landscape there is traditionally a long list of programs that have produced waves of great teams and All-Americans. While many might hesitate to put Army in that category, only four schools, Notre Dame, Ohio State, Oklahoma and USC, have produced more Heisman Trophy winners than the Black Knights.

The lethal rushing combination of Felix "Doc" Blanchard and Glenn Davis first brought Heisman glory to West Point following the 1945 and 1946 seasons. Not only did the backfield duo both gain the nation's top individual award and earn All-American status three years; they helped lead the Cadets to three consecutive (1944-46) national championship claims. Let's take some time to look at these three Army stalwarts:

USMA Heisman Winners—DOC BLANCHARD 1945,
GLENN DAVIS 1946, PETE DAWKINS 1958.

USMA Statue Featuring Heisman Trophy Winners & Coach Blaik

Doc Blanchard

Blanchard became the first junior to win the award. He was known
as "Mr. Inside" because of his punishing running style delivered by
his six-foot, 200-pound plus frame. Oddly enough Blanchard only
entered West Point after being rejected from the Navy's V-12
program because he was considered overweight and because he had a
vision problem.

Whatever vision problems Blanchard had, Army Legendary Coach
Earl Red Blaik never lost sight of how the South Carolina native
struck fear into Army opponents.

"Doc Blanchard was the best built athlete I ever saw: 6 feet and 208 pounds at his peak, not a suspicion of fat on him, with slim waist, atlas shoulders, colossal legs," Blaik wrote in his book "You Have to Pay the Price."

For a big man, 'Doc' was the quickest starter I ever saw, and in the open he ran with the niftiness as well as the speed of a great halfback...."

Glenn Davis

The dynamic duo of Glenn Davis and Doc Blanchard Time Magazine.

The perfect complement to Doc Blanchard's power running style was Glenn Davis who was dubbed "Mr. Outside" for his ability to shed tacklers with his blazing speed. In his first year as a varsity regular, the California native led the nation in scoring in 1944 while averaging an amazing 11.1 yards-per-carry.

"He was emphatically the greatest halfback I ever knew," Coach Blaik wrote. "He was not so much a dodger and side-stepper as a blazing runner who had a fourth, even fifth gear in reserve, could change direction at top speed and fly away from tacklers as if jet-propelled."

When the dust had settled after their final year at Army in 1946, both players had combined to score an NCAA record of 97 touchdowns and 585 points while leading the Black Knights to a 27-0-1 record.

When considering their Heisman impact, Blanchard and Davis still rank as the most dominating backfield tandem of all time. The pair ranked an amazing 2-3 in 1944, 1-2 in 1945 and 1-4 in the 1946 Heisman balloting.

While Davis had much in common with his running mate Blanchard, it paled in comparison to a bond he would later develop with another Heisman winner. Davis married Yvonne Ameche, the widow of Wisconsin's Alan Ameche who won the award in 1954. Another love interest of Glen Davis was Hollywood starlet Elizabeth Taylor, who he dated prior to marrying actress Terry Moore.

Another similar comparison to Blanchard is the fact that both Heisman winners donated their trophies to their high schools. Davis' resides at Bonita High in Laverne, CA., while Blanchard's spent many years at St. Stanislaus High School in Bay St. Louis, Miss. The trophy resided at Davis' high school until it was washed away by Hurricane Katrina.   Davis is buried at West Point near his former Army head coach, Red Blaik.

Pete Dawkins Army's 3rd Heisman winner in 1958.

Pete Dawkins

Not only did the 1958 season produce Army Heisman winner Pete Dawkins, but it was also the Black Knights last undefeated season. Dawkins totaled 12 touchdowns during the season as he combined his rushing, receiving and kick returning skills to account for 1,216 total yards. Dawkins' tackling of the Heisman Trophy was just one of his many accomplishments as the rambling Cadet ranked 10th in his 1959 graduating class of 499.

Following his career at West Point, Dawkins snubbed the NFL's Baltimore Colts and studied at Oxford University as a Rhodes Scholar instead. Displaying the same leadership that he did on the field and in the classroom, Dawkins became the youngest Brigadier

General on active duty in the U.S. Army at the age of 43. Pete Dawkins was a Rhodes scholar at Oxford and later earned a PhD. from Princeton. He was awarded two bronze stars for valor in Vietnam and retired as a Brigadier general. He finished his "business" career as a high-ranking executive with Citibank in New York.

It may not be the Coolest Pep Rally in College Football…but…

The Army West point Black Knights may not have the coolest pre-game tradition in College Football. When you go to an Army Home game, you might miss it but if you get to go, it should be a lot of fun.

In 2007 for example, the Dave Matthews Band played for Army football — at two free shows. It was a victory before the game was even played. The U.S. Military Academy beat out Air Force, Navy and more than 100 other colleges that participated in the World's Loudest Pep Rally contest to win a visit from the rock star. Matthews played for Cadets Nov. 14 and 15, 2007

Cadet 2nd Class Garrison Haning [right] asks Dave Matthews a question during the meet-and-greet before the Wednesday night concert at West Point. Cadet 2nd Class Roderic O'Connor listens. (Photo Credit: Eric Bartelt)

"Congratulations! We'll see you in November," Matthews, 40, said in a videotape that was to be shown to Cadets at West Point's mess hall before the event. The videotape itself was exciting.

Cadets at the storied Hudson Valley academy won the contest by submitting invitations by text messages or postings at attblueroom.com. AT&T sponsored the contest. What a neat idea.

Cadets showed off their hip-hop moves in one posted video, while others made direct pleas to Matthews, such as "West Point NEEDS someone to ROCK our stonewalled campus."

WEST POINT, N.Y. (Army News Service, Nov. 19, 2007) -- The U.S. Military Academy was rocking Wednesday and Thursday nights as Cadets, faculty and other local community members packed Eisenhower Hall for two nights of free concerts by the Dave Mathews Band.

The concerts, billed as "The World's Loudest Pep Rally," were the result of a competition by colleges and universities across the country. AT&T sponsored the contest, which encouraged students from participating schools to each send up to 50 online invitations per day, via a Web site, asking Dave and the band to perform at their school.

West Point -- a service academy with a student body of just over 4,000 -- competed with powerhouses like Iowa State University, the University of Maryland, the University of Nebraska and countless others. Lucky for the Cadets, the contest was based on the number of votes submitted relative to student population, and the USMA student population was up to the challenge.

Matthews performs at free Cadets Concert

The initial voting began with only a few Cadets. Cadet 2nd Class Jeff Caslon, a "Dave" fan who found the contest, recruited his classmate Luke Gebhart to start sending text messages and set out to spread the word through the Corps of Cadets.

During the second week of the contest, Cadets Caslen and Gebhart approached the director of Cadet Activities, Lt. Col. Craig Flowers, about what would happen if the cadet corps was successful in winning the contest. Once the DCA was on board, the rest of the corps got heavily involved. The DCA and the USCC Chief of Staff's office began sending e-mails out to the brigade reminding everyone to vote and West Point jumped from 12th place to 2nd place overnight.

"I think we were pumped to win this competition because West Point isn't a big college like the other ones,"

Cadet Caslen said. "We've gotten looked over on things before, and this fired the Corps up even more."

Thanks to the sheer tenacity and competitive nature of the Cadets and the Long Gray Line, West Point was in first place within two days of the first brigade-wide e-mail.

When the other service academies saw Army's success, they jumped on the bandwagon. The Air Force Academy even managed to edge into first place for three days, mid-contest. But by the close of voting Oct. 15, West Point was solidly in first place and Air Force and Navy were 2nd and 3rd, respectively. And while the Cadets are excited about their victory, they aren't the only ones with high hopes for the "World's Loudest Pep Rally."

"To be invited by a school in this sort of way is unusual, and I think all of us are just really excited about it," Dave Matthews said during an exclusive interview. "I think it was the Cadets who are the ones who brought us here and the reason we're coming is because it was the Cadets who made it happen.

"When the audience is responsible for you being there, it's different than just having tickets available," he added. "Everyone shares the same humility and awe and eagerness to put on a hell of a [show], well, as good a show as we can."

In 2003, Dave Matthews gave an acoustic performance at West Point, but this was his first Ike Hall performance with the entire band.

"The whole experience last time, from top to bottom [was great]. [I was so impressed with] just how gracious everyone was," Dave Matthews said. "It was just unusual how respectfully we were treated. "It was really inspiring to us," he added.

Army's Black Knights were 3-5 when Dave Matthews got the concert gig. Things are changing every year for Army football. A few recorded words from Red Blaik would be the next best thing to Dave Matthews?

Chapter 2 The United States Military Academy

One of the Beautiful Sites on USMA Campus

The West Point short story

Founded in 1802, West Point is our nation's oldest service academy. Graduates of West Point "serve this nation honorably, sharing a strong sense of purpose, pride, and satisfaction that comes from meaningful service to others."

Attending the United States Military Academy is a wonderfully unique and challenging experience. West Point is a four-year college with a mission to develop leaders of character for our army—leaders who are inspired to careers as commissioned officers and lifetime service to the nation. The students of West Point (called Cadets) are selected from the most talented, energetic, and well-rounded young people in the country. Located on 16,000 acres in the scenic Hudson Valley region of New York State, West Point is conveniently situated just fifty miles north of New York City. The year-round pageantry and tradition make the Military Academy a national treasure and a popular tourist spot. People come from all over the world to see Cadets in action, and there is so much to see.

Prominent Graduates

Most of you will recognize most of these names as they are truly famous historical figures in many ways:

Robert E. Lee, 1829
Ulysses S. Grant, 1843
George Goethals, 1880
John J. Pershing, 1886
Douglas MacArthur, '03
George Patton, '09
Omar Bradley, '15
Dwight D. Eisenhower, '15
Matthew Ridgway, '17
Leslie Groves, '18
Maxwell Taylor, '22
Creighton Abrams, '36
Doc Blanchard, '47
Glenn Davis, '47
Alexander Haig, Jr., '47
Brent Scowcroft, '47
Frank Borman, '50
Fidel Ramos, '50
Edward White, '52
H. Norman Schwarzkopf, '56
Peter Dawkins, '59
Mike Krzyzewski, '69

The West Point Mission

United States Military Academy West Point

The mission is simple:

"To educate, train, and inspire the Corps of Cadets so that each graduate is a commissioned leader of character committed to the values of Duty, Honor, Country and prepared for a career of professional excellence and service to the Nation as an officer in the United States Army."

Chapter 3 Michie Stadium at West Point

Michie Stadium, Dedicated to an Army Hero

Michie Stadium is dedicated to the memory of Dennis Michie (1870–1898), who was instrumental in starting the football program while a cadet at the Academy. A member of the Class of 1892, Michie organized, managed, and coached the first football team at West Point in 1890.

Six years after graduation, he was killed in Cuba during the Spanish–American War. There have been several renovations since the stadium's first game in October 1924, when Army defeated Saint Louis, 17–0.

Dennis Michie

Blaik Field at Michie Stadium West Point NY

Michie Stadium is an outdoor football stadium on the campus of the U.S. Military Academy in West Point, New York. The home field for the Army Black Knights, it opened 94 years ago in 1924 and has a current seating capacity of 38,000.

The stadium sits at the upper portion of campus, directly west of Lusk Reservoir. The field is at an elevation of 335 feet (102 m) above sea level and runs in the traditional north-south configuration, with the press box above the west sideline. Due to the view offered by its location overlooking the Hudson River and the Neo-Gothic architecture of the campus below, it was rated as Sports Illustrated's #3 sports venue of the 20th century.

Michie Stadium, splendid in its scenic beauty and long recognized as one of the most popular stadiums in the nation, will celebrate its 94th season as the home of Army football during the 2017 campaign.

Over the years, the venerable stadium has received its share of plaudits as one of the most desired locations in which to watch a college football game. Recently, noted football analyst Mel Kiper Jr. of ESPN.com hailed the Academy's game day atmosphere as among the most inspirational in the country.

In addition, renowned sports periodicals Sports Illustrated and The Sporting News have heaped lofty praise upon the historic arena by listing it among their top all-time venues.

A new FieldTurf playing surface was installed during the summer of 2008, along with plans to complete a state-of-the-art video board before the start of the 2008 campaign. These enhancements ensure that the venerable facility will maintain its lofty status for years to come.

Construction of the $7 million Hoffman Press Box was completed in the spring of 2003. The new press box houses a full-service media operations center with state-of-the-art radio and television broadcast booths.

Work on the $40 million Kimsey Athletic Center, just outside the south end zone, was also concluded in the spring of 2003. The facility houses state-of-the-art locker rooms, coaches' offices, athletic training facilities, equipment rooms, meeting rooms and the Kenna Hall of Army Sports, a large display area that will chronicle Army's vast athletics history. Construction of Randall Hall, the project's second phase, was completed this past summer.

The entire stadium annex is the jewel of an aggressive athletic facilities renovation plan that has seen recent major improvements to Gillis Field House, Shea Stadium, Johnson Stadium at Doubleday Field, Clinton Field and Malek Courts. The acclaimed Lichtenberg Tennis Center just completed its fifth full academic year. In the spring of 2002, Army dedicated the Gross Sports Center, which provides the Army gymnastics team with a state-of-the-art home while also lending extra indoor space for the Black Knights' basketball programs.

Realizing the need for a permanent athletic field as Army's football program continued to assert itself nationally, West Point officials selected a patch of meadow land adjacent to Lusk Reservoir and within the shadow of historic Fort Putnam. Construction of Michie Stadium was completed in 1924, just in time for Army's 35th football campaign.

In 91 previous campaigns in Michie Stadium, the Black Knights have compiled a remarkable record of 326-156-7.

The Black Knights posted more home wins than any previous Army team while forging a perfect 6-0 mark at Michie in 1996, the 28th undefeated home campaign in Academy grid annals. In addition to 28 unblemished seasons, there have been two undefeated but tied campaigns at Michie. Following a 14-14 tie in the "Dedication Game" in the home finale of 1924, the Cadets won 39 straight contests in Michie Stadium, spanning more than six seasons.

Only 15 Division I-A stadiums, and just six located east of the Mississippi River, are older than fabled Michie Stadium. The original stadium structure was formally dedicated to the memory of Dennis Mahan Michie, who was instrumental in starting the game of football at the U.S. Military Academy in 1890. It was Michie who organized, managed and coached the first football team in history at West Point.

There have been several facelifts since that first game in 1924 when Army defeated Saint Louis University 17-0.

Temporary East stands and upper stands were added before construction of permanent East stands was completed in 1962. In the summer of 1969 an upper deck on the West side was added, boosting the seating capacity to 41,684. Capacity has since been adjusted to 38,000. Army's most prolific attendance came in 1972 when the Black Knights averaged a record 41,123 fans. Army ranked among the nation's attendance leaders in 2000, averaging 38,516 per game, or 96.5 percent of Michie Stadium's capacity.

A major change occurred on the playing field in 1977 when AstroTurf replaced the natural grass surface. The artificial turf greatly reduced maintenance costs and guaranteed the Army team an excellent practice facility for use all fall while providing for multiple uses. SuperTurf replaced the AstroTurf in 1984, which was in turn replaced by AstroTurf 8 in 1992. Since 2008, the playing surface has been FieldTurf. This replaced AstroPlay, which had been used since 2001. The stadium's playing field was natural grass until AstroTurf was installed in 1977.

Blaik Field

In honor of legendary mentor Earl "Red" Blaik, Army christened the Michie Stadium playing surface "Blaik Field" in 1999. Blaik, a gridiron innovator, compiled an 18-year Army record of 121-33-10 and brought Army its only three national championships (1944, 1945, 1946). The winningest coach in Army annals, Blaik is enshrined in the College Football Foundation Hall of Fame.

In the spring of 2002, Army dedicated the Gross Sports Center, which honored the dedication in grand style, trouncing Ball State 41-21

Army–Navy Game

Michie Stadium has hosted the Army–Navy Game only once, in 1943 during World War II, after it was played at Thompson Stadium at Annapolis the year before. Neither Army nor Navy have played at an on-campus facility since very early in the rivalry, since teams' home stadiums are not nearly large enough to accommodate the crowds and media that usually attend the rivalry games. Their rivalry game is normally played at a neutral site between the campuses on the East Coast, usually in Philadelphia in early December.

Chapter 4 First Five Coaches of Army;s Football Teams 1890-1896

Michie,   Coach #1
Williams   Coach #2
Bliss   Coach #3
Graves   Coach #4
Dyer   Coach #5

Year	Coach	Record	Conf	Record
1890	Dennis Michie	0-1-0	Indep	0-1-0
1891	Henry Williams	4-1-1	Indep	4-1-1
1892	Dennis Michie	3-1-1	Indep	3-1-1
1893	Laurie Bliss	4-5-0	Indep	4-5-0
1894	Harmon Graves	3-2-0	Indep	3-2-0
1895	Harmon Graves	5-2-0	Indep	5-2-0
1896	George Dyer	3-2-1	Indep	3-2-1

1890 First Army Navy Game (Only game this season) Notice no protective gear

The 1890 season was unique in many ways. First of all, it was Army's first football season. Second, it is the only season that Army played just one game, and Third, it was the season in which the inaugural Army-Navy game was played – the only game.

Army's football program began on November 29, 1890, when Navy challenged the Cadets to a game of the relatively new sport. Navy defeated Army at West Point that year, but Army avenged the loss in Annapolis the following year.

The academies still clash every December in what is traditionally the last regular-season Division I college-football game. The 2016 Army–Navy Game marked Army's overcoming its fourteenth consecutive loss to Navy, defeating the Midshipmen in a great game W (21-17).

From 1944 to 1950, the Cadets had a phenomenal run which included all wins against Navy--57 wins, 3 losses and 4 ties. During this time span, Army won three national championships.

Army's football team reached its pinnacle of success during the Second World War under coach Earl Blaik when Army won three consecutive national championships in 1944, 1945 and 1946, and produced three Heisman trophy winners: Doc Blanchard (1945), Glenn Davis (1946) and Pete Dawkins (1958). Past NFL coaching greats—Vince Lombardi (Packers) and Bill Parcells (Giants et al) were Army assistant coaches early in their careers.

The football team plays its home games at Michie Stadium, where the playing field is named after Earl Blaik. Cadets' attendance is mandatory at football games and the Corps stands for the duration of the game. At all home games, one of the four regiments marches onto the field in formation before the team takes the field and leads the crowd in traditional Army cheers.

For many years, Army teams were known as the "Cadets." In the 1940s, several papers called the football team "the Black Knights of the Hudson." From then on, "Cadets" and "Black Knights" were used interchangeably until 1999, when the team was officially nicknamed the Black Knights.

Between the 1998 and 2004 seasons, Army's football program was a member of Conference USA, but starting with the 2005 season Army reverted to its former independent status. Army competes with Navy and Air Force for the Commander-in-Chief's Trophy.

On November 29th, 1890, over 125 years ago, Army hosted Navy at West Point on the Plain in their very first football game. Navy beat Army 24-0 that day.

Army did not take too long to learn how to win. The Cadets came back the next year with a 32-to-16 win.

Before it had lived for five years, the classic rivalry almost died an early death in 1894, when, for mostly stupid reasons, both academies were forbidden to play anything but HOME games.

One of the greatest football fans of the ages was Teddy Roosevelt. At the time, TR was Assistant Secretary of the Navy. After an appeal to bring back the games that was made to Theodore Roosevelt, the game was re-instated in 1899. Some bureaucrat in Washington had taken four good years away from the rivalry.

Since 1899, with just a few interruptions that should not have been scheduled, it's been "game on" ever since.

Few may know this but in the pre-Super Bowl era, Army-Navy was widely considered to be THE game. I can remember cozy up on the couch with my dad in his favorite chair watching the Army Navy game in the 1950's on our 1956 B/W Admiral Console TV.

Usually played on neutral ground in Philadelphia, the game quickly became a magnet for Presidents. Harry Truman was a frequent fan, and John F. Kennedy attended in 1962.

In the period of mourning following his assassination the very next year, it was Jacqueline Kennedy who urged that the game go on, as her late husband was a great fan.

Navy won 21-to-15, in a game also remembered for featuring the very first instant replay ... a CBS Sports innovation, as it happens. Sadly enough, that game cannot be replayed now as it was erased long ago.

After 117 games in the series, Navy currently leads the series with 60 wins to Army's 50, with seven ties. In the 2016 game, another president was in attendance. This was president elect Donald Trump. He was in the crowd for the 117th match

President-elect Donald Trump waved to the crowd and pumped his fist as he arrived in the first quarter of the Saturday December 10, 2016 edition of The Army-Navy game

Navy had won 14 straight contests in the rivalry, but Army's underdog Black Knights prevailed 21-17, in a fourth-quarter comeback that came weeks after Trump's stunning victory over Hillary Clinton.

Trump spent the first half of the game in the box of David Urban, a West Point graduate and one of his Republican advisers in battleground Pennsylvania, and the second half in the box of retired Marine Lt. Col. Oliver North, a graduate of Annapolis.

The 1890 Army-Navy-Game was the first game and the first Army Navy Game

This game which, since 1890, comes almost like clockwork in late November or early December, does not have the same national championship implications it once did during some of the 127 seasons of Army football. Some think that the rise of the National Football League has a lot to do with that, as elite young athletes now are choosing major colleges as a path to the professional game rather than one of the service academies as a path to serving their country. And there is nothing wrong with that.

The U.S. Armed Forces have fought for centuries to allow all Americans the right to choose whatever profession they desire. So, most of the players in the 118th version of the rivalry to be played in 2017 are more likely to end up at Fort Bragg than with the 49ers— a choice they've proudly made.

Still, the contest has produced its share of extremely talented players, including Heisman Trophy winners Roger Staubach (Navy, 1963), Joe Bellino (Navy, 1960), Pete Dawkins (Army, 1958), Glenn Davis (Army, 1946) and Felix "Doc" Blanchard (Army, 1945).

Entering this afternoon's matchup at FedEx Field in Landover, Md., the Midshipmen led the series 60-50-7 and lost the most recent contest.

As we go through each season we will pick ten in which we amplify the abbreviated coverage of arguably the 10 greatest games in the history of this historic rivalry featuring players who all eventually will end up on the same team.

1890 First Coach & Player Dennis Michie

In their inaugural season, the Army Cadets football team represented the United States Military Academy in the 1890 college football season. In its first season fielding a team in intercollegiate football, the Cadets compiled a 0–1-0 record with just one game played.

Football had begun being played on campus at the Academy in 1889, but only one inter-class match game was played that year. During the 1890 season, the Cadets played only one official football game, on the West Point grounds. In this historical game, the Army team lost to the Navy team, L (0-24). Navy's Midshipmen were the only players to score in the kickoff game to a long-time series of great Army–Navy Games.

Even though it was a first for Army, there was a lot of pre-game publicity. A week before the game, the New York Times reported that the planned match "is beginning to assume almost national proportions."

During the game, Army's quarterback Kirby Walker was knocked out of the game four times, the last time being carried off the field and to the hospital in an unconscious state. As you can see, in those days there was no protective headgear.

After the victory, Navy Cadets in Annapolis "fired twenty-four great guns, and then paraded the streets with horns." If the score were reversed, Army would have been doing some powerful celebrating also. As it is, the Cadets would have to wait just one more year in order to get back at Navy for the loss.

A 20-year-old Army player, Dennis Michie, was the coach and the captain of the 1890 Army football team. Michie is often listed as the team's head coach because he served the purpose for the team. He actually put in a year as head coach in 1892. Dennis Michie was the lightest player on the team at 142 pounds. He had a wonderful career at the Academy but his life ended too soon.

Lieutenant Michie was killed in 1898 during the Spanish–American War. It is a stark reminder of the Army's mission of preserving liberty and democracy. Army's home football stadium, Michie Stadium, was dedicated in his honor when it opened in 1924. With just one game played, no Army Cadets were honored on the 1890 College Football All-America Team.

LIEUTENANT DENNIS M. MICHIE.

Dennis Michie –Army's 1st functioning Head Football Coach

1891 Coach Henry Williams

The Army Cadets football team represented the United States Military Academy in the 1891 college football season. It was their second season of intercollegiate football. They were coached by

Henry Williams in his first of just one year. The team played as an independent (no conference) and had a nice record of 4-1-1.

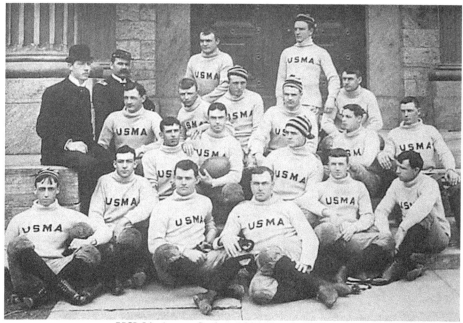

USMA Army Cadets 1891 Football Team

This was technically Army's first season fielding a team in intercollegiate football, the Cadets had compiled a 0–1-0 record with just one game played in 1890. And, so, in this, the first full season of Army football, the Cadets compiled a highly respectable 4–1–1 record.

<<< Coach Williams

Army outscored its opponents by a combined total of 80 to 73. The Cadets opened the season with a 10–6 victory over Fordham– the first win in Army football history. In the final game of the season, the Cadets defeated the Navy Midshipmen by a 32 to 16 score in the second annual Army–Navy Game.

Army's head coach in 1891 was 22-year-old Henry L. Williams, who had played football at Yale. Williams remained at the Academy only one year. He later served as head coach at Minnesota or 22 years and was inducted into the College Football Hall of Fame.

Not having been playing long enough to get noticed, no Army Cadets were honored on the 1891 College Football All-America list.

Games of the 1891 Season

In its first full length season, Army began its season at home at the Plain, its more or less makeshift football field at West Point NY. Fordham was the first official opponents in 1891 and the Cadets prevailed W (10-6. On Oct 31, having tasted victory and liking it, the Cadets played another home game against was tea known as the Princeton "B" team and though the team played well, all It could manage was a tie T (12-12). At home again on Nov 7, with a 1-0-1 record, Army beat Stevens Tech in a nail -biter W (14-12).

Playing home at the Plain again against Rutgers on Nov 14, the Cadets lost their first game of the season as they were overpowered by the Scarlet Knights, L (6-27). Next up at home on Nov 21 was the Schuylkill Navy AC and Army won W (6-0). Then, on Nov 28, in the final game of the season, the Cadets played their first away game at Worden Field in Annapolis MD. Against the Navy Midshipmen.

Army made up for last year's disappointing loss with a big win W (32-16) to finish with a nice 4-1-1 record.

1892 Coach Dennis Michie

The Army Cadets football team represented the United States Military Academy in the 1892 college football season. It was their third season of intercollegiate football. They were coached for the second time in their short span of playing intercollegiate football by Coach Dennis Michie. Playing as an independent, the team had another nice record of 3-1-1.

<< Coach Dennis Michie

Michie Led the team well with just one loss, shutting out three of their five opponents, and they outscored all opponents by a combined total of 90 to 18. In the third annual Army–Navy Game, the Cadets lost to the Midshipmen by a 12 to 4 score.

No Army Cadets were honored on the 1892 College Football All-America Team. It is worthy to note that Dennis Michie, who was captain of the Army football team in 1890 and 1891, and who technically was the coach in 1890, was the bona fide head coach of the 1892 team. Michie, as noted previously, was killed in 1898 during the Spanish–American War. Army's home football stadium, Michie Stadium, was dedicated in his honor when it opened in 1924.

Games of the season

The season opened at the Plain, on the campus of the US Military Academy in West Point NY on October 8 at home against Wesleyan. The Cadets and Wesleyan tied in this game T (6-6). At home on Oct 22, the Cadets shut-out Stevens Tech in a big game W (42-0). On Oct 29 at home, Army shut out Trinity W (24-0).

On Nov 19, at home, the Cadets defeated the Princeton "B" team W (14–0). In the final game of a short season, at home, the Cadets failed in an attempt to gain a repeat win from Navy and lost to the Midshipmen L (4–12) before an attendance of 3,000.

1893 Coach Laurie Bliss

The Army Cadets football team represented the United States Military Academy in the 1893 college football season. It was their fourth season of intercollegiate football. They were coached by Laurie Bliss, shown in a picture from his Yale playing days. As an independent football entity, the team had a losing record of 4-5-0

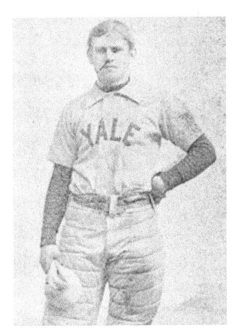

<< Coach Laurie Bliss

In their first and only season under head coach Laurie Bliss, the Cadets compiled a 4–5-0 record and were outscored by their opponents by a combined total of 109 to 84. In the annual Army–Navy Game, the Cadets lost to the Midshipmen by a 6 to 4 score. No Army Cadets were honored on the 1893 College Football All-America Team.

Games of the season

The season opened with a close loss at the Plain, on the campus of the US Military Academy in West Point NY on Sept 30 at home against the Volunteer AC L (4-6). On Oct 7 at home, the Cadets defeated Lafayette in a shutout W (36-0). On Oct 14 again at home, Army lost to Lehigh L (0-18). On Oct 21, the Cadets beat Amherst W (12-4). Yale was a tough team in the 1890's as Walter Camp was so adept at football, he was building the rule book. On Oct 28, at home, the Cadets were beaten by Yale in a shutout L (0-28).

All games were played at the Plain until Dec 2 when Army would travel to Worden Field in Annapolis MD for the Army Navy Game, won by Navy again L (406). On Nov 4, the Cadets beat Union, W (6-0). Then, on Nov 11, Army defeated Trinity. The Cadets finished the season with two losses. The first loss was a blowout on Nov 18 v L (4-36) against Princeton. The next was the Army-Navy Game.

1894 Coach Harmon Graves

The Army Cadets football team represented the United States Military Academy in the 1894 college football season. It was their fifth season of intercollegiate football. They were coached by Harmon Graves in his first of two seasons as head coach of Army. Harmon Graves, is shown in the below picture. As an independent football entity, the team had a winning record of 3-2-0.

<< Coach Harmon Graves

In their first season under head coach Harmon Graves, the Cadets compiled a 3-2 record and outscored their opponents by a combined total of 95 to 22. 1 The Army was not played in 1894 because of the rule about no away games. No Army Cadets were honored on the 1894 College Football All-America Team. All 1896 games were played at home.

The season opened on Oct 6 with a shutout win W (18-0) at the Plain, on the campus of the US Military Academy in West Point NY at home against Amherst W (18-0). In this short five-game season, the Cadets won every other game. On Oct 13, their first loss was a shutout against Brown L (0-10) On Oct 20, the Cadets picked up a shutout win v MIT W (42-0).

On Oct 27, the Cadets were defeated in a close game against Yale L (5-12). On Nov 3, the Army Cadets shut out Union for a nice win W (30-0). No Army-Navy game was held in 1894.

1895 Coach Harmon Graves

The Army Cadets football team represented the United States Military Academy in the 1894 college football season. It was their sixth season of intercollegiate football. They were coached by Harmon Graves in his first of two seasons as head coach of Army. As an independent football entity, the team had a winning record of 5-2-0.

In their second season under head coach Harmon Graves, the Cadets compiled a 5-2 record, shut out five of their seven opponents by a combined total of 141 to 32. It was a good year.

Because of away game restrictions, the Army-Navy Game was not played in 1895. On November 2, 1895, Army lost to Yale by a 28 to 8 score in what one press account called the greatest and most exciting game of football ever played on the West Point grounds."
No Army Cadets were honored on the 1895 College Football All-America Team.

Almost all games were played at home. The season opened on Oct 6 with a big shutout win W (50-0) at the Plain, on the campus of the US Military Academy in West Point NY at home against Trinity W (50-0). After a loss to Harvard L (0-4) on Oct 12, the Cadets won two shutouts in a row.

Oct19, Tufts W (35-0); On Oct 26, Dartmouth, W (6-0). On Nov 2, in a closer game than the score, Yale beat the Cadets L (8-28). Army finished with two more shutout wins. The first on Nov 16 v Union W (16-0) The next was an exception away game against Brown in Newburgh NY W (26-0) on Nov 23.

1896 Coach George Dyer

The Army Cadets football team represented the United States Military Academy in the 1895 college football season. It was their seventh season of intercollegiate football. They were coached by George Dyer in his first and last season as head coach of Army.

George Dyer is shown in the below picture. As an independent football entity, the team had a winning record of 3-2-1.

The Cadets compiled a 3-2-1 record, shut out five of their seven opponents by a combined total of 93 to 45 to 32. It was a so-so year.

Because of away game restrictions, the Army–Navy Game was not played in 1896. No Army Cadets were honored on the 1896 College Football All-America Team.

All games were played at home. The season opened on Oct 3 with a big shutout win W (50-0) at the Plain, on the campus of the US Military Academy in West Point NY at home against Tufts W (27-0). After a loss to Princeton, L (0-11) on Oct 17, the Cadets won a game, lost one, then tied one and then won again to close the season.

Oct24, Union, W (44-0); On Oct 31, Yale, Dartmouth, W (6-0). On Nov 2, in a closer game than the score, Yale beat the Cadets L (2-16). Then Wesleyan on Nov 7, T (12-12), finishing up with Brown, W (8-6) on Nov. 21.

Chapter 5 Next Seven Army Coaches from 1897-1907

Koehler   Coach # 6
Kromer   Coach # 7
Nolan   Coach # 8
King   Coach # 9
Boyers   Coach #10
Smither   Coach #11
Graves   Coach #12

Year	Coach	Record	Conf	Record
1897	Herman Koehler	6-1-1	Indep	6-1-1)
1898	Herman Koehler	3-2-1	Indep	3-2-1)
1899	Herman Koehler	4-5-0	Indep	4-5-0
1900	Herman Koehler	7-3-1	Indep	7-3-1
1901	Leon Kromer	5-1-2	Indep	5-1-2
1902	Dennis Nolan	6-1-1	Indep	6-1-1
1903	Edward King	6-2-1	Indep	6-2-1
1904	Robert Boyers	7-2-0	Indep	7-2-0
1905	Robert Boyers	4-4-1	Indep	4-4-1
1906	Henry Smither	1-0-0	Indep	1-0-0
1906	Ernest Graves	2-5-1	Indep	2-5-1
1907	Henry Smither	6-2-1	Indep	6-2-1

1897 Army Team Picture Coach Herman Koehler

1897 Coach Herman Koehler

The Army Cadets football team represented the United States
Military Academy in the 1897 college football season. It was their
eighth season of intercollegiate football. They were coached by
Herman Koehler in his first of four seasons as head coach of Army.
Herman Koehler is shown in the below picture. As an independent
football entity, the team had an excellent record of 6-1-1.

**<<Coach Herman
Koehler**

The Cadets compiled a
6-1-1 record, shut out
five of their seven
opponents by a
combined total of 194 to
41. It was a fine year.

Because of away game
restrictions, the Army-
Navy Game was not
played in 1897. The
Cadets suffered their
only loss against
Harvard by a 10 to 0
score and played Yale
to a 6–6 tie. The Army–
Navy Game was not
played in 1897.

Three Army Cadets
were honored on the
1897 College Football
All-America Team.
Halfback William Nesbitt received second-team honors from Walter
Camp. Quarterback Leon Kromer received second-team honors from
the New York Sun. Tackle Wallace Scales received second-team
honors from Walter Camp and The New York Sun.

All games were played at home. The season opened on Oct 3 with a big shutout win W (38-6) at the Plain, on the campus of the US Military Academy in West Point NY at home against Trinity. On Oct 9, the Cadets defeated Wesleyan W 12-9). After a loss to Harvard L (0-10) on Oct 16, the Cadets shut-out Tufts W (30-0)

On Oct30, the Cadets tied Yale T (6-6) and were more than ready when they walloped Lehigh on Nov 6 W (48-6). On Nov 13, the Cadets beat Stevens Tech W (18-4) and then Army finished the season against Brown with a nice W (42-0) shutout on Nov 20.\

1898 Coach Herman Koehler

The Army Cadets football team represented the United States Military Academy in the 1898 college football season. It was their ninth season of intercollegiate football.

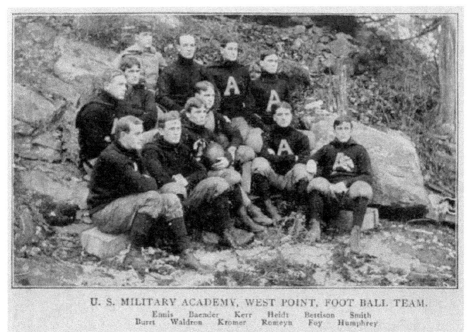

U. S. MILITARY ACADEMY, WEST POINT, FOOT BALL TEAM.
Ennis   Baender   Kerr   Heidt   Bertlson   Smith
Buret   Waldron   Kromer   Romeyn   Foy   Humphrey

1898 Army Cadets Football team

They were coached by Herman Koehler in his second of four seasons as head coach of Army. As an independent football entity, the team had a winning record of 3-2-1.

The Cadets compiled a 3-2-1 record, shut out five of their seven opponents by a combined total of 90-51. It was an OK year.

Because of away game restrictions, the Army–Navy Game was not played in 1897. The Cadets' two losses came against undefeated co-national champion Harvard and Yale. The Army–Navy Game was not played in 1898.

The Cadets really played tough football against tough opponents. They suffered their only loss against National Champion Harvard by a 10 to 0 score and played co-champion Yale to a 6–6 tie. The Army–Navy Game stupidly was not played in 1898.

Army was no longer an also-ran. Army players were from this point on always contenders for national honors. The Army teams got strong early and stayed that way for many years.

Four Army Cadets were honored on the 1898 College Football All-America Team. Fullback Charles Romeyn was a consensus first-team All-American, receiving first-team honors from Caspar Whitney and the New York Sun. Quarterback Leon Kromer, tackle Robert Foy, and end Walter Smith were recognized as third-team All-Americans by Walter Camp.

All Army games again, because of unreasonable demands on opponents were played at home. Thus, there were fewer games as should have been on the Army schedule.

The 1898 season opened on Oct 3 with a big shutout win W (40-0) at the Plain, on the campus of the US Military Academy in West Point NY at home against Tufts. On Oct 8, the Cadets defeated Wesleyan W (27-8). After a loss to Harvard L (0-28) on Oct 15, the Cadets shut-out Lehigh W (18-0)

On Oct 29, the Cadets lost to Yale L (0-10) and were more than ready on Nov 5 when they put a run attack together to keep a tough Princeton squad at bay in a tie T (5-5).

1899 Coach Herman Koehler

The Army Cadets football team represented the United States Military Academy in the 1899 college football season. It was their tenth season of intercollegiate football. They were coached by Herman Koehler in his third of four seasons as head coach of Army. As an independent football entity, the team had a losing record of 4-5-0.

The Cadets compiled a 4-5-0 record, were outscored by their opponents by a combined total of 100 to 57. It was a negative year overall.

Because the away game restrictions were lifted, the Army–Navy Game was played again as a matter of course from 1899 onward. In this version of the annual Army–Navy Game, the Cadets defeated the Navy by a 17 to 5 score. Army had become a powerful player on the national stage.

As noted, Army was no longer an also-ran. Army players were from several years prior to 1899, always contenders for national honors. The Army teams got strong early and stayed that way for many years.

Because 1899 was a weak year overall for Army, like the olden days, there were no Army Cadets honored on the 1899 College Football All-America Team.

Even though restrictions were lifted, scheduling of games is not an instantaneous art and so all Army games again, because of prior unreasonable demands on opponents, were played at home. Thus, there were still fewer games as should have been on the Army schedule.

The 1899 season opened on Oct 2 with a big shutout win W (22-0) at the Plain, on the campus of the US Military Academy in West Point NY at home against Tufts. On Oct 7, the Cadets lost to Penn State L (0-6) After a loss to Harvard L (0-18) on Oct 14, the Cadets were shut-out by Princeton L (0-23).

On Oct 28, the Cadets defeated Dartmouth W (6-2) and then Army lost to Yale L (0-24). Then, the Cadets lost to Columbia L (0-16) and came back against Syracuse W (12-6) The season finale against Navy was on Dec 2 at a neutral site because of the anticipated crowd – Franklin Field in Philadelphia. Army beat Navy W (17-5) and so in 1899, the bus ride home was much more pleasant for the Cadets and fans than the Midshipmen and their fans.

1900 Coach Herman Koehler

The Army Cadets football team represented the United States Military Academy in the 1900 college football season. It was their eleventh season of intercollegiate football. The 1900 team is shown below:

1—Phillips; 2—Kromer; 3—Sterling, Mgr ; 4—Davis; 5—Koehler; 6—Williams; 7—Clark; 8—Farnsworth , 9—Phipps; 10—Casad; 11—Boyers; 12—Hackett; 13—Zehl; 14—Nichols; 15—Burnett ; 16—Bettison ; 17—Smith, Capt.; 18—Bunker ; 19—Goodspeed; 20—Finn.
Photo by Pach Bros.

WEST POINT MILITARY ACADEMY FOOT BALL TEAM.

The team was again coached by Herman Koehler in his fourth and final year of four seasons as head coach of Army. As an independent football entity, the team had a winning record of 7-3-1.

The Cadets compiled a 7-3-1 record, shut out seven opponents (including a scoreless tie with Penn State), and outscored all opponents by a combined total of 109 to 68.

Army end Walter Smith was recognized by the NCAA as a consensus first-team player on the 1900 College Football All-America Team, having received first-team honors from Caspar Whitney and third-team honors from Walter Camp. Tackle Edward Farnsworth also received third-team honors from Camp.

The Army–Navy Game was played again as a matter of course. In this version of the annual Army–Navy Game, played at Franklin Field in Philadelphia, Navy defeated the Cadets L (7-11).

Even though away-games were permitted, scheduling of games did not yet catch up to the waiving of the restrictions. Consequently, other than the Navy game at Franklin Field, all Army contests were played at home at the Plain. Army played eleven games in 1900.

The 1900 season opened on Sept 29 with a low scoring shutout win W (5-0) at the Plain, on the campus of the US Military Academy in West Point NY at home against Tufts. On Oct 6, the Cadets tied Penn State in a scoreless game T (0-0). Next, the Cadets shut out Trinity W (28-0) before facing Lasalle on Oct 17 W (11-) and then Harvard. L (0-29) on Oct 20. After the expected loss to this very strong Harvard team, Army shut out Williams on Oct 27 in a low-scoring game W (6-0).

On Nov 3, the Cadets were beaten by a tough Yale Squad L (0-18) Then on Nov 7, the Cadets shut out Rutgers W (23-0). Three days later, against Hamilton, Army won another close shutout W (11-0). On Nov 17, the Cadets beat Bucknell in a close match W (18-0)

The season finale against Navy was on Dec 1 at a neutral site because of the anticipated crowd – Franklin Field in Philadelphia. The Cadets lost to the Midshipmen L (7-11) at Franklin Field. At the time, Franklin Field was comparatively huge with a capacity for 30,000.

1901 Coach Leon Kromer

The Army Cadets football team represented the United States
Military Academy in the 1901 college football season. It was their
twelfth season of intercollegiate football.

1901 Army Cadets Football Team

The team was coached by Leon Kromer in his first and only year as
head coach of Army. As an independent football entity, the team had
a winning record of 5-1-2.

The Cadets compiled a 5-1-2 record, shut out four opponents, and
outscored all opponents by a combined total of 98 to 22. The team's
only loss was by a 6 to 0 score against an undefeated Harvard team
that has been recognized as a co-national champion for the 1901
season. The Cadets also tied with Yale (5–5) and Princeton (6–6). In
the annual Army–Navy Game, the Cadets defeated the Midshipmen
by an 11 to 5 score.

Two members of the 1901 Army team have been inducted into the
College Football Hall of Fame: quarterback Charles Dudley Daly
and tackle Paul Bunker. Both are also recognized by the NCAA as
consensus first-team players on the 1901 College Football All-

America Team. Daly received first-team honors from Walter Camp, Caspar Whitney, the New York Post and The Philadelphia Inquirer. Bunker received first-team honors from Camp and the New York Post and second-team honors from Whitney.

Even though away-game limitations were called off, scheduling of games still had not yet caught up to the waiving of the restrictions. Consequently, other than the Navy game at Franklin Field, all Army contests were played at home at the Plain. Army played just eight games in 1901.

The 1901 season opened on Oct 5 with a shutout win W (22-0) at the Plain, on the campus of the US Military Academy in West Point NY at home against Franklin & Marshall. On Oct 12, the Cadets defeated Trinity (CT) W (17–0). Then, on Oct 19, #1 Harvard came in and the Cadets almost pulled it off but were defeated L (0-6). The Cadets then beat Williams on Oct 26 W (15-0). In another tough battle against one of the toughest teams in the nation, Army tied Yale on Nov 2 T (5-5).

Another tough team, Princeton came to West Point on Nov 9 and worked for a tie against the Cadets T (6-6). On Nov 23, the Cadets then shut out the always tough Penn Quakers W (24-0)

The season finale against Navy was on Nov 30 at a neutral site because of the anticipated crowd which approached 30,000. Franklin Field in Philadelphia was the venue. In this contest, the Cadets beat the Midshipmen W (11-5) in a tough but convincing battle. Harvard was the only loss for the entire season.

President Roosevelt ar 1901 Army Navy Game (Roosevelt loved Football)

1902 Coach Dennis Nolan

The Army Cadets football team represented the United States Military Academy in the 1902 college football season. It was their

thirteenth season of football. They were coached by Dennis Nolan in his first and only year as head coach of Army. As an independent football entity, the team had a winning record of 6-1-1.

<< Coach Nolan

The Cadets compiled a 6-1-1 record, shut out five of eight opponents, and outscored all opponents by a combined total of 180 to 28. The team's only loss was by a 14 to 6 score against Harvard. The Cadets also defeated Syracuse by a 46 to 0 score and tied with an undefeated Yale team that has been recognized as a national co-champion. In the annual Army–Navy Game, the Cadets defeated the Midshipmen by a 22 to 8 score.

Two members of the 1902 Army team were inducted into the College Football Hall of Fame: quarterback Charles Dudley Daly and tackle Paul Bunker. During the 1892 college football season, the selectors were Caspar Whitney (CW) Harper's Weekly (HW) and the Walter Camp Football Foundation (WC). Whitney began publishing his All-America Team in 1889, and his list, which was considered the official All-America Team, was published in Harper's Weekly from 1891 to 1896

And, so, in addition to the two inductees, five members of the squad were honored by one or both of Walter Camp (WC) and Caspar Whitney (CW) on the 1902 College Football All-America Team. They are: Bunker (WC-1, CW-1); Daly (WC-3); center Robert Boyers (WC-2, CW-1); tackle Edward Farnsworth (CW-2); and fullback Henry Torney (WC-3

Even though away-game limitations were called off, scheduling of games still had not yet caught up to the waiving of the restrictions. Consequently, other than the Navy game at Franklin Field, all Army contests were played at home at the Plain. Army played just eight games in 1902.

The 1902 season opened on Oct 4 with a shutout low-score win W (5-0) at the Plain, on the campus of the US Military Academy in West Point NY at home against Tufts. On Oct 11, the Cadets shut out Dickinson W (17–0). Then, on Oct 18, #1 Harvard came in and the Cadets played well but Harvard played a bit better L (6-14). The Cadets then shut-out Williams on Oct 25 W (28-0). In another tough battle against one of the toughest teams in the nation, Army tied Yale on Nov 1 T (6-6).

The Union Team came to West Point on Nov 8 and were shut out and walloped good by the Cadets W (56-0. Then, on Nov 15, the Cadets shut out the Syracuse Orangemen in a great offensive display W (46-0).

The season finale against Navy was on Nov 29 at a neutral site because of the anticipated crowd which approached 30,000. Franklin Field in Philadelphia was the venue again. In this contest, the Cadets beat the Midshipmen W (22-8) in a tough but convincing match. Harvard again was the only loss for the entire season.

1903 Coach Edward King

<< Coach Edward King

The Army Cadets football team represented the United States Military Academy in the 1903 college football season. It was their fourteenth season of intercollegiate football. They were coached by Edward King in his first and only year as head coach of Army. As an independent football entity, the team had a winning record of 6-2-1.

The Cadets compiled a 6-2-1 record, shut out five of their nine opponents, (including a scoreless tie with Colgate), and outscored all opponents by a combined total of 164 to 33. The team's only losses were to Harvard (5–0) and Yale (17–5). These two teams typically competed year after year for the mythical National Championship.

In an intersectional game, the Cadets defeated Chicago by a 10 to 6 score. In the annual Army–Navy Game, the Cadets, behind quarterback Horatio B. Hackett, defeated the Midshipmen by a huge 40 to 5 score.

Three members of the squad were honored by one or both of Walter Camp (WC) and Caspar Whitney (CW) on the 1903 College Football All-America Team. They are: guard Napoleon Riley (WC-2); halfback Edward Farnsworth (CW-2); and fullback Frederick Prince (CW-2).

The 1903 season opened on Sept 26 with a scoreless tie T (0-0) at the Plain, on the campus of the US Military Academy in West Point NY at home against Colgate. On Oct 3, the Cadets shut out Tufts W (17–0). On Oct 10, the Cadets shut out Dickinson W (12-0). Then, on Oct

17, the always-tough Harvard squad came in to the Plain and the Cadets played well but Harvard played just a bit better, shutting out the Cadets L (0-5). The Cadets then faced another tough team, Yale and played well in defeat L (5-17).

On Oct 31, the Cadets shut out Vermont W (32-0). This was a warm-up game for Manhattan on Nov 7, in this game the Cadets walloped the Manhattan squad in a big shutout W (48-0). The Cadets did well in an intersectional game on Nov 14 v Chicago, pulling out a nail-biter win W (10-6).

The season finale against Navy was on Nov 28 again at a neutral site because of the anticipated crowd which always approached 30,000. Franklin Field in Philadelphia was the venue again because of proximity and size of stadium. In this match, the Cadets overwhelmed the Midshipmen W (40-5) in a one-sided match. Harvard and Yale were the only losses for the entire season. Army kept getting closer to beating these two great teams of the 1900's.

Having studied the history of many teams from their first game to their last, I always seemed to find the teams having sluggish seasons in the beginning and it was not until they hired a long-term coach that the team began to settle into winning.

Army is an enigma regarding this theory. The Cadets longest term coach at this point was Herman Koehler at just four years. Here we are in just the fourteenth season and the Army Cadets were on their third one-year coach in a row and yet they were not only winning games, they were almost knocking off perennial champs, such as Harvard, Yale, Princeton, and Penn.

Before all the trickery and sophisticated play-calling that came from years of coaching, Army was whipping its opponents with first-year coaches. Why? Maybe there is something in a soldier's blood that makes them, all things being equal, fight lots harder for the victory. That's what I think. How about you?

1904 Coach Robert Boyers

The Army Cadets football team represented the United States Military Academy in the 1904 college football season. It was their fifteenth season of intercollegiate football. They were coached by Robert Boyers in his first of two years as head coach of Army. As an independent football entity, the team had a winning record of 7-2-0.

The Cadets compiled a 7-2-0 record, shut out five of their nine opponents, (including a scoreless tie with Colgate), and outscored all opponents by a combined total of 136 to 27. The team's only losses were to Harvard (4–0) and Princeton (17–5). In the annual Army–Navy Game, the Cadets defeated the Midshipmen by an 11 to 0 score.

Five members of the squad were honored by one or both of Walter Camp (WC) and Caspar Whitney (CW) on the 1904 College Football All-America Team. They are: center Arthur Tipton (WC-1, CW-1); back Henry Torney (CW-1); end Alexander Garfield Gillespie (WC-2); halfback Frederick Prince (CW-2); and tackle Thomas Doe (WC-3)

Other than the Army-Navy Game, all games were played at The Plain on the Campus of the US Military Academy in West Point, NY.

The 1904 season opened on Oct 1 with a shutout against Tufts W (12-0). The next game on Oct 8 was another shutout against Dickinson, W (18-0) Then, on Oct 17, the always-tough Harvard squad came in to the Plain and the Cadets played well but Harvard played just a bit better, shutting out the Cadets L (0-5). The Cadets then faced another tough team, Yale and played well just like in the past but this time their efforts resulted in the Cadets' first win ever against Yale W (11-6).

On Oct 29, the Cadets shut out Williams W (16-0). This was a warm-up game for Princeton on Nov 5, but good fortune left the Cadets at the Williams game as Princeton beat Army L (6-12) in a nail-biter on Nov. 5. On Nov 12, the Cadets got back all their moxie and thumped NYU in a big shutout W (41-0). On Nov 19, the Cadets squared off against the Syracuse Orangemen, and brought home the W (21-5).

The season finale against Navy was on Nov 26 again at a neutral site because of the anticipated crowd which always approached 30,000. Franklin Field in Philadelphia was the venue again because of proximity and size of stadium. In this match, the Cadets held the Midshipmen scoreless while scrounging up 11 points to salt away the game W (11-0).at Franklin Field in Philadelphia, PA.

1905 Coach Robert Boyers

The Army Cadets football team represented the United States Military Academy in the 1905 college football season. It was their sixteenth season of intercollegiate football. They were coached by Robert Boyers in his second and last of two years as head coach of Army. As an independent football entity, the team had a break-even record of 4-4-1. In 1905, Coach Boyer and the many Army fans unhappily learned that Army could be beaten more than a few times in a season. It was a lesson well-learned. The next year, would find another head coach manning the squad.

The Cadets compiled a 4-4-1 record, shut out three opponents, and outscored all opponents by a combined total of 104 to 60. The team's big losses were to Virginia Tech, Harvard, Yale, and the Carlisle Indians. In the annual Army–Navy Game, the Cadets and the Midshipmen played to a 6-6 tie.

Halfback Henry Torney was honored as a consensus first-team player on the 1905 College Football All-America Team.

Other than the Army-Navy Game, all games were played at The Plain on the Campus of the US Military Academy in West Point, NY.

The 1905 season opened on Sept 30 with a shutout against Tufts W (18-0). The next game on Oct 7 was another win against Colgate, W (1860) Then, on Oct 14, VPI defeated the Cadets L (6-16). Following this unexpected loss, the always-tough Harvard squad came in to the Plain and the Cadets played well again but Harvard played just a bit better again, shutting out the Cadets L (0-6). The Cadets then faced another tough team, Yale and played well just like in the past but this time their efforts were not good enough as the Yalees defeated the Cadets L (0-20) in a well-played game by Yale.

On Nov 11, the Cadets lost to the Carlisle Indians in a very close match L (5-6). After recovering from this loss, the Cadets took it out by shutting out Trinity W (34-0). On Nov 25, the Cadets squared off against the Syracuse Orangemen, and brought home another Win a shutout W (17-0).

The season finale against Navy was on Nov 26 again at a neutral site because of the anticipated crowd which always approached 30,000. University Field in Princeton NJ was the venue for the first time because of proximity and size of stadium. In its heyday, this stadium's maximum capacity was 20, 000. In this match, the Cadets held the Midshipmen to six points but the Midshipmen also held the Cadets to 6 points as the game ended in a tie T (6-6)

1906 Coach Ernest Graves

The Army Cadets football team represented the United States Military Academy in the 1906 college football season—their seventeenth season of intercollegiate football. 1906 team is shown below:

1—Phillips; 2—Kromer; 3—Sterling, Mgr. ; 4—Davis; 5—Koehler; 6—Williams; 7—Clark; 8—Farnsworth, 9—Phipps; 10—Casad; 11—Boyers; 12—Hackett; 13—Zehl; 14—Nichols; 15—Burnett; 16—Bettison; 17—Smith, Capt.; 18—Bunker; 19—Goodspeed; 20—Finn.
Photo by Pach Bros.

WEST POINT MILITARY ACADEMY FOOT BALL TEAM.

They were coached by Henry Smither and Ernest Graves. For both, it was their time being head coach of Army. Both would be back to coach in other years. As an independent football entity, the team had a record of 3-5-1. In 1906, Coaches Smither and Graves' combined record was worse than their predecessor, though technically Smither was 1-0. Army fans unhappily learned again that the Cadets could be beaten more than a few times in a season. It was a lesson well-learned. The next year, Army would rehire Smither to take over the squad. He had a fine year in 1907.

Coaches Graves & Smither

The Cadets compiled a 3-5-1 record, shut out four opponents, and outscored all opponents by a combined total of 59 to 37. Henry Smither was the coach in just the first game of the 1906 season, and Ernest Graves, Sr., was the coach in games two through nine. Smither was relieved from duty following a 12–0 victory over Tufts in the season opener. Ernest Graves, Sr. served as head coach for the remaining eight games of the season, leading Army to a record of 2–5–1. Graves came back to coach again in the 1912 season.

The team's setbacks included losses to Harvard, Yale, and Princeton. In the annual Army-Navy Game, the Cadets lost to the 1906 Midshipmen by a 10 to 0 score.

Two Army players were honored by either Walter Camp (WC) or Caspar Whitney (CW) on the 1906 College Football All-America Team. They are tackle Henry Weeks (WC-3, CW-2) and guard William Christy (WC-3).

Other than the Army-Navy Game, which was played at Franklin Field in Philadelphia, all games were played at The Plain on the Campus of the US Military Academy in West Point, NY.

The 1906 season opened on Sept 29 with a shutout against Tufts W (12-0). The next game on Oct 6, was another shutout—this one against Trinity W (24-0) The next game on Oct 13, Colgate played the Cadets to a scoreless tie T (0-0). Then, on Oct 20, Army shut out Williams W (17-0). The Cadets looked like the season was under control with a 3-1 record after four games. The Williams' match would be the last win of the 1906 season as the Cadets went on a five-game losing streak to finish the season. The five losses were as follows:

On Oct 27, Harvard shut out the Cadets L (0-5). On Nov 3, Yale defeated the Cadets L (6-10) On Nov 10, Princeton turned a shutout against Army L (0-8).

On Nov 24, the Cadets squared off against the Syracuse Orangemen, and lost the match by an unusual score of L (0-4). The season finale against Navy was on Dec 1 at a neutral site because of the anticipated crowd which always approached 30,000. Franklin Field in Philadelphia PA was the venue. In this match, the Cadets held the Midshipmen to ten points but failed to score and were thus shut-out by Navy L (0-10).

1907 Coach Henry Smither

The Army Cadets football team represented the United States Military Academy in the 1907 college football season. It was their eighteenth season of intercollegiate football. They were coached by Henry Smither in his first and only full year as head coach of the Cadets. As an independent football entity, the team had a record of 6-2-1. In 1907 Coach Smither got his act together and had a nice season.

The Cadets compiled a 6-2-1 record, shut out six of their nine opponents, and outscored all opponents by a combined total of 125 to 24. The team's only two losses were to Cornell and to Navy in the annual Army–Navy Game.

1907 Army Cadets Football Team Coach Henry Smithers

Two Army players were honored by either Walter Camp (WC) or Caspar Whitney (CW) on the 1907 College Football All-America Team. They are guard William Erwin (WC-1, CW-1) and tackle Henry Weeks (WC-3, CW-2).

Other than the Army-Navy Game, which was played at Franklin Field in Philadelphia, all games were played at The Plain on the Campus of the US Military Academy in West Point, NY.

The 1907 season opened on Sept 29 with a shutout against Franklin & Marshall W (23-0). The next game on Oct 12, was another shutout—this one against Trinity W (12-0). On Oct 19, Yale and Army played to a scoreless tie T (0-0). The Cadets then shut out Rochester W (30-0) on Oct 26.

In the next game on Nov 2, the Cadets shut out Colgate W (6-0) Then, on Nov 9, the Cadets picked up their first loss of the season v Cornell in a close match L (10-14).

1907 Army Cadets in Action on the Plain

On Nov 23, the Cadets squared off against Syracuse, and defeated the Orangemen W (23-4) The season finale against Navy was on Nov 30 at a neutral site because of the anticipated crowd which always approached 30,000. Franklin Field in Philadelphia PA was the venue. In this match, the Midshipmen shut out the Cadets L (0-6)

Chapter 6 Coaches Nelly, Beacham, & Graves 1908-1912

Nelly   Coach #13
Beacham   Coach #14
Graves   Coach #12 (also coached in 1906)

Year	Coach	Record	Conference	Record
1908	Harry Nelly	6-1-2	Indep	6-1-2
1909	Harry Nelly	3-2-0	Indep	3-2-0
1910	Harry Nelly	6-2-0	Indep	6-2-0
1911	Joseph Beacham	6-1-1	Indep	6-1-1
1912	Ernest Graves	5-3-0	Indep	5-3-0

1908 Coach Harry Nelly

<<< Coach Harry Nelly

The Army Cadets football team represented the United States Military Academy in the 1908 college football season. It was their nineteenth season of intercollegiate football. They were coached by Harry Nelly in his first of three seasons as head coach of the Cadets. As an independent football entity, the team had a record of 6-1-2. In 1908 Coach Nelly had a nice season.

The Cadets compiled a 6-1-2 record, shut out five of their nine opponents (including a scoreless tie with Princeton), and outscored all opponents by a combined total of 87 to 21. The team's only loss was to Yale. In the annual Army–Navy Game, the Cadets defeated the Midshipmen by a 6 to 4 score

1, Hines, Asst. Mgr.; 2, Moss; 3, Dean; 4, Devore; 5, Kelly, Mgr.; 6, Bader; 7, Johnson; 8, Hyatt; 9, Benson; 10, Chamberlain; 11, Nix; 12, Carberry; 13, Walmsley; 14, Byrne; 15, Weir; 16, Philoon, Capt; 17, Grehle; 18, Stearns; 19, Pullen.
McManus, Photo.
UNITED STATES MILITARY ACADEMY, WEST POINT, N. Y.

1908 Army Cadets Football Team Coach Harry Nelly

Two Army players were honored by Walter Camp (WC) on his 1908 College Football All-America Team. They were center Wallace Philcon (second team) and end Johnson Philcon (third team). Philcon also received first-team honors from the Washington Herald, Chicago Inter Ocean, and Fred Crolius. In addition, tackle Daniel Pullen was selected as a first-team All-American by the New York World, Fielding H. Yost, T. A. Dwight Jones, and the Kansas City Journal.

Other than the Army-Navy Game, which was played at Franklin Field in Philadelphia, all games were played at The Plain on the Campus of the US Military Academy in West Point, NY.

The 1908 season opened on Oct 3 with a shutout against Tufts W (5-0). The next game on Oct 10, was another shutout—this one against Trinity W (33-0). On Oct 17, Yale defeated Army L (0-6). The Cadets then shut out Colgate W (6-0) on Oct 24.

In the next game on Nov 7, the Cadets defeated Springfield (MA) W (6-5). Then, on Nov 14, the Cadets tied their second game of the season T (6-6) against Washington & Jefferson. On Nov 21, the Cadets beat shut out Villanova W (25-0). Then on Nov 28, at franklin

Field, in the annual Army-Navy Game, in a real nail-biter, the Army defeated the Navy W (6-4).

1909 Coach Harry Nelly

The Army Cadets football team represented the United States Military Academy in the 1909 college football season. It was their twentieth season of intercollegiate football. They were coached by Harry Nelly in his second of three seasons as head coach of the Cadets. As an independent football entity, the team had a record of 3-2-0.

Coach Harry Nelly's 1909 Army Football Offense

The Cadets compiled a 3-2-0 record, shut out two of their five opponents, and outscored all opponents by a combined total of 57 to 32. The team's only losses were to Yale and Harvard. The Army–Navy Game was not played in 1909.

Tackle Daniel Pullen was selected by The New York Times as a second-team player on its 1909 College Football All-America Team. All games were played at The Plain on the Campus of the US Military Academy in West Point, NY.

The 1909 season opened on Oct 2 with a shutout against Tufts W (22-0). In the next game on Oct 9, the Cadets defeated Trinity W 17-6) On Oct 16, Yale shut-out Army L (0-17). The Cadets then shut out Lehigh W (18-0) on Oct 23. In the next game on Oct 30, Harvard shut-out the Cadets L (0-9). The Cadets played just five games and turned in a respectable 3-2 record, losing the big games to Yale and Harvard.

1910 Coach Harry Nelly

The Army Cadets football team represented the United States Military Academy in the 1910 college football season. It was their twenty-first season of intercollegiate football. They were coached by Harry Nelly in his third and last of three seasons as head coach of the Cadets. As an independent football entity, the team had a record of 6-2-0. In 1910 Coach Nelly had a nice season.

The Cadets compiled a 6-2-0 record, shut out five of their eight opponents, and outscored all opponents by a combined total of 96 to 12 – an average of 12.0 points scored and 1.5 points allowed. The Cadets' two losses came against 1910 national champion Harvard by a 6 to 0 score and to the Navy Midshipmen by a 3 to 0 score in the annual Army–Navy Game.

The 1910 season opened on Oct 8 with a shutout against Tufts W (24-0) In the second game of the season, on Oct 15, the Cadets pulled out all the stops and defeated a fine Yale team W (9-3). The next game on Oct 21, was another shutout—this one against Lehigh, W (28-0). On Oct 29, Harvard, defending National Champions came to the Plain and barely shut out the Cadets W (6-0)

In the next game on Nov 5, the Cadets shut out Springfield (MA) W (5-0). Then, on Nov 12, the Cadets defeated Villanova in a shutout W (13-0). tied their second game of the season T (6-6) against On Nov 19, the Cadets beat shut out Trinity W (17-0). Then on Nov 28, at Franklin Field, in the annual Army-Navy Game, in a real nail-biter, the Navy defeated the Army L (0-3)

1911 Coach Joseph Beacham

The Army Cadets football team represented the United States Military Academy in the 1911 college football season. It was their twenty-second season of intercollegiate football. They were coached by Joseph Beacham in his first and only season as head coach of the Cadets. As an independent football entity, the team had a record of 6-1-1. In 1911 Coach Beacham had a nice season.

The Cadets compiled a 6-1-1 record, shut out five of their eight opponents (including a scoreless tie with Georgetown), and outscored all opponents by a combined total of 88 to 11 – an average of 11.0 points scored and 1.4 points allowed. The Cadets' only loss came against the Navy Midshipmen by a 3 to 0 score in the annual Army–Navy Game.

The season opener for 1911 was on Oct 7 with a Cadet shutout against Vermont W (12-0) In the second game of the season, on Oct 14, the Cadets shut out Rutgers by a score of W (18-0). The next game on Oct 21, was a great shutout against powerhouse Yale W (6-0). The next shutout was on Oct 28, against Lehigh W (20-0) Then, on Nov 4, the Cadets and Georgetown played to a scoreless tie T (0-0).

From here, working on an undefeated season, the Cadets took on Bucknell and defeated the Bisons, W (20-2). The, on Nov 18, keeping the season clean of losses, Army beat Colgate W (12-6). The heartbreaker came on November 25. Going into the annual Army-Navy Game undefeated, the Cadets got their first big blemish in the last game of the season in a nail biter at Franklin Field. They lost to Navy's Midshipmen L (0-3).

1912 Coach Ernest Graves

The Army Cadets football team represented the United States Military Academy in the 1912 college football season. It was their twenty-third season of intercollegiate football. They were coached by Ernest Graves in his first and only season in his second stint as head coach of the Cadets. As an independent football entity, the team had a record of 5-3-0.

The Cadets compiled a 5-3-0 record. They shut out two of their eight opponents The Cadets offense scored 108 points, while the defense allowed 59 points. On November 9, Army battled the Carlisle Indian Academy, which featured legendary athlete Jim Thorpe.

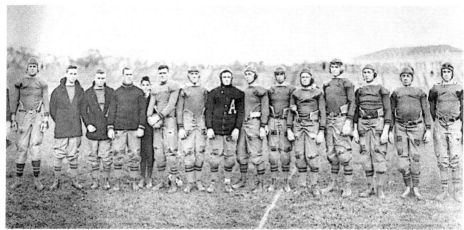

Dwight D. Eisenhower (3rd from left) and Omar Bradley (far right) were members of the 1912 West Point football team.

In 1912, the value of a touchdown was increased from five to six points. The value of the points after TD remained an extra end zone was also added. Before the addition of the end zone, forward passes caught beyond the goal line resulted in a loss of possession and a touchback. The increase from five points to six did not come until much later in Canadian Football, and the touchdown remained only five points there until 1956.

The season opener for 1911 was on Oct 5. The Cadets shutout Stevens Tech W (27-0) In the second game of the season, on Oct 12, the Cadets shut out Rutgers by a score of W (18-0). The next game on Oct 21, was a close game in which Yale shutout the Cadets L (0-6). The next game shutout was on Oct 26, against Colgate W (18-7) Then, on Nov 9, the Cadets took on the Carlisle Indians with the gifted all-everything Jim Thorpe. Carlisle dominated the Cadets L (6-27).

From here, on Nov 16, the Cadets defeated Tufts W (15-6) and on Nov 23, Army followed this with a nice victory over Syracuse W (23-7). Going into the annual Army-Navy Game with two losses, the game was up for grabs. Navy hung in and shut out the Cadets L (0-6) in another nail biter at Franklin Field. They lost to Navy's midshipmen L (0-6.)

Chapter 7 Coaches Daly, Keyes, Mitchell & Daly 1913-22

Daly   Coach #15
Keyes   Coach #16
Mitchell   Coach #17

Year	Coach	Record	Conf	Record
1913	Charles Daly	8-1-0	Indep	8-1-0
1914	Charles Daly	9-0-0	Indep	9-0-0
1915	Charles Daly	5-3-1	Indep	5-3-1
1916	Charles Daly	9-0-0	Indep	9-0-0
1917	Geoffrey Keyes	7-1-0	Indep	7-1-0
1918	Hugh Mitchell	1-0-0	Indep	1-0-0
1919	Charles Daly	6-3-0	Indep	6-3-0
1920	Charles Daly	7-2-0	Indep	7-2-0
1921	Charles Daly	6-4-0	Indep	6-4-0
1922	Charles Daly	8-0-2	Indep	8-0-2

1913 Coach Charles Daly

The 1913 Army Team is shown below:

1, James Cooper Waddell; 2, John James McEwan; 3, Charles Curtiss Herrick; 4, Alexander Mathias Weyand; 5, Lawrence Bascum Meacham; 6, Woodfin Grady Jones; 7, Harold Francis Loomis, Mgr.; 8, Joseph James O'Hare; 9, Thomas Bernard Larkin; 10, John Forest Goodman; 11, Louis Alfred Merillat, Jr.; 12, Henry McElderry Pendleton, Asst. Mgr.; 13, Vernon Edwin Prichard; 14, Charles Calvert Benedict; 15, Hamner Huston; 16, John Prince Markoe; 17, Elbert Louis Ford, Jr.; 18, Paul Alfred Hodgson; 19, Thomas George Lanphier; 20, Walter Wood Hess, Jr.; 21, Leland Stanford Hobbs; 22, Benjamin Fiery Hoge, Capt.; 23, Walter Woolf Wynne; 24, John Hamilton Jouett; 25, Roscoe Barnett Woodruff; 26, Weldon Williamson Doe; 27, Frank William Milburn.

UNITED STATES MILITARY ACADEMY, WEST POINT, N. Y.

The Army Cadets football team represented the United States Military Academy in the 1913 college football season. It was their twenty-fourth season of intercollegiate football. They were coached by Charles Dudley Daly, one of the best coaches in Army history. Daly was in his first season of stint one of two stints of four seasons each as head coach of the Cadets. As an independent football entity, the team had a record of 8-1-0. It was a fantastic season.

<< Coach Charles Daly

The Cadets compiled an 8-1-0 record. They shut out five of their nine opponents, and outscored all opponents by a combined total of 253 to 57 – an average of 28.1 points scored and 6.3 points allowed. The Cadets' only loss was against Notre Dame by a 35 to 13 score. All-American Knute Rockne played on that Notre Dame team. In the annual Army–Navy Game, the Cadets defeated the Midshipmen by a 22 to 9 score.

More About Coach Daly

After earning football letters at West Point in 1901 and 1902, Charles Daly returned to the Academy for two separate coaching stints, guiding the Black Knight gridders from 1913 to 1916 and again from 1919 through 1922. During his eight campaigns along the Army sideline, the Black Knights amassed a sparkling .804 winning percentage, forging a record of 58-13-3.

Daly directed the Black Knights to undefeated seasons in 1914, 1916 and 1922. Army's perfect 9-0 mark in 1914 was the first in the program's history. Daly's Army teams defeated Navy five times in eight meetings. And, it was Daly roaming the sideline for the Black

Knights in 1913 when the Academy initiated its series with Notre Dame, beginning what would evolve into one of college football's most storied rivalries.

In 1951, Daly became the first player or coach from West Point to be enshrined in the College Football Hall of Fame, accepting his honor as part of the Hall's inaugural induction class. Daly was a founding member of the American Football Coaches Association and served as that organization's first president in 1922.

During his undergraduate playing days, which included stints as a quarterback at both Harvard and Army, Daly was named a first-team All-American four times (1898-1900 with the Crimson and 1901 at Army) before earning third-team plaudits at West Point in 1902.

Daly notably coached Army Football teams. He began his coaching career in American football with teams at Harvard before West Point. At West Point, as previously noted, he is known as one of the immortals. More specifically, he is known as the "Godfather of West Point Football.

He was coach to Dwight Eisenhower, Omar Bradley, Joseph Stilwell, Matthew Ridgway, James Van Fleet, George S. Patton and other American military luminaries of the 20th century. In 1921 he founded the American Football Coaches Association.

At West Point he was also an Assistant Professor of Military Science and Tactics from 1928 to 1934. An athletic field on the campus is named in honor of him.

In addition to the legacy Daly created on the gridiron, he also initiated a long-time family association with West Point that saw three of his sons, two grandsons and one great-grandson earn degrees from the Academy.

Here is a famous quote from Coach Daly:

A remarkable similarity exists between war and football. This is particularly manifest in their organization. In both war and football, we have the staff and the troops. In both we have the supply department, medical branch, and the instruction branch. In both, the importance of leadership is paramount. The principles of war laid down by Clausevitz are the principles of the application of force. Just so in football, we have exactly analogous principles of the application of force and a similar organization.

— Charles Dudley Daly, American Football

The Cadets opened the season against Stevens Tech at home as usual, and came away with a fine shutout W (24-0) In the second game of the season, on Oct 11, the Cadets shut out Rutgers (State University of NJ) by a score of W (29-0). The next game on Oct 18, against Colgate was a close match in which the Cadets barely prevailed W)7-6). Other than ND< this was the closest game to a loss all season for the Cadets. On Oct 25, the Cadets played the second closest game of the season other than ND as they squeaked by Tufts in a shutout win W (2-0).

Notre Dame found the money to get to Army from South Bend and they came home with a big payoff. Coach Jesse Harper had the best passer in the country with Gus Dorais, and he had the best end in the country with Knute Rockne. Notre Dame had a passing attack when other teams were just learning about the forward pass. If this were a ground game, the Cadets would have put in an undefeated season in 1913. Notre Dame passed big and won big L (13-35).

On Nov 8, Albright had no idea how good Army really was when they came to the Plain on Nov 8 and were beaten W (77-0) Next up for a smashing was Villanova, on Nov 15—a fine team but not up to the new-found power of Army Football W (55-0).

Then on Nov 22, Springfield (MA) played tough football but lost anyway to the Cadets W (14-7) After losing the prior two years to Navy in the traditional Army-Navy Game, the Cadets would not be stopped on Nov 29 in the last game of the season and Army beat Navy W (22-9). Army had a phenomenal 8-1 season, which set them up for one of the finest West Point Seasons of all time in 1914.

1914 Coach Charles Daly

The 1914 Army Team is shown below:

1, Pendleton, Mgr.; 2, Hess; 3, O'Hare; 4, Meacham; 5, Herrick; 6, Timberlake; 7, Tally; 8, Cruse, Asst. Mgr., 9, Merillat; 10, Larkin; 11, McEwan; 12, Weyand; 13, Butler; 14, Kelly; 15, Woodruff; 16, Britton; 17, Van Fleet; 18, Bradley; 19, Parker; 20, Ford; 21, Neyland; 22, Goodman; 23, Harmon; 24, Hodgson; 25, Coffin; 26, Prichard, Capt.; 27, Benedict; 28, Hobbs.

UNITED STATES MILITARY ACADEMY, WEST POINT, N. Y.

White, Photo.

The Army Cadets football team represented the United States Military Academy in the 1914 college football season. It was their twenty-fifth season of intercollegiate football. They were coached by Charles Dudley Daly. Daly was in his second season of stint one of two stints of four seasons each as head coach of the Cadets. As an independent football entity, the team had a record of 9-0-0. It was a phenomenal season. It was Army's best season to date.

The Cadets compiled an 9-0-0 record. They were undefeated and untied. They shut out six of their nine opponents, and outscored all opponents by a combined total of 219 to 20 – an average of 24.3 points scored and 2.2 points allowed. In the annual Army–Navy Game, the Cadets shut-out the Midshipmen 20 to 0.

The Cadets also defeated Notre Dame by a 20 to 7 score. The 1914 Army team was recognized as the 1914 national champion by the Helms Athletic Foundation, the Houlgate System, and the National Championship Foundation, and a co-national champion by Parke H. Davis.

The Cadets opened the season against Stevens Tech at home as usual, and came away with a blowout shutout W (49-0) In the second game of the season, on Oct 11, the Cadets shut out Rutgers (State University of NJ) by a score of W (13-0). The next game on Oct 18, against Colgate was a close match in which the Cadets pulled away and won handily W (21-7) On Oct 24, the Cadets played Holy Cross and did not permit a point in a fine shutout W (14-0).

Next up for a smashing was Villanova, on Oct 31—a fine team but not up to the new-found power of Army Football W (41-0). On Nov 7, the Cadets played the Fighting Irish of Notre Dame and this time, Army Was ready for Jesse Harper's Irish. Army dominated a close game and won the final score W (20-7) against what was then one of the finest football programs in the nation. f

Then on Nov 14, Maine came to play in the plain and were pushed back up country by the score of W (28-0). On Nov 21, Springfield (MA) played tough football but lost anyway to the Cadets W (13-6). The Army-Navy Game was back at Franklin Field in 1914 and Army shut-out Navy W (20-0). Army had a phenomenal 9-0-0 season, which brought many honors to the Daly coached Army Cadets. They simply had a great year.

1915 Coach Charles Daly

The Army Cadets football team represented the United States Military Academy in the 1915 college football season. It was their twenty-sixth season of intercollegiate football. They were coached by Charles Dudley Daly. Daly was in his third season of stint one of two stints of four seasons each as head coach of the Cadets. As an independent football entity, the team had a record of 5-3-1.

The Cadets compiled an 5-3-1. They shut out four of their nine opponents, and outscored all opponents by a combined total of 114 to 57. In the annual Army–Navy Game, the Cadets lost to the Midshipmen by a 14 to 0 score.

Dwight D. Eisenhower practice punting for Army in the 1915 season

The Cadets opened the season on Oct 2, with a tie T (14-14) against Holy Cross at home. In the second game of the season, on Oct 9, the Cadets shut out Gettysburg by a score of W (22-0). The next game on Oct 18, against Colgate was a close match in which Colgate shut out the Cadets L (0-13). Oct 23, the Cadets played Holy Cross and did not permit a point W (10-0).

Next up for a smashing was Villanova, on Oct 30—a fine team that rose to the occasion to defeat the Cadets L (13-16). On Nov 6, the Cadets played the Fighting Irish of Notre Dame and Notre Dame got the best of the Cadets in a close shutout L (0-7).

Then on Nov 13, Maine came to play in the plain and were shut out W (24-0). Springfield (MA) was next on Nov 20 as the Cadets won the game W (17-7). The Army-Navy Game was at The Polo Grounds again and Navy shut out Army W (14-0).

1916 Coach Charles Daly

The Army Cadets football team represented the United States Military Academy in the 1916 college football season. It was their twenty-seventh season of intercollegiate football. They were coached by Charles Dudley Daly. Daly was in his fourth season of stint one of two stints of four seasons each as head coach of the Cadets. As an independent football entity, the team had a record of 9-0-0. Army had a great season.

The Cadets compiled an 9-0-0. They shut out three of their nine opponents, and outscored all opponents by a combined total of 235 to 36. In the annual Army–Navy Game, the Cadets defeated the Midshipmen 15 to 7. The Cadets also defeated Notre Dame by a score of 30 to 10 and Villanova by a 69 to 7 score. The 1916 Army team was selected retroactively as the 1916 national champion by Parke H. Davis. Army itself has chosen not to claim this as a National Championship but it sure in fact was

The Army Navy Game 1916 Championship

The Cadets opened the season on Sept 30, with a low scoring shutout W (3-0) against Lebanon Valley at home on the Campus of West Point in NY. In the second game of the season, on Oct 7, the Cadets shut defeated Washington & Lee W (14-7). The next game on Oct 14, against Holy Cross was shutout W (17-0).

Army got its moxie back and began to wallop teams on the way to its undefeated and untied 1916 season. On Oct 21, the Cadets thumped Trinity in a shutout W (53-0). The following week on Oct 28, the Cadets routed Villanova W (69-7). The following week on Nov 4, the Cadets overpowered Notre Dame W 30-10).   On Nov 11, the Cadets defeated Maine W (17-3).

From the archives: ARMY CONQUERS NAVY, 15-7, AMID CHEERS OF 45,000;

Oliphant the Chief Figure in West Point's Victory at the Polo Grounds, makes a run of 83 yards. Then, Goodstein scores for the losers by turning a blocked kick into a touchdown. There were quite a few notables in the gay throng. But, President Wilson was Absent. Yet, the crowd included men Prominent in All Walks of Life.

– New York Times – Nov 26, 1916

More than 45,000 cheering spectators saw the Army football team defeat the Navy by a score of 15 to 7 at the Polo Grounds yesterday. Famous for its gala crowds, the annual contest never attracted a more brilliant assemblage, while spectacular playing, especially by Oliphant and Vidal, the Army stars, transformed the banks of the huge eclipse of the Brush stadium into a mass of shouting, flag-waving humanity. **Here is a great link to the original NY Times article: http://query.nytimes.com/mem/archive-free/pdf?res=9D04E1DA1F3FE233A25755C2A9679D946796D6CF**

Army Navy National Championship Game 1916

1917 Coach Geoffrey Keyes

1917 Army Football Team above and below

1, Jenkins; 2, Chapline; 3, Zimmerman; 4, Haaen; 5, Grey; 6, Barton; 7, Groves; 8, Holbrook; 9, Searby; 10, Ward; 11, Moore; 12, Rockafellow; 13, Gould; 14, Gilmartin; 15, Seibert, Mgr.; 16, Robinson, Asst. Mgr.; 17, Crouch; 18, Epes; 19, Richardson; 20, Lipman; 21, Manning; 22, Deminbey; 23, Bartlett; 24, Christiansen; 25, Yeager; 26, Watkins; 27, Marsden; 28, Ferenbaugh; 29, Springer; 30, Rundell; 31, Luce; 32, McQuarrie; 33, Shrader; 34, Stokes; 35, Oliphant, Capt.; 36, Knight; 37, Murrill; 38, Adams; 39, March; 40, York; 41, Major Keyes, Coach; 42, Badger; 43, Casey; 44, Kreber; 45, Monroe; 46, Johnson; 47, Estill; 48, Van de Graaff; 49, Stenzel; 50, Post; 51, Pulsifer; 52, Smith; 53, Hendricks.   Copyright, 1917, by White Studio, New York.

UNITED STATES MILITARY ACADEMY, WEST POINT, N. Y.

FOOTBALL, throughout the season of 1917, was followed by a particularly malevolent jinx, but the records show that he was pretty well foiled. First of all, the beginning of the season caught us unprepared. This happened because the War Department had ordered our schedule cancelled last spring and the ban was not removed until the time of the first call for candidates in September. The War Department still had its foot down on a Navy Game, and the premature cancellation of our schedule lost Pennsylvania and West Virginia from the list. These losses did not leave a very formidable schedule, but we were thankful to have prospects for some sort of a season.

The early graduation of '18 deprived us of Jones, Place, Hirsch, House and Timberlake, all "A" men; also Chapman, Jack Knight, Huff, Fleming and other lesser lights. In addition there was the gap left by Big Mac, Meacham, Gerhardt, Butler, Redfield and others of 1917. Thus the team had little resemblance to our last Navy wrecker. Despite these gaps we had enough good material, but, unfortunately, various causes prevented the use of all of it.

The greatest handicap, apparent from the first, was the lack of experienced coaches. The nation being at war, no officers could be specially detailed for this purpose. Moreover, with such poor Navy Game prospects, the Athletic Council

About the 1917 Team

The Army Cadets football team represented the United States Military Academy in the 1917 college football season. It was their twenty-eighth season of intercollegiate football. They were coached by Geoffrey Keyes in his first and only season as head coach of the Cadets. As an independent football entity, the team had a record of 7-1-0. Army had a great season.

The Cadets compiled an 7-1-0 record. shut out four of their eight opponents, and outscored all opponents by a combined total of 203 to 24. The Cadets' sole loss came to Notre Dame by a 7 to 2 score. The Army–Navy Game was not played during the 1917 season.

Halfback Elmer Oliphant was a consensus first-team player on the 1917 College Football All-America Team and was later inducted into the College Football Hall of Fame.

All Army games were played at The Plain on the Campus of the US Military Academy in West Point, NY.

The Cadets opened the season on Oct 6 with a shutout W (28-0) against Carnegie tech at home on the Campus of West Point in NY. In the second game of the season, on Oct 13, the Cadets shut out VMI W (34-0). In the next game on Oct 20, against Tufts the Cadets dominated W (26-3).

On Oct 27, the Cadets defeated Villanova W (21-7). The following week on Oct 28, the Cadets lost a close match to the Fighting Irish of Notre Dame coached by Jesse Harper, L (2-7). On Nov 10, the Cadets shut out Carlisle W (28-0).

Then on Nov 17, the Cadets walloped Lebanon Valley W (50-0). In the season finale without an Army Navy Game, the Cadets outlasted Boston College in a fine game W (14-7).

Army Football Coach Geoffrey Keyes 1917

1918 Coach Hugh Mitchell

<< Coach Hugh Mitchell

The Army Cadets football team represented the United States Military Academy in the 1917 college football season. It was their twenty-ninth season of intercollegiate football. They were coached by Hugh Mitchell in his first and only season as head coach of the Cadets. As an independent football entity, the team had a record of 1-0-0.

The Cadets compiled an 1-0-0. In the only game played by the Cadets in 1918, they defeated a team from Mitchel Army Air Service in New York.

World War I had created a major demand for soldiers and football was no longer the priority of the football athletes at the academy.

1919 Coach Charles Daly

The Army Cadets football team represented the United States Military Academy in the 1919 college football season. It was their thirtieth season of intercollegiate football. They were coached by Charles Dudley Daly. Daly was in his first season of stint two of two stints of four seasons each as head coach of the Cadets. (Daly had been Army's coach from 1913 to 1916 but Army regulations said he had to resign after four years.) As an independent football entity, the team had a record of 6-3-0.

The Cadets compiled an 6-3-0 record. They shut out five of their nine opponents, and outscored all opponents by a combined total of 140 to 38. In the annual Army–Navy Game, the Cadets lost to the Midshipmen by a 6 to 0 score. The Cadets also defeated Villanova by a 62 to 0 score, but lost to Notre Dame by a 12 to 9 score.

End Earl "Red" Blaik, who later went on to be a great Army Coach, was selected by Walter Camp as a third-team player on the 1919 College Football All-America Team.

The Cadets opened the season on Sept 27 with a shutout W (28-0) against Middlebury at home on the Campus of the USMA at West Point, In the second game of the season, on Oct 4, the Cadets shut out Holy Cross in a close game W (9-0). In the next game on Oct 11, against Syracuse, the Cadets could not keep up in the close game and lost to the Orangemen L (3-7).

On Oct 27, the Cadets shut out Maine W (6-0) The following week on Oct 28, the Cadets defeated Boston College W (13-0). On Nov 1, the Cadets beat Tufts W (24-13).

Then on Nov 8, the Cadets barely lost to big rival Notre Dame L (9-12). Notre Dame was coached by Knute Rockne in his second year. The Irish won the National Championship in 1919 with the famous George Gipp (The Gipper) doing a lot of the heavy lifting.

President Wilson attended the 1919 Army-Navy Game

On Nov 15, the Cadets pounded Villanova W (62-0). On Nov 29, at the Polo Grounds in NY, Army was shut out by Navy L (0-6)

The Midshipmen finished the season 6-1, while the Cadets ended up 6-3.

1920 Coach Charles Daly

The Army Cadets football team represented the United States Military Academy in the 1920 college football season. It was their thirty-first season of intercollegiate football. They were coached by Charles Dudley Daly. Daly was in his second season of stint two of two stints of four seasons each as head coach of the Cadets. (Daly was Army's coach from 1913 to 1916) As an independent football entity, the team had a record of 7-2-0.

The Cadets compiled a 7-2-0 record. They shut out five of their nine opponents, and outscored all opponents by a combined total of 314 to 47. Army excelled on Offense and Defense. In the annual Army–Navy Game, the Cadets lost to the Midshipmen by a 7 to 0 score. The Cadets also defeated Lebanon Valley College by a 53 to 0 score and Bowdoin College by an embarrassing 90 to 0 score.

The Cadets opened the season on Oct 2 with a shutout W (35=0) against Union at home on the Campus of the USMA at West Point, In the second game of the season, which ironically in all of my references says it was also played on Oct 2 v Marshall, the Cadets brought home a W (38-0) shutout. If I figure this one out by book printing time, I will make the change otherwise, I admit, I just do not know.

On Oct 9, the Cadets shut out Middlebury W (27-0). In the next game on Oct 16, against Springfield (MA) the Cadets prevailed W (26-7). On Oct 23, the Cadets beat Tufts quite handily W (28-6). On Oct 30, the visiting Fighting Irish from Notre Dame, coached by Knute Rockne defeated the Cadets L (17-27) The Irish always saw Army as its most formidable opponent.

On Nov 6, the Cadets shellacked Lebanon Valley in a big W (53-0) shutout. On Nov 13, in an unusual game against a first-time opponent, the Cadets played every minute of the game against Bowdoin and literally knocked the smithereens out of the visitors W (90-0).

On Nov 27, at the Polo Grounds in NY, Army was shut out by Navy in a close match L (0-7)

1921 Coach Charles Daly

The Army Cadets football team represented the United States Military Academy in the 1921 college football season. It was their thirty-second season of intercollegiate football. They were coached by Charles Dudley Daly. Daly was in his third season of stint two of two stints of four seasons each as head coach of the Cadets. (Daly was Army's coach from 1913 to 1916) As an independent football entity, the team had a record of 6-4-0.

The Cadets compiled a 6-4-0 record. They shut out five of their ten opponents, and outscored all opponents by a combined total of 217 to 65. In the annual Army–Navy Game, the Cadets lost to the Midshipmen by a 7 to 0 score. The Cadets also lost to Yale and Notre Dame, two rivals / nemeses /.

The Cadets opened the season on Oct 1 with a win against Springfield (MA) W (28-6) at home on the Campus of the USMA at West Point, In the second game of the season, which ironically in all of my references says it was also played on Oct 1 vs. New Hampshire, the Cadets lost a close game L (7-10). Like the prior year, if I figure this one out by book printing time, I will make the change otherwise, I admit, I just do not know. Too many references are the same. Army needs to clear this up.

On Oct 8, the Cadets shut out Lebanon Valley W (33-0). In the next game on Oct 8, against Middlebury, the Cadets won in a shutout W (19-0). Then, on Oct 15, the Cadets shut out Wabash quite handily W (21-0). On Oct 22, Army got out of the Plain in a real game at the Yale Bowl and were beaten in a close game v Yale L (7-14).

On Oct 29, Susquehanna got thumped by the Cadets W (53-0). After this great warm-up game, the next game was Knute Rockne's

Fighting Irish on Nov 5. The Irish shut out the Cadets L (0-28). The Irish never took an Army team for granted. On Nov 12, the Cadets whooped Villanova W (49-0). Despite the great big wins, when the Midshipmen came to play at the Polo Grounds, like this year, the Cadets burped a bit, played a fine game but lost the game in another nail-biter L (0-7).

1922 Coach Charles Daly

The Army Cadets football team represented the United States Military Academy in the 1922 college football season. It was their thirty-third season of intercollegiate football. They were coached by Charles Dudley Daly. Daly was in his fourth and last season of stint two of two stints of four seasons each as head coach of the Cadets. (Daly was also Army's coach from 1913 to 1916) As an independent football entity, the team had a record of 8-0-2. It was one of a rare number of times that and always well-playing Army had attained eight wins in a season.

The Cadets compiled an undefeated, twice tied 8-0-2 record. They shut out seven of their ten opponents, and outscored all opponents by a combined total of 228 to 27 – an average of 22.8 points scored and 2.7 points allowed. In the annual Army–Navy Game, the Cadets defeated the Midshipmen 17 to 14.

Two Army players were recognized as first-team players on the 1922 College Football All-America Team: guard Fritz Breidster and center Edgar Garbisch. Garbisch was later inducted into the College Football Hall of Fame.

Other than the Yale Game played at the Yale Bowl, and the Army-Navy Game, which was played at the Polo Grounds again in 1922, in New York, all Army games were played at The Plain on the Campus of the US Military Academy in West Point, NY.

The Cadets opened the season on Sept 23, with a shutout against Lebanon Valley W (12-0) at home on the Campus of the USMA at West Point, On Sept 30, the Cadets shut out Springfield (MA) W (35-0). In the next game on Oct 7, against Kansas, the Cadets won in a shutout W (13-0) On Oct 14, the Cadets beat Auburn W (19-6) On Oct 228 Army got out of the Plain in a real football game at the Yale Bowl and tied Yale T (7-7).

On Nov 4, New Hampshire was shut out by the Cadets W (33-0). After this warm-up game, the Cadets were really ready to put up a big score and they did against St. Bonaventure on Nov 4. The Cadets walloped the Bonnies in a shut out win W (53-0). Notre Dame was next on Nov 11 and they played the Cadets to a scoreless tie T (0-0) in a major defensive battle.

On Nov 18, the Cadets whooped Bates W (39-0). Despite the great big wins, when the Midshipmen came to play at any of the venues such as Franklin Field in Philadelphia PA , as in 1922, it was an exciting game. This year, the Cadets got the victory in another close match W (17-14).

Chapter 8 Coaches McEwan, Jones, & Sasse 1923-1932

McEwan   Coach #18
Jones   Coach #19
Sasse   Coach #20

Year	Coach	Record	Conf	Record
1923	John McEwan	6-2-1	Indep	6-2-1
1924	John McEwan	5-1-2	Indep	5-1-2
1925	John McEwan	7-2-0	Indep	7-2-0
1926	Biff Jones	7-1-1	Indep	7-1-1
1927	Biff Jones	9-1-0	Indep	9-1-0
1928	Biff Jones	8-2-0	Indep	8-2-0
1929	Biff Jones	6-4-1	Indep	6-4-1
1930	Ralph Sasse	9-1-1	Indep	9-1-1
1931	Ralph Sasse	8-2-1	Indep	8-2-1
1932	Ralph Sasse	8-2-0	Indep	8-2-0

1923 Coach John McEwan

<< Coach John McEwan

The Army Cadets football team represented the United States Military Academy in the 1923 college football season. It was their thirty-fourth season of intercollegiate football. They were coached by John McEwan in his first of three seasons as head coach of the Cadets. As an independent football entity, the team had a record of 6-2-1.

The Cadets compiled a 6-2-1 record. They shut out five of their nine opponents, and outscored all opponents by a combined total of 237 to 56. In the annual Army–Navy Game, the Cadets and the Midshipmen played to a scoreless tie.

The Cadets opened the season on Sept 29, with a shellacking shutout against Tennessee W (41-0) at home on the Campus of the USMA at West Point, On Oct 6, the Cadets shut out Florida W (20-0). In the next game on Oct 13, against Knute Rockne's Notre Dame at Ebbetts Field in Brooklyn, the Cadets were shut out in a close match L (0-13). On Oct 20, v Auburn, the Cadets defeated the Tigers W (28-6). On Oct 27, the Cadets walloped Lebanon Valley in a blowout shutout W (74-0).

For the third year in a row, Army got out of the Plain in another real football game at the Yale Bowl in New Haven Connecticut and lost to the Bulldogs, L (10-31). On Nov 10, the Cadets shut out Arkansas Tech W (44-0). Then, on Nov 17, it was Bethany at home defeated by the Cadets in a nice game W (20-6). On Nov 24 v. Navy at the Polo Grounds the Cadets played the Midshipmen to a scoreless tie T (0-0).

1924 Coach John McEwan

The Army Cadets football team represented the United States Military Academy in the 1924 college football season. It was their thirty-fifth season of intercollegiate football. They were coached by John McEwan in his second of three seasons as head coach of the Cadets. As an independent football entity, the team had a record of 5-1-2.

The Cadets compiled a 5-1-2 record. They shut out four of their eight opponents, and outscored all opponents by a combined total of 111 to 41. In the annual Army–Navy Game, the Cadets defeated the Midshipmen by a 12 to 0 score. The team's only loss came to undefeated national champion Notre Dame by a 13 to 7 score.

The Cadets opened the season on Oct 4, with a shutout victory over Saint Louis in the inaugural game for the brand new Michie Stadium on the Campus of the USMA at West Point, On Oct 11, the Cadets shut out Detroit W (20-0). In the next game on Oct 13, against Knute Rockne's National Champion Notre Dame squad, complete with the "immortal" Four Horsemen, at the Polo Grounds, the Cadets gave the Irish a run for their money but lost in a close match, L (7-13) before a huge crowd of 55,000.

On Oct 25, v Boston University, the Cadets defeated the Terriers, W (20-0). Then, on Nov 1, Army played Yale at the Yale Bowl in New Haven CT to a tie T (7-7). Nov 8, the Cadets defeated Florida's Gators at home, W (14-7). In the setup game for the Army-Navy annual battle, on Nov 15, the Cadets tied Columbia in a hard-fought contest T (14-14). Then, in the season finale, on Nov 29 v. Navy at Municipal Stadium • Baltimore, MD (Army–Navy Game), the Cadets shut out the Midshipmen W (12-0).

1925 Coach John McEwan

The Army Cadets football team represented the United States Military Academy in the 1925 college football season. It was their thirty-sixth season of intercollegiate football. They were coached by John McEwan in his third and last of three seasons as head coach of the Cadets. As an independent football entity, the team had a record of 7-2-0.

The Cadets compiled a 7-2-0 record. They shut out three of their nine opponents, the Cadets offense scored 185 points, while the defense allowed 71 points, On November 28, Army beat Navy by a score of 10–3.

The Cadets opened the season on Oct 3, with a nice victory over Detroit W (31-6) at Michie Stadium on the Campus of the USMA at West Point. On Oct 10, the Cadets defeated Knox W (26-7). In the traditional third game on Oct 17, it was pay-back time against Knute Rockne's prior National Champion Notre Dame squad at Yankee Stadium. The Cadets shut out the Irish by a good margin W (27-0).

On Oct 24, v St. Louis, the Cadets shut out the Billikens W (19-0). Then, on Oct 31, Army played Yale at the Yale Bowl in New Haven CT and were defeated by a score of L (7-28). On Nov 17, the Cadets defeated Davis & Elkins W (14-6).

On Nov 14, at Columbia's Baker Field, the Cadets were defeated by the Lions L (7-21). Then, in the season finale, on Nov 28 v. Navy at the Polo Grounds in New York, NY, the Cadets defeated the Midshipmen W (10-3)

Biff Jones takes over as Cadets head coach

A PROSPECTUS of the '26 season filled us with high hopes despite the fact that our coaching staff had migrated to the West. We had lost but one regular from 25's none too successful team, and felt that from a nucleus of ten experienced men, almost any coach could mold a winning combination. Also, this was the last season during which Plebes were to be eligible; so we anxiously awaited news of their prospects. As some famous general once said, everything went as planned. Our new material proved of exceptional ability, our regulars, with one or two exceptions, were free from serious injuries, and as a result, our team was good—one of the best. A hard schedule was successfully met, and for once the Army-Navy game was a football game besides being a national exhibit.

To sketch individual performance would be too great a task, but Biff Jones must be mentioned as a first year head coach who was unusually successful. Great credit is due the men who performed; as a collection of football players we hold them unequalled.

Capt. Jones, Coach   Hewitt, Captain

Biff Jones, a great coach, a Cadet favorite

Lawrence "Biff" Jones graduated from the U.S. Military Academy in 1917. He served in France as a Lieutenant of field artillery and returned to West Point in 1926 as head football coach, succeeding John McEwan.

His four-year record there was an impressive 30-8-2. His 1926 and 1927 teams lost but one game each, his 1928 Cadets but two.

In 1927, Jones did Army a great service when he brought Earl "Red" Blaik back to the Point as an assistant coach. Blaik worked for three years under Jones and would return years later to lift the Cadets to their highest success.

However, Jones moved on and enjoyed further success at Louisiana State, Oklahoma and Nebraska. He established himself as a serious, sound, hard- working mentor with a gift for organization.

In 1937, Jones retired from the Army as a Major.

Also in 1937, he left the Oklahoma Sooners to coach their rival, the Nebraska Cornhuskers, replacing coach Dana X. Bible.

Jones remained at Nebraska for five years and tallied a 28–14–4 mark. He led Nebraska to its first bowl game, the 1941 Rose Bowl, and also coached the second-ever televised college football game.

Jones left Nebraska in 1942 when he was called back to service as a colonel during World War II.

Later, he served as graduate manager at the Academy until June, 1948.

Playing career
1915–1916 Army Position: Tackle

Coaching career as Head Coach
1926–1929 Army 30-8-2
1932–1934 LSU 20-5-6
1935–1936 Oklahoma 9-6-3
1937–1941 Nebraska 28-14-4

Head coaching record Overall
87–33–15

Administrative career as Athletic Director
1935–1936 Oklahoma
1937–1942 Nebraska
1942–1948 Army

On or off the gridiron, Jones was always in command of the situation and never suffered from a lack of respect paid to him.

He was inducted into the College Football Hall of Fame in 1954, and the Nebraska Football Hall of Fame in 1971.

Jones married Elizabeth Trueman King, daughter of Mr. & Mrs. George Anderson King, in 1920, when he was a Captain in the Field Artillery at West Point. She was a graduate of Smith College.

1926 Coach Biff Jones

<< Coach Biff Jones

The Army Cadets football team represented the United States Military Academy in the 1926 college football season. It was their thirty-seventh season of intercollegiate football. They were coached by Biff Jones in his first of four seasons as head coach of the Cadets. As an independent football entity, the team had a record of 7-1-1.

The Cadets compiled a 7-1-1 record. They shut out four of their nine opponents, and outscored all opponents by a combined total of 240 to 71. In the annual Army–Navy Game, the Cadets tied with the Midshipmen at a 21 to 21 score. The team's only loss came to Notre Dame by a 7 to 0 score.

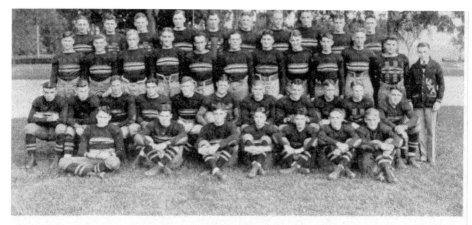

Left to Right, Top Row—Simonson, Morrell, Cagle, Dibb, Zimmerman, Waldrop, Dahl, Tobin, Kenny, Miller.   Second Row—Brentnall, Davidson, Landon, Muse, Elias, Lynch, Perry, Bunker, Harbold, Fletcher, Gilbreth, Holland, Mgr.   Third Row—Swonders, Seaman, Born, Hammack, Sprague, Hewitt, Capt., Wilson, Daly, Trapnell, Harding, Schmidt. Fourth Row—Conner, Wisner, Hutchinson, Eller, Meehan, Piper, Smidt.

Army Cadets 1926 A-Team Coach Biff Jones

The Army Cadets began the 1926 season at home on Oct 2, with a nice shutout victory over Detroit W (21-0) at Michie Stadium on the Campus of the USMA at West Point. On Oct 9, the Cadets defeated Davis & Elkins W (21-7). In the third game on Oct 16, Army defeated Syracuse W (27-21) in a very close match. On Oct 23, the Cadets shut out the Eagles of Boston College W (41-0). Then, on Oct 30, at the Yale Bowl, Army shut out Yale W (33-0).

On Nov 6 v Franklin & Marshall, the Cadets shut out the Diplomats W (55-0) in a major shellacking. Then, on Nov 13, Knute Rockne's Fighting Irish shut out army by a close score L (0-7). Then, on Nov 20, the Army pounded Ursinas in a shutout W (44-0). Then, in the season finale, on Nov 27 v. Navy at Soldier Field in Chicago, IL, the Cadets tied the Midshipmen T (21-21).

About the 1926 Army Navy Game

THE GREATEST ARMY–NAVY GAME
Thanks to Ray Schmidt
PAGE 9
https://forwhattheygave.com/2007/12/11/1926-football-team/

There was a time — more difficult to remember with each passing season — when the results of the annual gridiron showdown between the teams of West Point and Annapolis (that's Army and Navy) were followed by football fans across the country, and often carried significance in the race for mythical national honors. Yet even more so, the game and its surrounding pageantry represented the best moments of college football. No other rivalry in college football consistently created such anticipation at the host cities, and then actually came through with the color, the excitement, and the spectacle that was unmatched — with even a good football game on occasion.

From this long-running series there is one game that stands above the others as the greatest Army-Navy clash ever, and one of the best in the annals of all college football history. In the early 1940s, Esquire magazine conducted a poll and named the game "the greatest in history" to that time, while the long-time prominent coach, Clark Shaughnessy, selected it as one of the 12 greatest games of all-time. Shaughnessy described it as one game "seldom matched for brilliant and courageous individual play, and for daring and spectacular team strategy." It was of course the legendary 1926 Army-Navy showdown.

In those times, the service academies alternated years in selecting the site for their annual game, and during the 1920s bids were frequently received from several cities — usually always along the Eastern Seaboard. In late 1924, a group from Chicago — supported by U.S. Representatives Fred Britten and Martin Madden of Illinois — entered the bidding to host the 1925 Army-Navy game. The other cities seeking the game included Washington D.C., Philadelphia, Baltimore, and two different groups from New York (one representing the Polo Grounds and the other the relatively new Yankee Stadium). Chicago was under a handicap because of its distance from the two schools, and West Point officials (who would be selecting the 1925 site) were on record as opposing any site that would keep the Corps of Cadets away from the school overnight — a position endorsed by War Secretary John W. Weeks.

The 1925 game was ultimately awarded to the Polo Grounds — despite Yankee Stadium's larger seating capacity — but Chicago businessmen were soon preparing another bid for the 1926 game which would be selected by Naval Academy officials. Again, the Midwest city was challenged by New York, Baltimore, and Philadelphia, but this time it was better prepared The Chicago group announced its willingness to raise $100,000 for each academies' athletic fund, in addition to the approximately $600,000 which would be required to cover the expenses of bringing the teams and students to the game. Yet the Eastern cities continued in the role of the favorites.

Political pressure upon the academies intensified, as Midwest congressmen and service men's organizations turned up the heat. No stone was left unturned — in December 1925 the Chicago Herald-Examiner ran an editorial stating that an Army-Navy game in Chicago would "arouse in youthful civilian minds a new understanding of love of country and eager appreciation of what education at West Point and Annapolis means" — this at a time when many leaders of America were urging the need for much better preparedness and training for the nation's youth, given the recent experiences of World War I. In case patriotism didn't strike the right chord, the editorial declared that, "Those great schools are not the exclusive property of the East."

In the end, political pressure and big money carried the day — along with a stadium that could seat in excess of 100,000 ticket-buying fans — and so Annapolis officials awarded the 1926 game to Chicago.

The Midwest city had built mammoth Grant Park Stadium on the banks of Lake Michigan just south of the downtown area in 1925. Some football games had been played there that first season — including Northwestern's famous 3-2 win over Michigan in the mud — yet for 1926 the stadium was being renamed as "Soldier Field" in memory of World War I military personnel, and the Army-Navy game was selected as the formal dedication event.

Soldier Field was a U-shaped arena with a seating capacity of nearly 100,000, with many of the seats at the north end well beyond the gridiron itself. In anticipation of a large ticket demand for the Army-Navy clash, the Chicago Park Board was having temporary bleachers installed to close the open north end of the stadium — with no concern that these seats would be 30-40 yards beyond the goal posts.

After holding out the seats for the two visiting student bodies and numerous dignitaries, there remained 40,000 decent seats which were priced at either $15 or $10 each, with the binocular-type seats priced lower. A full house scaled at these prices would produce gate receipts of approximately $800,000.

To say the least, the demand for tickets was overwhelming, as over 600,000 ticket requests were received for the 100,000 seats available on sale. Placed in charge of the ticket sales was Colonel H.C. Carbaugh — a 65-year old Army veteran who normally served as supervisor of the Civil Service Department for Chicago's South Park Board Members of the public seeking tickets at times became so aggressive that it was necessary for Carbaugh to have body guards while at work, and police were assigned to protect the entrances to the Park's Administration Building.

Of course, it wouldn't be Chicago without some hint of corruption, and it came to light when U.S. Representative John J. Gorman from Chicago charged that the South Park Board was violating an earlier agreement with the Chicago-area congressmen by only providing them with a hundred tickets each. Gorman added that rumors abounded that each of the park commissioners was receiving 1200 tickets. E. J. Kelly, president of the South Park commissioners, replied that everything possible was being done to distribute the tickets fairly and no attention was being given to the complaints of the congressmen.

Two days before the game Navy's traveling party arrived aboard a special train via the Pennsylvania Railroad Coach Bill Ingram spurned a practice session at Soldier Field, and instead took his Middies to a workout on a secluded grassy island in the Sherman Park lagoon while guards protected all the bridgeways leading over the water. The Army team arrived soon afterward on the Michigan Central line, and Coach Biff Jones then drilled his charges at Soldier Field before the team headed for its accommodations at the South Shore Country Club.

The day before the game the visiting student bodies from the two academies were treated to a luncheon at Marshall Field's giant department store in downtown Chicago, after which the Cadets and midshipmen staged a big parade south on Michigan Avenue as they marched to Soldier Field for the formal dedication ceremony. Meanwhile, there was also a full slate of luncheons and parties planned to entertain the service personnel throughout the weekend.

Helping to fuel the already overheated college football fans of
Chicago was the fact that the two teams were among the nation's
elite for 1926 — Navy coming in with a record of 9-0-0 and Army at
7-1-0, with only a narrow 7-0 defeat to Notre Dame marring the
Cadets record. The Army team was slightly favored, and its
powerhouse included such great players as Chris Cagle, "Lighthorse"
Harry Wilson, Chuck Born, Gar Davidson, and Red Murrell; while
Navy countered with standouts such as Tom Hamilton, Frank
Wickhorst, Tom Eddy, and Whitey Lloyd.

When time for the kickoff finally arrived on November 27, 1926 —
amidst concerns over the many counterfeit tickets which had been
found in circulation — Soldier Field was jammed with
approximately 110,000 fans, with thousands more standing atop
every nearby building, water tower, and bridge that afforded any
hopes of a glimpse of the action. A New York Times writer surveyed
the scene from the rim of Soldier Field and reported that, "Looking
off over the top of the stadium, there was nothing to see but people."

It was later stated that over 18,000 automobiles had been parked
around the stadium, while Chicago taxi companies reported that they
had made approximately 20,000 separate trips out to the arena. The
massive crush of people and cars required the city to assign 1,350
police officers to direct traffic and maintain order. James Bennett of
the Chicago Tribune described it as "a multitude that was worthy of
the game."

It was a cold day along the Chicago lakefront, and, except for the sun
breaking through on one occasion, the game was played under a gray
and heavily clouded sky. Snow banks surrounded the field from an
earlier storm that had required 300 men to work the entire night
before the game shoveling off the seats of the stadium. Around the
rim of the stadium were large American flags which rippled in the
wintry breezes off Lake Michigan.

Army kicked off to open the game, and surprisingly, Coach Jones of
the Cadets had a half dozen of his first-string players on the sideline.
After the teams exchanged punts, the offensive fireworks began.
Starting from its 45-yard line, Navy began to mix an array of short

passes with its running attack. After several plays moved the ball to Army's 34, Jim Schuber of Navy faked an end sweep but instead rifled a long pass that Hank Hardwick plucked out of the air at the eight-yard line before being dragged down at the one. Two plays later Howard Caldwell blasted in for the touchdown, and Tom Hamilton's drop-kick made it 7-0, Navy.

Again, the teams returned to an exchange of possessions although Navy clearly held the upper hand, and writer Walter Eckersall later declared that "the Middies appeared unbeatable in the first quarter." Late in the period Navy began a drive from its 43-yard line and, after a penalty set them back to the 32, Hamilton connected on a pass to Schuber that was good for 23 yards. After a couple more plays, Coach Jones rushed the rest of his Army first string into the game just before the quarter ended with the Middies at the Army 22. Several plays later Schuber blasted in from one yard out for the TD, and Hamilton's PAT made it 14-0.

Later in the second quarter Army finally got its offense on track behind the hard running of Chris Cagle and Harry Wilson. Starting from their 37-yard line after a punt, the Cadets got rolling as Wilson broke off a dazzling change of pace run of 23 yards to the Navy 40.

Two plays later, Cagle swept around right end on a 21-yard gallop, and on the next snap Wilson slashed through the left side of the line and sailed 17 yards to Army's first touchdown. Wilson's placekick made it 14-7.

The next time Army had the ball it was unable to move, and so Red Murrell dropped back to his 20, from where he boomed a towering punt that came down to the Middies' Howard Ransford on the Navy 25. Attempting a running catch, Ransford fumbled the ball and the bouncing pigskin caromed off the foot of Army's Skip Harbold and toward the Navy goal line. Catching up with the ball near the 15, Harbold picked it up and rumbled toward paydirt, and despite falling down at the one, the weary cadet managed to squirm into the end zone for the touchdown. Wilson's PAT made it 14-14, and the wild first half soon came to a close.

After the gigantic throng had been entertained by a mock battle between students of the two schools, the second half got underway as

Army started from its 26 after Cagle's 20-yard runback of the kickoff. Several plays later Wilson swept around left end for a gain of 15 yards to the Navy 44, and on the next snap Cagle broke up the middle and dashed all the way for the touchdown that put Army ahead 21-14 after Wilson's PAT.

Despite the stunning comeback by the Cadets, the Middies returned to the attack. Both of the high-powered offenses fought back and forth until late in the third quarter when Navy started from its 43-yard line after a punt. Slowly the Middies headed up the field as the action moved into the fourth quarter. Hamilton completed two key passes to Alan Shapley on the drive, and Ransford chipped in a critical gain of eight yards for a first down at Army's 15. The 12-play drive was capped off in sensational fashion when Shapley swept around right end on a fourth down and three play for an eight-yard touchdown run. With the entire stadium holding its breath, Hamilton calmly drop-kicked the extra point to tie it at 21-21.

With just over seven minutes left to play, the surrounding gloom and darkness had gathered to the point where it was increasingly difficult for fans and writers in the press box to distinguish the players on the field. Still, Army mounted one last attempt at the win, starting from its 27-yard line after the following kickoff. On the second play of the series Wilson broke through left tackle for a 28-yard dash into Navy territory, and then he and Murrell alternated in pounding the Middies' line. Finally, checked just inside the 20, Wilson dropped back to attempt a place-kick from the 26. The ball was spotted directly in front of the goal posts, but incredibly Wilson's kick sailed just wide.

The final couple minutes were played in "almost total darkness," as the electric lights over the stadium's entrance tunnels and on the Scoreboard twinkled in the gloom. On the last play of the game Hamilton attempted a desperate pass for Navy, but the aerial was intercepted by (and here's where the darkness contributed to the confusion) either Wilson, Cagle, or Chuck Harding — depending on which game account you choose to accept. The runback was finally halted deep in Navy territory, and so the monumental battle ended in a 21-21 tie.

Combined with Notre Dame's shocking 19-0 loss to Carnegie Tech that same day, undefeated Navy's hard-earned tie gave its supporters plenty of ammunition to debate Stanford for the mythical national championship. Yet more significant was the 1926 game's place in football history. Walter Eckersall described it as "one of the greatest football games ever played," and it remains so to his day. No single game in college football history has ever so completely combined the color, spectacle, national media coverage, public popularity, and top-flight level of play as the Army-Navy battle of 1926 at Soldier Field. Robert Kelley of the New York Times defined the game's significance when he wrote that day: "Football had the greatest pageant, its high spot of color, and so did sport in the United States." http://www.la84.org/SportsLibrary/CFHSN/CFHSNv17/CFHSN v17n2e.pdf

1927 Coach Biff Jones

The Army Cadets football team represented the United States Military Academy in the 1927 college football season. It was their thirty-eighth season of intercollegiate football. They were coached by Biff Jones in his second of four seasons as head coach of the Cadets. As an independent football entity, the team had a record of 9-1-0.

The Cadets compiled a 9-1-0 record. They shut out six of their ten opponents, and outscored all opponents by a combined total of 197 to 37. In the annual Army–Navy Game, the Cadets defeated the Midshipmen by a 14 to 9 score. The team's only loss came to national champion Yale by a 10 to 6 score.

The season opener was played on Sept 24. Army began the 1926 season at home with a nice shutout victory over Boston University -- W (21-0) at Michie Stadium on the Campus of the USMA at West Point. On Oct 1, the Cadets shut-out Detroit W (6-0). In the third game on Oct 8, Army defeated Marquette W (21-12). On Oct 15, Army defeated Davis & Elkins W (27-6). Then, on Oct 22, at the Yale Bowl, Army was shut out by National Champion Yale L (6-10).

On Oct 29, v Bucknell the Cadets shut out the Bisons W (34-0). Then, on Nov 5, Army shut out Franklin & Marshall W (45-0). On

Nov 12, Army shut out the vaunted Knute Rockne coached Fighting Irish W (18-0) at Yankee Stadium L (0-7). Then, on Nov 20, the Army shut out Ursinas W (13-0) In the season finale, on Nov 27 v. Navy at the Polo Grounds in NY, NY, the Cadets beat the Midshipmen W (14-9)

1928 Coach Biff Jones

The Army Cadets football team represented the United States Military Academy in the 1928 college football season. It was their thirty-ninth season of intercollegiate football. They were coached by Biff Jones in his third of four seasons as head coach of the Cadets. As an independent football entity, the Army team had a record of 8-2-0.

The Cadets compiled an 8-2-0 record. The Cadets offense scored 215 points, while the defense allowed 79 points. The 1928 season was one of the few years in which Army did not play the Navy Midshipmen in the Army–Navy Game.

In the 1928 game versus Notre Dame, held at Yankee Stadium, with the score 0–0 at halftime, legendary Notre Dame coach Knute Rockne gave his "win one for the Gipper" speech (with reference to All-American halfback George Gipp, who died in 1920); Notre Dame went on to defeat Army, 12–6.

Army participated in the best-attended college football game at Yankee Stadium. The game was held on December 1, 1928, when Army lost to Stanford 26–0 before 86,000 fans.

They shut out six of their ten opponents, and outscored all opponents by a combined total of 197 to 37. In the annual Army–Navy Game, the Cadets defeated the Midshipmen by a 14 to 9 score. The team's only loss came to national champion Yale by a 10 to 6 score.

The season opener was played on Sept 29. Army began the 1926 season at home with a nice shutout victory over Boston University -- W (35-0) at Michie Stadium on the Campus of the USMA at West Point. On Oct 6, the Cadets battled for a close win against SMU W (14-13). In the third game on Oct 13, Army shut out Providence W

(44-0). On Oct 20 at Harvard's Harvard Stadium in Boston MA, the Cadets defeated the Crimson W (15-0).

On Oct 27, at Yale in the Yale Bowl New Haven CT, the Army beat Yale W (18-6). On Nov 3, at home, Army defeated DePauw W (38-12). On Nov 10, Army played a great game but were defeated by Knute Rockne's Fighting Irish L (6-12) in a very close tough played match. On Nov 17, the Army defeated Carleton W (32-7). In a first-time appearance for Nebraska at Michie Stadium, the Cadets defeated the Cornhuskers W (13-3). In the Season finale on December 1, without an Army-Navy Game, the Cadets were shut-out by the West-Coast Stanford Cardinal L (0-26) before 86,000 screaming fans at Yankee Stadium in the Bronx, NY.

1929 Coach Biff Jones

The Army Cadets football team represented the United States Military Academy in the 1929 college football season. It was their fortieth season of intercollegiate football. They were coached by Biff Jones in his fourth and last of four seasons as head coach of the Cadets. As an independent football entity, the Army team had a record of 6-4-1.

The Cadets compiled a 6-4-1 record. The 1929 game between Army and Notre Dame had the highest attendance in the series at 79,408.

The days of Army having it forever its way at home had come to an end. Army began to play as all other collegiate teams with both home games and away games. The preponderance of exceptions to Army playing at home hit five teams last year. Army chose to compete like all other teams with both home and away games.

The season opener was played on Sept 28. Army began the 1929 season at home with a nice shutout victory over Boston University -- W (26-0) at Michie Stadium on the Campus of the USMA at West Point. On Oct 5, the Cadets battled for a big score win against Gettysburg, W (33-7). In the third game on Oct 12, Army beat Davidson, W (23-7). On Oct 19 at Harvard's Harvard Stadium in Boston MA, the Cadets tied the Crimson T (20-20).

On Nov 2, at home, Army defeated South Dakota, W (33-6). On Nov 9, Army lost to Illinois, L (7-17). Then in a thunderous overpowering victory, the Cadets beat Dickinson at home, W (89-7) in a huge victory. On Nov 23, Ohio Wesleyan fought hard but list to Army by a score of W)19-6).

On Nov 30, the Cadets could not keep up with Notre Dame and lost in a shutout by a small score of L (0-7. Army played a great game but were defeated by Knute Rockne's Fighting Irish in a very close tough played match. On Dec 28, at Stanford in Stanford Stadium, Stanford, CA, Army lost its last game of 1929 L (13–34).

Because of Army regulations curtailing the tenure of head coaches to four years, the much beloved Biff Jones stepped down as head man at the end of the 1929 season, sporting an impressive 30-8-2 (.775) record. He was replaced by Ralph Sasse, another favorite.

In the last two years of Biff Jones at Army, the Cadets enjoyed another successful season in 1928 with eight wins but two losses - to Stanford and Notre Dame. However, Army regressed to 6-4-1 in 1929, partly because its star RB, Chris Cagle, injured his shoulder. After the season, Jones was removed from his post since the Army high command considered coaching football at the Academy just another four-year assignment for an officer.

Several years later, Jones would be assigned to the ROTC program at LSU at the request of Huey Long so that Biff could coach the Tigers.

Major Ralph Sasse replaced Jones and kept future coach Red Blaik on his staff along with another assistant, Gar Davidson, whom Blaik could not stand and who would prove to be his nemesis in his quest for the top job on the Plains. Under Sasse, Red became the disciplinarian of the staff, earning the unaffectionate nickname of "The Whip" from the players.

Ralph Irvin Sasse (July 19, 1889 – October 16, 1954) was an American football player, coach, college athletics administrator, and United States Army officer. He served as the head football coach at the United States Military Academy from 1930 to 1932 and at

Mississippi State College, now Mississippi State University, from 1935 to 1937, compiling a career college football record of 45–15–4.

1930 Coach Ralph Sasse

The Army Cadets football team represented the United States Military Academy in the 1930 college football season. It was their forty-first season of intercollegiate football. They were coached by Ralph Sasse in his first of three seasons as head coach of the Cadets. As an independent football entity, the Army team had a great record of 9-1-1.

The Cadets compiled an 9-1-1 record. They shut out seven of their eleven opponents, and outscored all opponents by a combined total of 268 to 22, an average of 24.4 points scored and 2.0 points allowed per game. In the annual Army–Navy Game, the Cadets defeated the Midshipmen by a 6 to 0 score. The team's only loss was by a 7 to 6 score against an undefeated national champion Notre Dame team in Rockne's final year as head coach.

<< Coach Ralph Sasse

The season opener was played on Sept 27. Ralph Sasse's Army squad began the 1930 season at home with a nice shutout victory over Boston University - - W (39-0) at Michie Stadium on the Campus of the USMA at West Point. On Oct 4, the Cadets battled for a big score shutout against Furman, W (54-0). In the third game on Oct 11, Army shut-out Swarthmore, W (39-0). On Oct 18 at Harvard's Harvard Stadium in Boston MA, the Cadets defeated the Crimson W (6-0).

On Oct 25, at the Yale Bowl in New Haven CT, Army tied Yale T (7-7). On Nov 1, Army defeated North Dakota at home W (33-6). Then on Nov 8, the Cadets defeated Illinois, W (13-0) In in a major scoring victory, the Cadets beat Kentucky Wesleyan at home W (47-2).

On Nov 22, Army shut out Ursinas at home W (18-0). At Soldier Field, Army and Notre Dame battled like there was no tomorrow. The game was almost a tie but ND pulled it off L (6-7) Army played a great game but were defeated by Knute Rockne's National Champion Fighting Irish in what was a very close tough played match. On Dec 13, at Yankee Stadium, in the Bronx, NY, the Cadets shut out the Midshipmen in a nail-biter game W (6-0).

1931 Coach Ralph Sasse

The Army Cadets football team represented the United States Military Academy in the 1931 college football season. It was their forty-second season of intercollegiate football. They were coached by Ralph Sasse in his second of three great seasons as head coach of the Cadets. As an independent football entity, the Army team had a great record of 8-2-1.

The Cadets compiled an 8-2-1 record. They shut out four of their eleven opponents, and outscored all opponents by a combined total of 296 to 72. In the annual Army–Navy Game, the Cadets defeated the Midshipmen by a 17 to 7 score. End Robert Sheridan broke his neck making a tackle in a 6 to 6 tie with Yale. The Cadets also defeated Notre Dame, 12 to 0. The team's only losses were to Harvard by a 13 to 14 score and to Pittsburgh by a 0 to 26 score.

The season home opener was played on Sept 27. Army began the 1931 season at home with a shooting shutout victory over Ohio Northern, W (60-0). As all home games, this match was played at Michie Stadium on the Campus of the USMA at West Point. On Oct 3, the Cadets battled for a big score win against Knox, W (67-6). In the third game on Oct 10, Army beat Michigan State at home, W (20-7). Then on Oct 17 Army lost in a close home battle with Harvard L (13-14).

On Oct 24, at the Yale Bowl in New Haven CT, Army tied Yale T (6-6). On Oct 31, Army shut-out Colorado College at home W (27-0). Then on Nov 7, the Cadets shut-out LSU at home W (20-0) In one of just two losses in 1931, the Cadets were shut out by Pittsburgh L (0-26). Army then defeated Ursinas at home W (54-6). After being beaten for several years in a row by Notre Dame, in this, the first year without Knute Rockne, the Army defeated Notre Dame W (12-0). On Dec 12, at Yankee Stadium, in the Bronx, NY, the Cadets shut out the Midshipmen W (17-7).

1932 Coach Ralph Sasse

The Army Cadets football team represented the United States Military Academy in the 1932 college football season. It was their forty-third season of intercollegiate football. They were coached by Ralph Sasse in his third and final season of three great seasons as head coach of the Cadets. As an independent football entity, the Army team had a great record of 8-2-0.

The Cadets compiled an 8-2-0 record. They shut out eight of their ten opponents, and outscored all opponents by a combined total of 261 to 39. In the annual Army–Navy Game, the Cadets defeated the Midshipmen by a 20 to 0 score. The Cadets also defeated Harvard, 40 to 0. The team's only losses were to Pittsburgh by an 18 to 13 score and to Notre Dame by a 21 to 0 score.

The season home opener was played on Oct 1. Army began the 1932 season at home with a shutout victory over Furman W (13-0). As all home games, this match was played at Michie Stadium on the Campus of the USMA at West Point. On Oct 8, the Cadets battled for a big shutout win against Carlton, W (57-0). In the third game on Oct 15, Army lost to Pittsburgh at home, L (13-18). Then, On Oct 22, Army shut out Yale at the Yale Bowl in New Haven CT. W (20-0).

On Oct 29, Army shut out William & Mary W (33-0). On Nov 5, Army won a big shut-out from powerhouse Harvard at Harvard Stadium in Allston MA W (46-0) Then on Nov 12, the Cadets shut-out North Dakota big-time at home W (52-0). On Nov 19, the Cadets shut out West Virginia Wesleyan W (7-0)

Notre Dame beat Army on Nov 26 at Yankee Stadium in the Bronx L (0-21) before 78,115 fans. Then, on Dec 32, at Franklin Field in Philadelphia PA, the Army Shut out the Navy W (20-0).

Sasse asks to be relieved of duty

Ralph Sasse's 1930 Cadet squad finished 9-1-1, the only loss coming to - who else? - Notre Dame. The 1931 season brought an 8-2-1 record, including a win over the Fighting Irish. However, the season was marred by the death of E Dick Sheridan in the fifth game. The tragedy deeply affected Sasse, who asked to be relieved after the 1932 season, which ended 8 up 2 down.

Chapter 9 Coaches Garrison Davidson & William Wood, 1933-1940

Davidson   Coach # 21
Wood   Coach # 22

Year	Coach	Record	Conference	Record
1933	Gar Davidson	9-1-0	Indep	9-1-0
1934	Gar Davidson	7-3-0	Indep	7-3-0
1935	Gar Davidson	6-2-1	Indep	6-2-1
1936	Gar Davidson	6-3-0	Indep	6-3-0
1937	Gar Davidson	7-2-0	Indep	7-2-0
1938	William Wood	8-2-0	Indep	8-2-0
1939	William Wood	3-4-2	Indep	3-4-2
1940	William Wood	1-7-1	Indep	1-7-1

1930-s Army Cadets Football

Garrison Hold Davidson replaces Ralph Sasse as Head Coach

Garrison Holt Davidson
Class of 1927

Hall of Fame Induction Class of 2014
Administrators / Football
l
Gar Davidson is a 1927 West Point graduate and is honored for a career that includes football accolades as a player, time spent as the head football coach and later, as Superintendent.

Davidson earned two varsity letters as a member of the football team and scored the first touchdown in Michie Stadium. He was also a part of a win and tie opposite Navy.

He was an assistant coach for the "plebe" team for two seasons, was the head coach of the "B" squad for one season and then moved on to head coach for the "plebe" team.

Davidson was the head football coach from 1933-37 and compiled a 35-11-1 mark, including a 3-2 record against Navy.

He later served as Senior Battalion Commander, was an instructor in the West Point Physics Department and worked for Leslie Groves building the Pentagon.

Davidson was selected by George Patton to be Deputy Engineer for Western Task Force Invasion of North Africa. He served as Seventh Army Engineer for the Sicilian Campaign, was an Assistant Division Command of the 24th Infantry and Commandant of the Command and General Staff College.

Davidson returned to West Point as the Superintendent from 1956-60 and retired in 1964 as a lieutenant general.

1933 Coach Gar Davidson

The Army Cadets football team represented the United States Military Academy in the 1933 college football season. It was their forty-fourth season of intercollegiate football. They were coached by Gar Davidson in his first of five fine seasons as head coach of the Cadets. As an independent football entity, the Army team had a great record of 9-1-0.

<< Coach GAR Davidson

The Cadets compiled a 9-1-0 record. They shut out seven of their ten opponents, and outscored all opponents by a combined total of 227 to 26. In the annual Army–Navy Game, the Cadets defeated the Midshipmen by a 12 to 7 score. In the final game of the season, the Cadets lost to Notre Dame by a 13 to 12. But for the one-point difference in this one game, Army would have been undefeated and untied in 1933

The season home opener was played on Sept 30. Army began the 1933 season at home with a victory over Mercer W (19-6). As all home games, this opening match was played at Michie Stadium on the Campus of the USMA at West Point. On Oct 7, the Cadets battled for a shutout win against VNI W (33-0). In the third game on Oct 14, Army shellacked Delaware in a shutout victory at home, W 52-0). Then, On Oct 21, Army shut out Illinois in a close game at Cleveland Ohio W (6-0).

On Oct 28, at the Yale Bowl in New Haven CT, the Cadets shut out the Bulldogs W (21-0). On Nov 4, Army won a big shut-out from

Coe at home W (34-0). Then on Nov 11, the Cadets shut-out
Harvard at Harvard Stadium in Allston MA, W (27-0). On Nov 18,
Army shut out the Pennsylvania Military College W (12-0)

In the big games of the year, operating with an undefeated and untied
record, next up was Navy in the Army-Navy Game. Then, on Nov
25, at Franklin Field in Philadelphia PA, the Army defeated the
Navy in a close match W (12-13). The next opponent on Dec 2was a
major rival and a spoiler--Notre Dame coached by Hartley Hunk
Anderson. Army was undefeated and untied and it was the last game
of the season. A win would mean a perfect record. The Irish beat the
Cadets on Dec 2 at Yankee Stadium in the Bronx by one point, L
(12-13) before 73,594 fans. It was a year that almost was.
Nonetheless it was a great year for Army.

1934 Coach Gar Davidson

The Army Cadets football team represented the United States
Military Academy in the 1934 college football season. It was their
forty-fifth season of intercollegiate football. They were coached by
Gar Davidson in his second of five seasons as head coach of the
Cadets. As an independent football entity, the Army team had a nice
record of 7-3-0.

The Cadets compiled a 7-3-0 record. They shut out five of their ten
opponents, and outscored all opponents by a combined total of 215
to 40. In the annual Army–Navy Game, the Cadets lost to the
Midshipmen by a 3 to 0 score. The Cadets also lost to Notre Dame
by a 12 to 6 score and to Illinois by a 7 to 0 score.

The Cadets opened the home season on Sept 29. Army began the
1934 season at home with a shutout victory over Washburn W (19-
0). As all home games, this opening match was played at Michie
Stadium on the Campus of the USMA at West Point. On Oct 6, the
Cadets commandeered a shutout win against Davidson W (41-0). In
the third game on Oct 13, Army shellacked Drake in a shutout
victory at home, W 48-0). On Oct 27, at the Yale Bowl in New
Haven CT, the Cadets defeated the Bulldogs W (20-12).

Then, On Nov 3, Army was shut out by Illinois at Memorial Stadium in Champaign, Illinois L (0-7) On Nov 10, at Harvard Stadium in Allston, MA, the Cadets beat the Harvard Crimson W (27-6). Then on Nov 17, at home, the Cadets shut-out the Citadel W (34-0).

Then, on Nov 24, at Yankee Stadium, in the Bronx, NY, Notre Dame Squeaked out a victory over Army L (6-12) before 73,594 fans. On Dec 1 in the Army-Navy Game, played at Franklin Field, Philadelphia, PA, the Midshipmen shut out the Cadets by a field goal L (0-3)

1935 Coach Gar Davidson

The Army Cadets football team represented the United States Military Academy in the 1935 college football season. It was their forty-sixth season of intercollegiate football. They were coached by Garrison H. Davidson in his third of five seasons as head coach of the Cadets. As an independent football entity, the Army team had a nice record of 6-2-1.

The Cadets compiled a 6-2-1 record. They shut out four of their nine opponents, and outscored all opponents by a combined total of 176 to 62. In the annual Army–Navy Game, the Cadets defeated the Midshipmen by a 28 to 6 score. The Cadets' two losses came against Mississippi State and Pitt. They played Notre Dame to a 6-6 tie.

Two Army players were recognized on the 1935 College Football All-America Team. End William R. Shuler received first-team honors from the Associated Press (AP). Halfback Charles R. Meyer received second-team honors from the United Press(UP) and North American Newspaper Alliance.

All Army home games that were not designated to be played on a neutral field--such as Soldier Field in Chicago, Yankee Stadium in the Bronx, or Franklin Field in Philadelphia, were played at Michie Stadium on the campus of the US Military Academy in West Point, New York.

The Army Home opener was on Oct 5. Army began the 1934 season at home with a low-scoring shutout victory over William & Mary W

(14-0). As all home games, this opening match was played at Michie Stadium on the Campus of the USMA at West Point.

On Oct 12, the Cadets overpowered Gettysburg for a high-scoring shutout victory W (54-0). In the third game on Oct 19, Army shut out Harvard at home W (13-0). On Oct 26, at the Yale Bowl in New Haven CT, the Cadets defeated the Bulldogs W (14-8).

Then, On Nov 2, Army was defeated at home by Mississippi State L (7-13). Then, On Nov 9 at Pitt Stadium, the Cadets were defeated by the Pittsburgh Panthers L (6-29). Then, on Nov 16, at Yankee Stadium, in the Bronx, NY, Notre Dame tied Army T (6-6) before 78114. On Nov 23 at home, Army shut-out Vermont W (34-0) Then in the season finale, on Nov 30 at Franklin Field in Philadelphia, in the annual Army-Navy Game, the Cadets defeated the Midshipmen W (28-6)

1936 Coach Gar Davidson

The Army Cadets football team represented the United States Military Academy in the 1936 college football season. It was their forty-seventh season of intercollegiate football. They were coached by Garrison H. Davidson in his fourth of five seasons as head coach of the Cadets. As an independent football entity, the Army team had a record of 6-3-0.

The Cadets compiled a 6-3-0 record. They shut out their opponents in three of nine games and outscored their opponents by a combined total of 238 to 71. In the annual Army–Navy Game, the Cadets lost to the Midshipmen by a 7 to 0 score. The Cadets' other two losses came against Colgate and Notre Dame.

Army opened at home on Oct 3 with a shutout victory over Washington & Lee W (28-0)). As all home games, this opening match was played at Michie Stadium on the Campus of the USMA at West Point. On Oct 10, at Baker Field in New Your, NY, Army defeated Columbia W (27-16). In the third game on Oct 17, at Harvard stadium in Allston, MA, Army shut out Harvard at W (32-0). On Oct 24, Army shut-out Springfield (MA) at home W (33-0)

On Oct 31, Army lost to Colgate at home L (7-14). Then, On Nov 7, Army dominated Muhlenberg at home W (54-7). On Nov 14, at Yankee Stadium in the Bronx, the Cadets were defeated by the Fighting Irish of Notre Dame L (6-20) before 74,423. Then, on Nov 21 Army overpowered Hobart at home W (51-7). Then came the Army-Navy-Game on Nov 28. This game was played at Municipal Stadium in Philadelphia. The Midshipmen defeated the Cadets L (0-7)

1937 Coach Gar Davidson

The Army Cadets football team represented the United States Military Academy in the 1937 college football season. It was their forty-eighth season of intercollegiate football. They were coached by Garrison H. Davidson in his fifth and last of five seasons as head coach of the Cadets. As an independent football entity, the Army team had a record of 7-2-0.

The Cadets compiled a 7-2-0 record. They had five games in which the defense gave up just one touchdown and of course they pitched a shutout in the Army-Navy game. Other than that, there were no shutouts. Army was terrific on offense and outscored their opponents by a combined total of 176 to 72. In the annual Army–Navy-Game, the Cadets defeated the Midshipmen by a 6 to 0 score. The Cadets' two losses came against Yale and Notre Dame.

On Oct 2, Army opened at home with a W (21-6) victory over Clemson. As all home games, this season opener was played at Michie Stadium on the Campus of the USMA at West Point. On Oct 9 at home, Army defeated Columbia in a close match W (21-18). In the third game on Oct 16, at the Yale Bowl in New Haven, CT, Army was defeated by Yale L (7-17) in a close match. On Oct 23, Army bested Washington (MO) big-time by a score of W (47-7). On Oct 30, Army defeated a tough Virginia Military Academy (VMI) at home W (20-7).

On Nov 6, at Harvard Stadium in Allston, MA, the Cadets defeated the Crimson W 7-6. On Nov 18, at Yankee Stadium in the Bronx, the Cadets were shut out in a tight game by the Fighting Irish of Notre Dame L (0-7) before 76,359 fans. On Nov 27 in the Army-

Navy-Game, played at Municipal Stadium in Philadelphia. The Cadets shut out the Midshipmen W (6-0)

1938 Coach Gar Davidson

The Army Cadets football team represented the United States Military Academy in the 1938 college football season. It was their forty-ninth season of intercollegiate football. They were coached by William Wood in his second of three seasons as head coach of the Cadets. As an independent football entity, the Army team had a record of 8-2-0.

The Cadets compiled an 8-2-0 record. They shut out three of ten opponents and outscored their opponents by a combined total of 243 to 95. In the annual Army–Navy Game, the Cadets defeated the Midshipmen by a 14 to 7 score. The Cadets' two losses came against Columbia and Notre Dame.

On Sept 24, Army got its season rolling at home with a shutout win W (32-0) victory over Wichita. As all home games, this season opener was played at Michie Stadium on the Campus of the USMA at West Point. On Oct 1 at home, Army defeated VPI in a shutout / blowout W (39-0) In the third game on Oct 8 at home, Army was beaten in a close match by Columbia L (18-20). On Oct 15, at Harvard Stadium in Allston, MA, the Cadets defeated the Crimson W (20-17)

On Oct 22, at home v Boston University, the Cadets shut out the Terriers W (40-0). On Oct 29, at Yankee Stadium in the Bronx, the Cadets were defeated in a tough fought game by the Fighting Irish of Notre Dame L (7-19) before 76,338 fans. On Nov 5 Army defeated a tough Franklin & Marshall team at home W (20-12). The Next team to take on the Army was Chattanooga who were defeated at Michie Stadium W (34-13). The Cadets then defeated Princeton W (19-7) on Nov 19. This all lead to the season finale – The Army-Navy-Game in Municipal Stadium in Philadelphia PA in which Army defeated Navy W (14-7)

1939 Coach William Wood

<< Coach William Wood

The Army Cadets football team represented the United States Military Academy in the 1939 college football season. It was their fiftieth season of intercollegiate football. They were coached by William Wood in his second of three seasons as head coach of the Cadets. As an independent football entity, the Army team had a record of 3-4-2.

The Cadets compiled a 3-4-2 record. They outscored their opponents by a combined total of 106 to 105 – just one point—very unusual for Army. In the annual Army–Navy Game, the Cadets lost to the Midshipmen by a 10 to 0 score. The Cadets' three other losses came against Yale, Notre Dame, and Harvard. It was a poor year overall for Army.

It was not a great offensive or defensive season for the Army Cadets. This was a truly unusual season but it would set the stage for a worse season the following year and it would make all Army fans clamor for two years from now when the immortal Red Blaik came to town on the coaching side.

On Sept 30, Army got off to a winning start in its season opener against Furman, W (16-7). As all home games, this season opener was played at Michie Stadium on the Campus of the USMA at West Point. On Oct 7 at home, Army defeated Centre in a close match W (9-0) In the third game on Oct 14 at Columbia's Baker Field in New York, the Cadets and the Lions played to a tie T (6-6). Then, on Oct 21, at the Yale Bowl in New Haven CT, the Bulldogs defeated the Cadets L (15-30).

On Oct 22, at home v Ursinas, the Cadets defeated the Bears W (46-13). The really tough teams were next to be played. On Oct 29, at Yankee Stadium in the Bronx, the Cadets were shut out in a tough game by the Fighting Irish of Notre Dame L (0-14) before 75,632 fans.

On Nov 11 Army was shut out by a tough Harvard squad at Harvard's Stadium in Allston, MA. L (0-15). On Nov 18, just before the Army Navy game, the Cadets and the Penn State Nittany Lions played at Michie Stadium to a tie T (14-14). This all lead to the season finale – The Army-Navy-Game in Municipal Stadium in Philadelphia PA in which Navy's Midshipmen shut out Army's Cadets L (0-10).

1940 Coach William Wood

The Army Cadets football team represented the United States Military Academy in the 1940 college football season. It was their fifty-first season of intercollegiate football. They were coached by William Wood in his third and final year of three seasons as head coach of the Cadets. As an independent football entity, the Army team had a record of 1-7-1, which is one of the team's all-time worst records. This would-be Wood's last year as coach before Red Blaik saved the day.

Was it Wood's fault?

Nobody from what I have researched faults William Wood for this poor year or the last poor year. Neither do they overly credit him for the fine first year he had with an 8-2-0 record. After all, in a day when colleges were hiring full-time professionals, Army had been making do with part-timers whose full-time role was being a commissioned officer. Such was the case with Coach William Wood.

The game was quickly changing from football to war at the US Military Academy when the big war was brewing in Europe. After having secured the neutrality of the Soviet Union (through the August 1939 German-Soviet Pact of nonaggression), we may all remember from our history books that Germany started World War II by invading Poland on September 1, Britain and France responded by declaring on Germany on September 3. This was the beginning of World War II

The US spent a lot of time from 1920 to 1941 analyzing its involvement in World War I. In the years after World War I many Americans quickly reached the conclusion that their country's participation in that war had been a disastrous mistake, one which should never be repeated again. During the 1920s and 1930s, therefore, the US pursued a number of strategies aimed at preventing war. In this end over time, a number of Neutrality acts had been passed to help prevent the US from engaging in such a horrific entanglement ever again.

When Hitler's Germany began the war in 1939 war with Germany on the one hand, and Britain and France on the other, President Franklin D. Roosevelt dutifully went back to American law and he invoked the Neutrality Acts. However, in his heart, Roosevelt believed this was a fundamentally different war from World War I.

Germany, he believed (and most Americans agreed with him) was in this case a clear aggressor. Without sending troops into battle, Roosevelt therefore sought to provide assistance for the Allies. He was not prepared to have the US enter the war. He began by asking Congress to change the neutrality laws so that the US could make arms sales to the Allies. Later on, after German forces overran France, the president asked Congress for a massive program of direct military aid to Great Britain—an initiative that Roosevelt dubbed "Lend-Lease." In both cases the legislature agreed to FDR's proposals, but only after intense debate.

How involved should the US become? After all, we had an ocean separating us from the war. This issue of involvement in the "European war" deeply divided America for over two years.

On the one hand, Roosevelt and the so-called "internationalists" claimed that a program of aid to Great Britain and other countries fighting against Germany would make actual U.S. participation in the war unnecessary. On the other hand, there were those, who were called "isolationists," who wanted nothing to with foreign entanglements of war. They believed that the president's policies were making it increasingly likely that the country would wind up in another disastrous foreign war—just like World War I. The fear of such a war was real for sure as only twenty-years had passed.

As 1939 turned into 1940 and then 1940 turned into 1941, and as 1942 was approaching, the US debate on the war continued until some other country, namely Japan "woke up a sleeping giant." This debate was still raging when Japanese aircraft attacked Pearl Harbor on December 7, 1941. At this point it was clear that, like it or not, the United States would be a full participant in the Second World War.

From the first inkling of war, especially from 1939 onwards, as important as football was for the service academies, protecting the US from aggression was a much more important mission. It affected everything and football was not an exception.

However, the US Army football team being successful had some bearing on the pride of the US Army servicemen. And, so after not paying much attention to coaching for so many years, the Army Brass knew that for the sake of the Army and the Country and for Army Football, they had to change their coaching philosophy.

After William Wood showed the Brass how bad a football team can get when it is not a priority, the Brass knew things had to change big-time. Luckily, Red Blaik was in the Army coaching pipeline as a former Cadet gridiron star.

Until Blaik was appointed coach in 1941, as noted, the teams of the Army's United States Military Academy at West Point usually had been coached for a tour of duty by a career officer for four years or less at a time. The officer, was assigned to the team in much the same manner as he might be posted to Fort Leonard Wood as supply officer.

But when Blaik was lured from Dartmouth, he came with his own set of rules, and Army Brass were mostly happy to play by them. For the first time, a coach was permitted to hire a professional staff and was automatically bestowed the rank of full colonel. He was also appointed athletic director, and systemized recruiting began at Army. The USMA had entered the era of big-time college football.

There are those of us Army fans who think that the same hard look at Army's football prowess needs to be reexamined today. It seems that Army is well on its way with a great 2016 and more to come in 2017. Can Jeff Monken be the new Red Blaik. Many of us on the fan line sure hope so.

Did hiring Red Blaik work? You bet it did. Hold on to your hats as after we purge this last bad chapter of early Army football from our innards, we get to be entertained through one of the finest periods of football in any American College. The United States Military Academy in the Red Blaik years made itself well known. Hold on… we'll be there soon. Let's look a little more at the scenario into which Red Blaik found himself before we finish this season.

War and Remembrances from Army-Navy Series

December 08, 1991 | By Robert Markus, Chicago Tribune.

The following includes excerpts from this great article from 1991 about what it was like to play football and be at war.

According to retired Col. Morris Herbert, head of the academy's association of graduates, of the 19 players on the Army team in a particular 1941 game (Army-Navy) that we will cover in the next chapter, six would become general officers; five would be killed in action.

Murphy, who retired a two-star general and now lives in Colorado Springs, remembers the main topic of conversation at West Point that winter-how quickly their training would be accelerated.

In previous wars, they knew, the four-year curriculum had been truncated by as much as two years. Murphy, it turned out, graduated on schedule that May. Succeeding classes were put on a three-year cycle for their diplomas.

As for the Army-Navy game itself, that 1941 game was the last in Philadelphia until after the war. It marked the debut of Army graduate Earl Blaik as coach, but that wouldn't be enough to keep Navy from scoring a 14-6 victory.

In time, Blaik would lead Army to incredible heights of glory. He had come to Army after a 45-0 loss to Cornell followed by a 48-0 defeat to Columbia convinced academy officials they needed a professional coach.

Until then, recounts Col. Morris, "They always had part-time coaches. The guy who coached from 1938-1940, Bill Wood, was a cavalry captain who would come back to the Point each fall to coach the team."

When Blaik arrived for his first spring practice, the story goes, he was in the midst of telling his squad that most football games are lost because of poor line play.

Seeing one player who appeared to be half asleep, Blaik barked out:

``Mister, where are most football games lost?``

``Right here at West Point, sir,`` came the answer.

Morris, who at 14 had seen his first Army-Navy game that year, explains why the game was moved from Philadelphia.

``They were afraid that having both cadet corps in one stadium at one time would be too inviting a target,`` he said.

``So in 1942, the game was at Annapolis. The cadet corps did not go to the game, so half of the midshipmen were ordered to root for Army. They sang the Army songs and cheered the Army cheers, though I doubt their hearts were in it.

``The next year the game was at the Point, and half the corps had to cheer for Navy.``

The 1940 Season with Coach Wood

The Cadets compiled a 1-7-1 record. They were outscored by their opponents by a combined total of 197 to 54. It was the first season since 1899 in which an Army football team had been outscored by its opponents. In the annual Army–Navy Game, the Cadets lost to the Midshipmen by a 14 to 0 score. The Cadets also suffered blowout defeats to Cornell (45-0) and Penn (48-0). It was a very poor year overall for Army.

No Army players were honored on the 1940 College Football All-America Team. Three weeks after the end of the 1940 season, the War Department ordered coach Wood back to active troop duty and named Earl Blaik as head coach for the 1941 season. The War Department had been paying attention to the football success of the Cadets. Though the Draft was in play, it was not a good recruiting tool to have an inept football team and so Army took the proper corrective action. Nobody really knew how great the team would become.

On Oct 5, Army got a look at just how poor this season would be as they played Williams and barely beat this 3rd level team (Division III of today). W (20-19). Williams should have won the game.
As all home games, this season opener was played at Michie Stadium on the Campus of the USMA at West Point. This October 5 game was the first and it would be the last win of the season for the Cadets. Without laboring over all the losses and ties, we'll simply list the games from this year which we soon hope to forget completely. Though there were some bright spots, such as the close game v #2 Notre Dame L (0-7) there were not many

October 5   Williams, Michie, W (20-19
October 12   Cornell, Michie L (0–45)
October 19   Harvard, Harvard Stadium in Allston, MA T (6–6)
October 26   Lafayette, Michie, L (0–19)
November 2 Notre Dame Yankee Stadium, Bronx, NY L 0–7
November 9 Brown, Michie, L 9–13
November 16 Penn, Franklin Field, Philadelphia, PAL (0–48)
November 23 Princeton, Palmer Stadium • Princeton, NJ L (19–26)
November 30 Navy, Municipal Stadium • Philadelphia, PA L (0–14)

Chapter 12 Coach Red Blaik 1941 - 1958

Blaik   Coach # 23

Year	Coach	Record	Conference	Record
1941	Red Blaik	5-3-1	Indep	5-3-1
1942	Red Blaik	6-3-1	Indep	6-3-1
1943	Red Blaik	7-2-1	Indep	7-2-1
1944	Red Blaik	9-0-0	Indep	9-0-0
1945	Red Blaik	9-0-0	Indep	9-0-0
1946	Red Blaik	9-0-1	Indep	9-0-1
1947	Red Blaik	5-2-2	Indep	5-2-2
1948	Red Blaik	8-0-1	Indep	8-0-1
1949	Red Blaik	9-0-0	Indep	9-0-0
1950	Red Blaik	8-1-0	Indep	8-1-0
1951	Red Blaik	2-7-0	Indep	2-7-0
1952	Red Blaik	4-4-1	Indep	4-4-1
1953	Red Blaik	7-1-1	Indep	7-1-1
1954	Red Blaik	7-2-0	Indep	7-2-0
1955	Red Blaik	6-3-0	Indep	6-3-0
1956	Red Blaik	5-3-1	Indep	5-3-1
1957	Red Blaik	7-2-0	Indep	7-2-0
1958	Red Blaik	8-0-1	Indep	8-0-1

Coach Red Blaik with offensive stars Doc Blanchard and Glenn Davis

Earl "Red" Blaik was everything Americans would expect a graduate of the United States Military Academy to be: an officer, a gentleman, and a winner: as West Point's head football coach from 1941 through 1958, he was one of the best coaches ever.

In his 18 years at West Point, he coached two national champions (most credit Army with three national championships—a tie with ND in 1946) and six unbeaten teams. Even more important than his 166 wins, though, was the example of leadership he provided at a place where leadership is prized.

In the mid-1940s, coincidental with the arrival of Red Blaik, Army football became one of college football's greatest dynasties. It was a tumultuous time for America, amid World War II, and college football had been shaken up like every other part of life. Some schools stopped playing. The great basketball powerhouse, Gonzaga, for example, had a nice football program going into World War II.

Like many colleges, their football program went on hiatus during World War II (in April 1942). After the war, the administration decided not to resume it. The program had been in some financial difficulty prior to the war and it seemed like a good idea at the time to forego the sport at Gonzaga.

There were more and more young men heading to combat and other roles to support the war effort. Many top players flocked to military training centers before heading overseas. And, of course, many great players chose to come to West Point. Army football had been strong before and after World War I under great coaches such as Charles Daly and Biff Jones. Army football had a storied rivalry with Notre Dame dating back to 1913 when Rockne and Dorais played for the Irish.

But in the post Rockne era, something happened to Army. From 1932-43, Army failed to beat Notre Dame, managing only two ties. That soon changed under the tutelage of Blaik. Football was maturing as an American sport and strategies were ever so much more important to have successful seasons.

Blaik was already an accomplished football master when he came to Army. It was not an easy decision for him. As a West Point grad, he made a difficult decision to leave Dartmouth, where he had gone 45-15-4 in seven seasons, finishing seventh in the AP poll in 1937. After three solid seasons back at West Point, Blaik's Black Knights went 27-0-1 from 1944-46. It was unexpected and wonderful. Army was beating everybody during the war including the Germans and the Japanese.

Army became undisputed national champions the first two years. In 1944, they didn't allow more than a TD in a game and beat Notre Dame 59-0 and Navy 23-7. In 1945, Army beat then-No. 2 Notre Dame 48-0 and then the Cadets whooped #2 Navy 32-13. In '46, Notre Dame had one of the most talented teams ever, with the war over, and the two battled to a 0-0 tie. The Fighting Irish were voted to be the # 1 college team in the final AP poll when Army barely hung on for a 21-18 win over 1-8 Navy.

Army had a 9-0-1 Army and were recognized by the CFB Research Group as champions and by the Helms group for a tie with Notre

Dame. Notre dame's record was 8-0-1 and their support by AP gave the Irish the consensus championship but many consider Notre Army as having a share of the gold that year. ND backers included the National Championship Foundation, AP Poll, Helms (tie).

The below photo shows some action in what is now referred to as the 1946 championship of ND V Army. Let's examine it briefly

This opportune photo above is considered by the football scholars and pundits as the defining play of 1946's "Game of the Century." In this play as you can see clearly in the photo, Notre Dame's Bill Gompers turned the corner on 4th down and headed for Army's goal line. But alas, he did not make it. In fact, he did not even reach the 2-yard line for a first down. In this game, there were no other serious scoring threats, and so this "Game of the Century," ended in a 0-0 stalemate.

Yes it was 1946 and it had been a little more than a year since the war had ended. Army had two in a row and ND had their best team, perhaps ever... Nonetheless, without cell phones or TV and a 24-hour news cycle, somehow everybody in the country knew this game was coming. Many have said that never before had a game been hyped as much as this meeting of #1 Army and #2 Notre Dame. Other games had been called "Game of the Century" in the past, but this was the first to be widely described as such by the press nationwide before the game.

Army had been kicked around by ND for years and now with two in a row under their belts, Army was confident that it could beat ND a third time. Hey, the Army Cadets were the 2-time defending national champion. They came into the game with a 25-game winning streak. They had whooped Notre Dame 59-0 and 48-0 the previous 2 years. But it was a different ND team this particular year. Frank Leahy, ND's coach, other coaches, and a number of players were now back from the war, and when last this group of were on campus, Notre Dame had beaten Army and had won the 1943 mythical national championship (MNC).

This game had the top greats from the period playing together on the same field. The game featured 3 Heisman Trophy winners, 3 Outland Trophy winners, and 10 Hall of Famers, not counting the Hall of Fame coaches on each side. Notre Dame claims MNCs for 1943, 1946, 1947, and 1949, and Army claims MNCs for 1944, 1945, and 1946. This was a true clash of the titans, an intersection of 2 of the greatest runs in college football history: Army going 27-0-1 1944-1946 and Notre Dame going 36-0-2 1946-1949.

Army kept its spot at #1 after the scoreless tie, but when they struggled to beat 1-8 Navy 21-18 in their final game, Notre Dame passed them up for the #1 ranking in the final AP poll. Above the picture, we showed how all of the organizations listed in the NCAA Records Book see the 1946 mythical national championship (omitting math/computer ratings, which are not generally accepted as MNCs). Both ND and Army have a right to their claims for a national championship. Since there were no official agencies like we have today, most consider that ND and Army shared the 1946 Mythical National Championship.

Army's three-year peak was nearly unmatchable, with Heisman winners Doc Blanchard and Glenn Davis sharing the backfield, but it wasn't the end of Blaik's success. While Notre Dame was getting tougher and tougher with Frank Leahy back in football action, Army was doing well with Red Blaik but ND's 36-0-2 record to 1949 was also unmatched.

With Blaik as the master, and a strict disciplinarian, nobody expected what happened to Army. An academic cheating scandal in 1951 ripped apart Blaik's team. Blaik's son was part of the scandal and he was forced to leave the Academy. Blaik persevered and after just a couple down years, including Blaiks's only losing season of 18, Army football bounced back.

Red Blaik ended his career on a high note in 1958, coaching an 8-0-1 team that finished third in the AP poll and featured Heisman winner Pete Dawkins, making it the last national powerhouse West Point football team.

In his career, Earl "Red" Blaik coached three Heisman winners and eight top-10 teams at Army, with two undisputed national championships and claims to share the '46 title as well. To enhance his legacy, Blaik produced an astounding coaching tree, headlined by five-year assistant Vince Lombardi. Now, we get to look at the action in those eighteen years, so hold on folks, we're just a few text lines away. Enjoy!

1941 Coach Red Blaik

The Army Cadets football team represented the United States Military Academy in the 1941 college football season. It was their fifty-second season of intercollegiate football. They were coached by Earl "Red" Blaik in his first of eighteen seasons as head coach of the Cadets. As an independent football entity, the Army team had a record of 5-3-1.

The Cadets compiled a 5-3-1 record. They outscored their opponents by a combined total of 105 to 87. The season represented a four-game improvement on the prior year's record of 1-7-1. In the annual Army–Navy Game, the Cadets lost to the Midshipmen by a 14 to 6 score. The Cadets also lost to Harvard and Penn and played Notre Dame to a scoreless tie.

Army halfback Hank Mazur was selected by Life magazine as a third-team player on the 1941 College Football All-America Team.

<< Coach Blaik

Gen. Douglas MacArthur in background pic.

On Oct 4, Army got off to a winning start in its season opener against The Citadel, W (19-6) It had been a whole season since Army had won its last game. All home games, just like this season opener were played at Michie Stadium on the Campus of the USMA at West Point. On Oct11 at home, Army defeated VMI in a close match at home, W (27-20). In the third game on Oct 18 at the Yale Bowl in New Haven, CT, Cadets beat the Bulldogs W (20-7). Then, on Oct 25, at the Yale Bowl in New Haven CT, the Bulldogs defeated the Cadets L (15-30). On Oct 25, at home, the Cadets shut out Columbia W (13-0).

Army was 4-0 with a great start when the meat of their schedule came up beginning on Nov 1 at Yankee Stadium in the Bronx, NY v the #6 ranked Fighting Irish of Notre Dame before 75,226 fans, the Cadets played ND to a scoreless tie T (0-0) showing that this Blaik-coached team had a lot of mettle.

The first loss did not come until Nov 8 when the Cadets went to Massachusetts to Harvard Stadium to play the Crimson and they were set back by a score of L (6-20). On Nov 15 Army got its second loss against a tough Penn at Franklin Field in Philadelphia PA L (7-14)

On Nov 26, Army got its moxie back when it beat a tough West Virginia team at home W (7-6) in a nail-biter. All of this lead to the most important game of the year for Army—its season finale – The Army-Navy-Game played in Municipal Stadium in Philadelphia PA. Navy's Midshipmen outgunned Army in this close match L (6-14).

Army had recovered and Army fans could expect about seventeen more great years before it had to worry about consistently winning again.

1942 Coach Red Blaik

The Army Cadets football team represented the United States Military Academy in the 1942 college football season. It was their fifty-third season of intercollegiate football. They were coached by Earl "Red" Blaik in his second of eighteen seasons as head coach of the Cadets. As an independent football entity, the Army team had a record of 6-3-1.

The Cadets compiled a 6-3-1 record.

After a long drought, Army again began pitching shutouts. This year there were two with more to come in future years. Army was back in control on offense and defense. They outscored their opponents by a combined total of 149 to 74. In the annual Army–Navy Game, the Cadets were shut out by the Midshipmen by a 14 to 0 score. The Cadets also lost to Penn and Notre Dame. Soon Army will be winning against all schools—big and small.

Army had a great team as reflected by the honors received. Four Army players were honored on the 1942 College Football All-America Team. Tackle Robin Olds was selected as a first-team player by Grantland Rice for Collier's Weekly. Tackle Francis E. Merritt was selected as a second-team player by both the Central Press Association (CP) and the Newspaper Enterprise Association (NEA) and was later inducted into the College Football Hall of Fame. Halfback Henry Mazur was selected as a second-team player by the

International News Service (INS). End James Kelleher was selected as a third-team player by the Sporting News and NEA.

On Oct 4, Army got off to a winning start in its season opener against Lafayette with a shutout W (14-0). All home games, were played at Michie Stadium on the Campus of the USMA at West Point. On Oct 10 at home, Army defeated Cornell W (28-8) and then traveled the short distance the following week to Baker Field in New York, NY to defeat Columbia W (34-6).

On Oct 24, at Harvard Stadium in Allston MA, Army Shut out the Crimson W (14-0). Next, on Oct 31 at Franklin Field in Philadelphia, the Cadets were shut out by the Penn Quakers L (0-19). Then, on Nov 7, the big rival Notre Dame Fighting Irish came to Yankee Stadium in the Bronx, NY and shut out the Cadets L (0-13).

On Nov 14, at home the Cadets defeated VPI W (19-7). Then feeling pretty good about themselves, Army crushed Princeton W (40-7 at Yankee Stadium. In the game that always counts, the Cadets came up short again against Navy at Thompson Stadium in Annapolis. Because the Army Brass did not want both service academies in the same stadium, Navy attended the game but Army did not. Half of the Navy guys learned the Army fight songs and took the places of their comrades in the other branch. The Cadets lost the game by a shutout despite all those fine Navy cheers, L (0-14)   i

The Cadets played VMI in a close match at home, W (27-20). In the third game on Oct 18 at the Yale Bowl in New Haven, CT, Cadets beat the Bulldogs W (20-7). Then, on Oct 25, at the Yale Bowl in New Haven CT, the Bulldogs defeated the Cadets L (15-30). On Oct 25, at home, the Cadets shut out Columbia W (13-0).

Army had more than recovered and Army fans had an air of confidence about each season and each game in each season forward.

1943 Coach Red Blaik

The Army Cadets football team represented the United States Military Academy in the 1943 college football season. It was their fifty-fourth season of intercollegiate football. They were coached by

Earl "Red" Blaik in his third of eighteen seasons as head coach of the Cadets. As an independent football entity, the Army team had a record of 7-2-1. Army had begun to win the big ones. This year, the Cadets were the #11 ranked team in the country. Not bad so close to being rock bottom. Wait until 1944 for some real National Level fireworks!

The Cadets compiled a 7-2-1 record. Firing shutouts right and left, the Cadets shut out five of their ten opponents, and outscored all opponents by a combined total of 299 to 66. Wow! In the annual Army–Navy Game, the Cadets lost to the Midshipmen by a 13 to 0 score. The Cadets also lost to Notre Dame by a 26 to 0 score, but won convincing victories over Colgate(42-0), Temple (51-0), Columbia (52-0), and Brown (59-0). The fans and alums were most upset by the Navy losses but had confidence that it would end soon. It did.

As noted but worth repeating, after a long drought with two shutouts last year, Army had again begun to pitch shutouts. This year there were five with many more to come in future years. Army was back in the saddle on both offense and defense. Soon it would show even more so.

Army kicked off its 1943 season On Sept 25 with a nice shutout win at home against Villanova W (27-0) All Army home games, were played at Michie Stadium on the Campus of the USMA at West Point. On Oct 2 at home, Army shut out Colgate, W (42-0) and then invited Temple who traveled the short distance from Philadelphia to Michie the following week on Oct 9 to be shellacked W (51-0) by the Cadets. The following week at Baker Field in New York, the Cadets walloped Columbia W (52-0).

On Oct 23, at the Yale Bowl in New Haven CT, the #2 ranked Cadets whooped the Yale Bulldogs W (39-7). Moving to the big Franklin Field, #2 Army tied #6 Penn T (13-13) Harvard Stadium in Allston MA, Army Shut out the Crimson W (14-0). Next, on Oct 31 at Franklin Field in Philadelphia, the Cadets were shut out by the Penn Quakers L (0-19). Then, on Nov 7, the big rival Notre Dame Fighting Irish came to Yankee Stadium in the Bronx, NY and shut out the Cadets L (0-13).

Frank Leahy's #1 ranked Notre Dame team of 1943 had been buzzing around the country picking off all opponents like they had not brought a defense. On Nov 16, Notre Dame showed up at Michie Field in full regalia, ready for a big win against their nemesis Army. Red Blaik was still fine tuning the Cadets and though they played very well against the Irish. It was not good enough as ND went home with the W but for Army it was L (0-26). Yankee Stadium was alive with excitement as 75,121 fans cheered Army and Notre Dame for a great game.

The United States Air Force was not an entity in 1943 but it was on its way. It was created on September 18, 1947, and its academy became the best training ground for pilots and navigators and other Air-personnel in the world, representing of course, the United States of America

So, when I saw that on Nov 13 this fine football season, that Army had played USNTS Sampson, I figured it was an Air Force operation to-be. They were tough enough to field a football team of their own good enough to take on Red Blaik's soon to-be National Champions. Army had a tough time with these upstarts but pulled out the win for Blaik at Michie on Nov 13, W (16-7). On Nov 20, Brown came to Michie to get in a good game but got a lot more. They got thumped / shut out by an enlivened Army corps who enjoyed the W (59-0) shootout.

Despite all the good Army play this year, Navy was still a formidable opponent in its baddest of years. This was not one of those. Playing for the first time at Michie Stadium with the Army contingent doing the Navy cheers and the Navy service absent from the game completely, Navy must have loved the sweet Army voices and were invigorated to win the game by shutout v Army L (0-14) Good day for Navy! Bad day for Army! But wait 'til next year!!!!!

1944 Coach Red Blaik

The Army Cadets football team represented the United States Military Academy in the 1944 college football season. It was their fifty-fifth season of intercollegiate football. They were coached by Earl "Red" Blaik in his fourth of eighteen seasons as head coach of the Cadets. As an independent football entity, the Army team had a perfect record of 9-0-0. Army had learned to win the big ones.

This year, they won everything big to small to all things in-between. This year, the Cadets were the #1 ranked team in the nation Not bad for a team that four years prior was at the bottom. This year, thanks to the Brass's faith in Red Blaik, the Army celebrated with some live National Level fireworks with a consensus National Championship.

The Cadets compiled a 9-0-0 perfect record. Firing shutouts right and left, the Cadets shut out four of their ten opponents, and outscored their opponents 504 points to 35 points. At the season's end, the team won a national championship. The team captain was Tom Lombardo. Showing the guts of the Army team in all kinds of action, in 1950, Lombardo was killed in action during the Korean War.

Dewitt Tex Coulter was All American as tackle via UP2, Glenn Davis, Halfback, and Doc Blanchard fullback were All American by just about everybody's standards such as AAB, AP, FN, INS, NEA, SN, UP, LK, etc. Army had a great team and great players and a great coach.

Army began its 1944 season on Sept 30 with a whomping shutout of North Carolina W (46-0) All Army home games, were played at Michie Stadium on the Campus of the USMA at West Point. On Oct 7 at home, Army shellacked Brown W (59-7) and then invited Pittsburgh to travel to Michie the following week on Oct 14 to be whacked W (69-7) by the Cadets. The following week at Michie, the @2 ranked Cadets thumped the Coast Guard W (76-0) Army was not trained to hear the cry of "Uncle" from its opponents. Duke looked like a championship team at the Polo Grounds in NY compared to all others who so far had met the onslaught of the Cadet Offense and the quick closes of the West Point Defense. Army did need to work to dispose of Duke W (27-7)

Army scores were never so high because Army had never been quite this good and this was reflected on Nov 4 at Michie v Villanova in a shutout rout W (83-0). No team at Army had ever shellacked Notre Dame until Red Blaik came to town. Red's Cadets beat the Tar out of ND at Yankee Stadium in the Bronx, NY as big as a win v ND could ever be W (59-0).

As good as Penn was, their great team looked like mush meat at Franklin Field when on the same field with Army in 1944. The vaunted Penn got thumped just like everybody else W (62-7). Ya got to give it to the Navy. Despite all the thumping, shellacking, whomping and outright devastating opponents by large scores, Navy kept its pride. They lost big-time to Army but by a respectable W (23-7). For Army, the navy win was the sweetest of the season.

Army was as good as it gets in 1944.

Great day for Army! Bad day for Navy and it was not about to change the next year.

1945 Coach Red Blaik

The Army Cadets football team represented the United States Military Academy in the 1945 college football season. It was their fifty-sixth season of intercollegiate football. They were coached by Earl "Red" Blaik in his fifth of eighteen seasons as head coach of the Cadets. As an independent football entity, the Army team had a perfect record of 9-0-0 for the second year in a row. Hard as it is for most humans to believe, this is the same record that Army posted last year and it is not a duplicate. That's how good the Army team had gotten because of Red Blaik and the Army Brass loosening up on items in the agenda that were not football oriented.

Army had already learned to win the big ones. This year, they won everything again. The Cadets were the #1 ranked team in the nation

The Cadets compiled a 9-0-0 perfect record. The Cadets shut out five of their nine opponents, and they outscored their opponents 412 points to 46 points. At the season's end, the team won a national championship.

Doc Blanchard won the Heisman Trophy in 1945.

Army began its 1945 season on Sept 30 with a shutout of Louisville AAF, W (32-0). This home opener and all Army home games, were played at Michie Stadium on the Campus of the USMA at West

Point. On Oct 6 at home, Army shellacked and shut out Wake Forest W (54-0) and then invited Michigan to Yankee Stadium for a neutral game. The Cadets beat the Wolverines W (28-7) On Oct 20, #1 Army played against the Melville PT Boats in a big win W (55-13). On Oct 27, the Cadets beat Duke at the Polo Grounds in NY W (48-13)

On Nov 3, the Cadets defeated Villanova at home at Michie in a blowout W (54-0). The Cadets had blowout fever as they kept it up another week this time blowing Notre Dame out of Yankee Stadium W (48-0). On Nov 17, the Cadets pounced on the Penn Quakers in at Franklin Field a big rout W (61-0). In the Army Navy-Game on Dec 1, Army defeated Navy in a tough game but the score was very convincing as to who the best was in the battle of the service academies. W (32-13). Army, for the second year in a row, 1945, was as good as it gets.

Dec 1 was a great day for Army! It was a bad day for Navy and it was not about to change the next year.

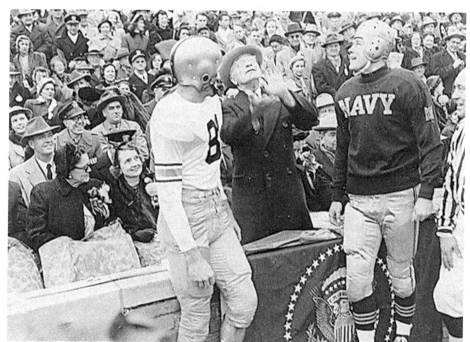

President Truman Tossing the Coin Army Navy Game 1945

1946 Coach Red Blaik

The Army Cadets football team represented the United States Military Academy in the 1946 college football season. It was their fifty-seventh season of intercollegiate football. They were coached by Earl "Red" Blaik in his sixth of eighteen seasons as head coach of the Cadets. As an independent football entity, the Army team had an undefeated record of 9-0-1 with a tie to spoil it from being perfect.

The Cadets spent most of the season as the #1 ranked team in the nation. The Cadets compiled a 9-0-1 undefeated record. The Cadets shut out five of their nine opponents, and they outscored their opponents 263 points to 80 points. At the season's end, the team came in #2 according to AP. The squad was also recognized as national champions for the 1946 season by several selectors. The 1946 Army vs. Notre Dame football game at Yankee Stadium is regarded as one of college football's Games of the Century. 1946 college football season.

The 1946 NCAA football season finished with the Notre Dame Fighting Irish crowned as the national champion in the AP Poll, with the United States Military Academy named as national champion in various other polls and rankings. In history, most observers give both teams credit as National Champions. Their 0-0 head to head battle proved both teams were great.

Glenn Davis won the Heisman Trophy in 1946.

The 1946 Army football season began later in September earlier later than usual on Sept 21 with a shutout of Villanova, W (35-0) This home opener and all Army home games, were played at Michie Stadium on the Campus of the USMA at West Point. On Sept 28, at home, Army defeated Oklahoma W (21-7). On Oct 5. On Oct 12 at Michigan Stadium in Ann Arbor, MI, the #2 Cadets defeated the #4 Wolverines W (20-13). On Oct 19, at home, the Cadets defeated the Columbia Terriers W (48-14)

On Oct 26, at the Polo Grounds in NY City, NY, the Cadets shut out the Duke Blue Devils, W (19-0). home, Army then shut out West Virginia by the same score W (19-0) a week later on Nov 2.

On Nov 9 at Yankee Stadium in the Bronx, NY. the Cadets and the Fighting Irish played what many call the best college football game in history. If you like high scoring games, you would not like this game but if you like tough, smash-mouth football, this was the best game ever. It was a battle of #1 Army coached by the immortal Red Blaik, v #2 Notre Dame coached by the immortal Frank Leahy. Neither team would give an inch—literally and the game wound up in a scoreless tie T (0-0).

On Nov 16, the Cadets still ranked #1 after the tie, defeated the #5 ranked Penn Quakers W (34-7). At the end of the season, Navy was all that mattered to Army and the Cadets had a real tough game against the Midshipmen but prevailed by the close score of W (21-18). At Philadelphia's Municipal Stadium in PA.

1947 Coach Red Blaik

The Army Cadets football team represented the United States Military Academy in the 1947 college football season. It was their fifty-eighth season of intercollegiate football. They were coached by Earl "Red" Blaik in his seventh of eighteen seasons as head coach of the Cadets. As an independent football entity, the Army team had a record of 5-2-2.

The Cadets compiled a 5-2-2 record. They shut out four of their nine opponents, and they outscored their opponents 220 points to 165 points. At the season's end, the team came in #11 in the National standings.

The Black Knights offense scored 220 points, while the defense allowed 165 points. At season's end, the team ranked eleventh in the National standings.

On Sept 27, the 1947 Army football season began with a light shutout over Villanova W (13-0). This home opener and all Army home games, were played at Michie Stadium on the Campus of the USMA at West Point. After a week off, the Illini of Illinois met the Cadets in Yankee Stadium and played to a scoreless tie T (0-0). On Oct 4, my wedding anniversary, the Cadets blew out the Colorado Buffalos at home in a shootout W (47-0). On Oct 18, at home, Army shutout

VPI in a fine win W (40-0). Then, playing a tough Columbia team, at Baker Field in New York, on Oct 25, the Cadets could not bring home the win in a very tough loss L 20-21)

On Oct 26, at the Polo Grounds in NY City, NY, the Cadets shut out the Duke Blue Devils, W (19-0). home, Army then shut out West Virginia by the same score W (19-0) a week later on Nov 2.

On Nov 1 at home v Washington & Lee, the Cadets put their offense in gear and whooped the generals in a shootout W (65-13). After a heartbreaking 0-0 tie the prior year at Yankee Stadium, Frank Leahy's Notre Dame squad was back at Yankee Stadium and they were ranked #1 in the nation. They were preparing to play the #1 ranked team, Army on Nov 8. This year, Leahy got the best of Blaik as ND defeated the Cadets L (7-27) before 59,171. Penn, a recent add-on team to the Army schedule was as tough as it gets for many years and 1947 was no exception. The Penn Quakers and the Army Cadets played to a low scoring tie T (7-7).

On Nov 29, Army had hit the end of its scheduled season and it was time for the raison d'etre (reason for being). This of course was the traditional season finale v the Midshipmen of Navy. Navy was all that mattered to Army and the Cadets had a real tough game against the Midshipmen but managed to shut them out W (21-0) in Philadelphia's Municipal Stadium in PA.

1948 Coach Red Blaik

The Army Cadets football team represented the United States Military Academy in the 1948 college football season. It was their fifty-ninth season of intercollegiate football. They were coached by Earl "Red" Blaik in his eighth of eighteen seasons as head coach of the Cadets. As an independent football entity, the Army team had an undefeated record of 8-0-1.

The Cadets compiled an 8-0-1 record. They shut out two of their nine opponents, and they outscored their opponents 294 points to 89 points. At the season's end, the team came in #6 in the National standings.

During the season, head coach Earl Blaik implemented a two-platoon system, using specialists strictly for offense and defense. Offensive coach Gillman left Army after the season to become the head coach at the University of Cincinnati.

The 1948 Army football season began with a shutout over Villanova W (28-0). This home opener and all Army home games, were played at Michie Stadium on the Campus of the USMA at West Point. On Oct 2, at home, Army won by a blowout over Lafayette W (54-7). Then, on Oct 9, at Illinois Memorial Stadium in Champaign IL, the Cadets barely defeated the Illini W (26-21) but brought home the win nonetheless. On Oct 16, Harvard was back on the schedule at #5 Army. The Cadets got the best of the Crimson W (20-7)

On Oct 23, #5 ranked Army defeated # 12 Cornell at Schoellkopf Field at Cornell W (27-6)) On Oct 30, the Cadets ripped apart VPI at home W (49-7). On Nov 6, unranked Stanford played Army and were shut out at Yankee Stadium in the Bronx, NY, W (43-0). Next up on Nov 13, in a very good Army year was a tough team, Penn, playing at Franklin Field, Philadelphia PA. The Cadets beat the Quakers in a tough battle W (26-20).

As happens just about every year, after a good or bad season, Army gets to play in the Army-Navy-Game. This year, the game was played on Nov 27 in Philadelphia Municipal Stadium in Phila., PA. Army was undefeated but that did not matter to Navy and they pulled out all the stops and the Midshipmen were able to tie the Cadets in a tough encounter T (21-21).

Going into the game undefeated, one must ask what impact the tie to Navy had on the Red Blaik team's opportunities for another National Championship. Well, we know it did not help one bit, no matter how tough a game it was.

1949 Coach Red Blaik

The Army Cadets football team represented the United States Military Academy in the 1949 college football season. It was Army's sixtieth season of intercollegiate football. They were coached by Earl "Red" Blaik in his ninth of eighteen seasons as head coach of the

Cadets. As an independent football entity, the Army team had an undefeated and untied record (perfect) of 9-0-0.

The Cadets compiled a 9-0-0 record. Is that not impressive in its frequency? They shut out two of their nine opponents, and they outscored their opponents 354 points to 68 points. Army was phenomenal and had a perfect record but it was not good enough for those calling the shots. At the season's end, the team came in #4 in the National standings. You cannot do much better than a perfect record.

Arnold Galiffa was the starting quarterback. Blaik had picked him ahead of his own son, Bob. Johnny Trent was the team captain. The Cadets won the Lambert-Meadowlands Trophy as the best college team in the East. At season's end, Red Blaik confessed that he thoughts of retiring. Why no National Championship with a perfect record? They are not too easy to come by. Red Blaik was simply a great coach. Even he wondered what was wrong with "perfect." Looking at the schedule, one must conclude that the teams Army played were not slackers.

The 1949 Army football season began with a blowout on Sept 24, over Davidson, W (47-7) This home opener and all Army home games, were played at Michie Stadium on the Campus of the USMA at West Point. On Oct 1, at home, Army won by a blowout over Penn State by the same exact score W (47-7). Feeling good about winning, the Army Cadets took on the #1 ranked Michigan team in Michigan Stadium on Oct 8, and put a hurt on the Wolverines creating a W 21-7) victory for Army. On Oct 15, at Harvard's Harvard Stadium in Boston MA, the Cadets beat the Crimson in a shootout W (54-14).

On Oct 22, #2 ranked Army defeated Columbia at home W (63-6). Then, on Oct 29, at home, #2 Army beat VMI w (40-14). On Nov 5, at home, the Cadets shut out Fordham W (35-)

Next up on Nov 12, in another very good Army year a tough Penn Team showed up and demanded to be played. This game was at Franklin Field, Philadelphia PA. The Cadets beat the Quakers in another tough battle W (14-13).

Regardless of how Army or Navy played through any season, either can have a fan/alumni resurrection with a victory over the other in the Army-Navy-Game. This year, the game was played on Nov 26 in Philadelphia Municipal Stadium in Philadelphia, PA. Army was undefeated but that did not matter to Navy and the Midshipmen tried to do what it could to shape the game's eventuality. Since Army dominated by a shutout win of W (38-0). I am really not sure what Navy could have done to look better other than to have been able to play better against a phenomenally tough Army team/

Going into this game undefeated, one must ask what impact a great win over Navy had on the Red Blaik team's opportunities for another National Championship. Well, we know it did not happen and many wonder to this day, Why Not? To Army, Red Blaik was like Knute Rockne was to Notre Dame. And, form a guy who studied both; he should have been. Blaik, who retired in 1958, is recognized as is Rockne, as one of college football's true immortals.

1950 Coach Red Blaik

The Army Cadets football team represented the United States Military Academy in the 1950 college football season. It was Army's sixty-first season of intercollegiate football. They were coached by Earl "Red" Blaik in his tenth of eighteen seasons as head coach of the Cadets. As an independent football entity, the Army team had a great, almost perfect record of 8-1-0. Try and do better yourself.

The Cadets compiled n 8-1-0 record. Considering how frequently Earl Blaik brought in a great team, that is another impressive record. They shut out five of their nine opponents, and they outscored their opponents 267 points to 40 points. Bob Blaik, the son of the coach, was the starting quarterback.

Army had a phenomenal one-loss (to Navy) record and the team did quite well finishing #5 in the Coaches' poll and #2 in the AP poll. Nothing including a championship level record mattered in the Army-Navy Game. All Army's great record did was make a poor Navy team ((2-6 going into the game) want to play better and they did. They topped the Cadets L (2-14), finishing their season at 3-6.

During this season, Tom Lombardo, the captain of the 1944 Army team, was killed in action in Korea. Two weeks before the Army–Navy Game, Johnny Trent, the captain of the 1949 Army team, was killed in action. Trent, and Arnold Galiffa, the starting quarterback of the 1949 Army team, has officers in the Army, had been sent with the Eighth Army to Korea. With President Harry S. Truman in attendance, Navy beat Army by a score of 14–2.

It was the first time Navy had beaten Army since 1943. Tough teams meet tough challenges. Tough soldiers always play to win but sometimes, despite their best, they are stopped from achieving. There are many heroes in the Army and the Navy and in the graves that hold the bones of those brave men, who gave it all up for God and country.

The 1950 Army football season began with a shutout on Sept 30, over Colgate, W (28-0) This home opener and all Army home games, were played at Michie Stadium on the Campus of the USMA at West Point. On Oct 7, at home, Army won by a wide margin over Penn State W (41-7). With a 2-0 undefeated record, the Cadets took on the Wolverines of Michigan at Yankee Stadium in the Bronx, NY on Oct 14, and prevailed W (27-6). Harvard was no longer a world-class football team but they were tough enough when the Crimson suffered a major blowout at the hands of the Cadets W (49-0) on Oct 21.

On Oct 28, a top-ten ranked Army team shut out Columbia at Baker Field, NY, W (34-0). Then, on Nov 4, a very tough Penn Quakers team was challenged and beaten at Franklin Field in Philadelphia, PA by the Cadets W (28-13). On Veterans Day, Nov 11, a National Holiday for all, especially Army Veterans, the Cadets whooped New Mexico in a blowout, W (51-0). Stanford, always a tough opponent, hosted the Cadets at Stanford and played a close match but lost nonetheless W (7-0).

Army had sailed through its second undefeated season in a row, except for one thing. The Cadets had to meet the poorly playing Midshipmen at Municipal Stadium for a season finale on Dec. 2. With a really lousy 2-6 record few pundits gave Navy a chance to avoid an embarrassment at the hands of Army. The Cadets were big favorites but then again, this was the Army-Navy Game when all bets are off. Navy kept Army in a hole the entire game and the Cadets blew an opportunity for being undefeated two years in a row simply because a stubborn Navy team would not let them win. Navy prevailed L (2-14))

1951 Coach Red Blaik

The Army Cadets football team represented the United States Military Academy in the 1951 college football season. It was Army's sixty-second season of intercollegiate football. They were coached by Earl "Red" Blaik in his eleventh of eighteen seasons as head coach of the Cadets. As an independent football entity, the Army team had its worst season under coach Red Blaik 2-7-0, their legacy immortal coach. It proved just one thing. Even Red Blaik was human.

The Cadets compiled a 2-7-0 record. Considering how frequently Earl Blaik brought in a great team, this was a major anomaly. at is another impressive record. The Cadets offense scored 116 points, while the defense allowed 183 points. There were no shutouts either way in 1951.

From the moment Army lost to Navy in 1950 after going undefeated, Coach Blaik was agitated by the loss. He held on to the agitation long after Army suffered the loss to Navy in 1950—well into the off-season. Blaik had another peeve that really frosted him. Around Army guys all his career, he was upset over the dismissal of General Douglas MacArthur.

Sam Galiffa, who was part of the 1949 team, and who, at the time was a decorated aide to General Matthew Ridgway, arranged for members of the Army coaching staff to come to Japan in the off-season to visit the troops.

Vince Lombardi and Doug Kenna first visited Tokyo and conducted several football clinics for the troops stationed there. Although defensive coordinator Murray Warmath helped the discharged players relocate to other schools, it was his last year at Army. He left at the end of the season to become the head coach for Mississippi State.

Red Blaik ultimately had more to worry about than the Navy loss. The Cadets, working hard to become soldiers in the shortest route possible, engaged in a massive honor code academic violation. It was revealed in the spring of 1951. There were accusations that football players were distributing unauthorized academic information to help assure that their "brothers" made it through the rigors and got their commissions.

This travesty was reported to Colonel Paul Harkins on April 2. It was later revealed that Red Blaik's son, Bob, was part of the honor code violation. On August 3, the violations were announced and several athletes were implicated in the scandal. Army Cadets do their best at all times to avoid black marks on themselves and the Academy. They did not get away with this one.

Joseph P. Kennedy spoke to assistant coach Doug Kenna, and he helped pay the way for several discharged players to attend Notre Dame. Bob Blaik, son of the Coach, left Army for Colorado College. Of the players that were discharged, three went on to careers in the National Football League: Al Pollard, Gene Filipski and Ray Malavasi. Malavasi also become head coach of the Los Angeles Rams. The message is that without the gradebook, the season would have been lost healthier than 2-6.

With such top Army talent playing for other colleges after the scandal, the makeshift team that was assembled was clean of honor violations, but their lack of strong talent was still a reminder of the reason why Army was in the doldrums in 1951. After losing several games to Ivy League schools, Army's scrappy team defeated Columbia for its first win. The team received a congratulatory note for this effort from General Douglas MacArthur. There would be few accolades this season.

In week 6 of the season, the Cadets played the great NY Giant Halfback Frank Gifford, who was a mainstay of the USC Trojans squad. The game, which Army lost by a respectable score, 28-6, was played at Yankee Stadium.

Going into the Army–Navy game, the Cadets had a very poor record of 2 wins and 6 losses. This was Blaik's only losing season at Army. In the Army–Navy game, Navy scored two touchdowns before Army even ran an offensive series. Army could not keep up with Navy and the Cadets were thumped by the aggressive Midshipmen W (42-7). Red Blaik coached a 2-7 team and it really was about as good a season as any coach could have made it.

Army kicked off the 1951 season with its first of seven kicks in the behind. This one came from Villanova on Sept 29, L (7-21). This home opener and all Army home games, were played at Michie Stadium on the Campus of the USMA at West Point. On Oct 6, at Dyche Stadium in Evanston, IL, Army lost to Northwestern L (14-20). On Oct 13, with a 0-2 winless record, the Cadets took were beaten by Harvard L (21-22) at Harvard Stadium in Boston, MA.

On Oct 27, Army defeated Columbia at home W (14-9) for its first win of the campaign. This was followed on Nov 3, with another defeat L (6-28) at Yankee Stadium, Bronx, NY, against USC. On, Nov 10, the Army defeated The Citadel W (27-6) giving the Army its second and last win of the season. Then, before the Army-Navy Game, On Nov 17, at Penn in a game played in Franklin Field in Philadelphia, PA, the scrappy Cadets were beaten by the tough Quakers L (6-7).

Army was at the end of its worst season in the Red Blaik Era. No matter how bad the Army-Navy loss of 1950 was for the psyche of Red Blaik and Army, this season was a killer. It was as if a big magic marker had erased a big part of the playing squad and Army was dared to compete. They competed and nobody pushed them over— well nobody other than Navy. So now in the final game of the year, there was hope that this scrappy group of courageous Cadets would find something from a season of Blaik coaching and at least look good. It did not happen as Navy loved beating Army as bad as it could and the Midshipmen would not let go until they had a big victory over Army L (7-42). Navy did everything but shut out Army in this game but it sure tried to do so. Army does not forget easily.

1952 Coach Red Blaik

The Army Cadets football team represented the United States Military Academy in the 1952 college football season. It was Army's sixty-third season of intercollegiate football. They were coached by

Earl "Red" Blaik in his twelfth of eighteen seasons as head coach of the Cadets. As an independent football entity, the Army team had its second worst season under coach Red Blaik 4-4-1, their legacy immortal coach. It proved just one thing. Even Red Blaik was human.

The Cadets compiled a 4-4-1 record. After having the better players on his 1950 team stripped from ever becoming upperclassmen, Blaik had himself an unwanted rebuilding year in 1952. It was not so bad as 1951, which had set the bottom of the troth for Army. Yet, it was not so good so nobody was cheering Army while the Cadets were losing four games, gaining zero shutouts, and suffering two shutouts on the way to a medsa medsa season.

After a 2-7 season, Army got back on the winning side of its games, right from its opening day on Sept 27 at South Carolina at home W (28-7). All Army home games were played at Michie Stadium at West Point NY. The good winning feelings from an opening day victory had not quite set in when on Oct4, the #7 USC Trojans defeated the unranked Cadets and shut them out clean as a whistle, L (0-22).

Recovering again, Army defeated Dartmouth W (37-7) at home on Oct 11. Then, on Oct 18, the Cadets found the need again to recover after being defeated by the Panthers of Pittsburgh L (14-22) at home. Then, On Oct 25, in a tough game, Columbia played the Army to a tie T (25-25).

On Nov 1, the Cadets pounded the VMI Keydets W (42-14) at home and then traveled to Grant Field in Atlanta GA to take on the #3 ranked Georgia Tech Bulldogs in a losing effort L (6-45). Then, it was off to Franklin Field in Philadelphia on Nov 15, to play the Penn Quakers and grab a nice win in a very close match W (14-13).

Nobody in New York State was looking for a loss against the Midshipmen in the Army Navy Game but that is exactly what Navy delivered at Municipal Field in Philadelphia PA. Army and Navy played well but Navy won the game in a nail-biter L (0-7).

1953 Coach Red Blaik

The Army Cadets football team represented the United States Military Academy in the 1953 college football season. It was Army's sixty-fourth season of intercollegiate football. They were led by Coach Earl "Red" Blaik in his thirteenth of eighteen seasons as head coach of the Cadets. As an independent football entity, the Army team had another fine season under coach Red Blaik 7-1-1,

The Cadets compiled a 7-1-1 record. After his 1952 building year, the building was done, and the Red Blaik Army team was ready to kick butt. Not sure if "Kick Butt" was an appropriate Army slogan but the fans did not care. Army was back. The Cadet fans were cheering for Army while the Cadets were winning most of their games. The Army Cadets finished the season by winning the Lambert-Meadowlands Trophy, awarded to the top college team in the East.

The Cadets had lost six players, including Freddie Myers, to academic ineligibility. The Cadets defeated Furman 41–0, the team's first shutout since the 1951 scandal, and the goings became bright.

After a tough loss to Northwestern, the Cadets were undefeated for the rest of the season. In a scoreless tie against the Tulane Green Wave, future Green Bay Packer Max McGee played exceptionally for Tulane. After too many years in a row of losses to Navy, in the Army-Navy game, Army's 20–7 victory over Navy was embraced and celebrated as it was the first since 1949.

The turning point of the season was an October victory over #7 ranked Duke University. Duke had the great named players such as Red Smith and Worth (A Million) Lutz. Tommy Bell ran up the middle and got his due. Quarterback Pete Vann switched the ball to his left hand, and made a southpaw pass. Red Smith was tackled by Bob Mischak in the final minutes of the game. Mischak ran 73 yards to make the tackle catching up eight yards of separation to save a touchdown.

Inspired by Mischak, Army held Duke inside the one-yard line, took over on downs, and eventually won the game. " Army had gotten the sludge behind them and had begun enjoying football again…And, the results wowed in the scores for Red Blaik's team produced throughout this great season.

"When Bob Mischak made that unlikely play, what Blaik called "a marvelous display of heart and pursuit," the Army football team regained its soul." Direct quote from Maraness.

Army restarted its football season program for 1953 on September 26 against Furman at home with a great shutout win W (41-0). All Army home games were played at Michie Stadium in West Point NY as was this season's opener. In the second game, the Cadets rolled out to play at Dyche Stadium in Evanston IL against a very tough Northwestern team and it they got beaten for the only time in 1953 L (20-23) On Oct 10, v Dartmouth at home, the Cadets shut out the Big Green W (27-0). In a nail-biter on Oct 17 vs. Duke at the Polo Grounds in New York, NY, the Cadets skimmed by the Blue Devils W (14–13). Next was Oct 24 at home vs. Columbia, the Cadets beat the Lions W (40–7).

The following week on Oct 31 at Tulane in a game played at Tulane Stadium in New Orleans, LA, the Cadets managed a tie against the Green Wave. On Nov 7 at home, Army defeated NC State W (27–7). Then, on Nov 14, the Cadets traveled to Franklin Field, Philadelphia, PA to beat the Penn Quakers W (21–14).

The season-making or breaking encounter with the Midshipmen in the Army-Navy Game on Nov 28 at Municipal Stadium, Philadelphia, PA, Army put Navy away W (20–7)

1954 Coach Red Blaik

The Army Cadets football team represented the United States Military Academy in the 1954 college football season. It was Army's sixty-fifth season of intercollegiate football. They were led by Coach Earl "Red" Blaik in his fourteenth of eighteen seasons as head coach of the Cadets. As an independent football entity, the Army team had another fine season under coach Red Blaik 7-2-0.

The Cadets compiled a 7-2-0 record. Army outscored all opponents by a combined total of 325 to 127. In the annual Army–Navy Game, the Cadets lost to the Midshipmen by a close 27 to 20 score. The Cadets also lost to South Carolina by a 34 to 20 score in the first game of the season.

Army began the 1954 football season on September 25 against South Carolina at home with a loss to the Gamecocks L (20-34). All Army home games by default were played at Michie Stadium in West Point NY as was this season's opener. On Oct 2, at Michigan Stadium • Ann Arbor, MI, the Cadets defeated the Wolverines W (26–7). On Oct 9, the Cadets got the show in gear as they pitched a blow-out against the Dartmouth Big Green at home W (60-6). After an extra week's rest, on Oct 23 at Columbia in Baker Field, New York, NY, Army won handily in a blow0ut W (67–12).

On Oct 30, in as close a battle as you can have, Army beat Virginia at home, W (21-20). Then, on Nov 6 at the Yale Bowl in New Haven CT, for the first game in twelve years (1943), the Cadets whooped the Bulldogs W (48-7). On Nov 13, at Franklin Field in Philadelphia, the Cadets shut out the Penn Quakers W (35-0).

On Nov 27, with a 7-1 record, Army played the #6 ranked Navy Midshipmen at Municipal Stadium Philadelphia, PA in the annual (Army–Navy Game). The game was close but it resulted in an Army loss L (20–27).

1955 Coach Red Blaik

The Army Cadets football team represented the United States Military Academy in the 1955 college football season. It was Army's sixty-sixth season of intercollegiate football. They were led by Coach Earl "Red" Blaik in his fifteenth of eighteen seasons as head coach of the Cadets. As an independent football entity, the Army team had another fine season under coach Red Blaik 6-3-0.

The Cadets compiled a 6-3-0 record. Army shut out two opponents and outscored all opponents by a combined total of 256 to 72. In the annual Army–Navy Game, the Cadets defeated the Midshipmen by a score of 14 to 6. The Cadets also lost to Michigan, Syracuse, and Yale. No Army players were honored on the 1955 College Football All-America Team.

Army got its 1955 football season started on September 24 against Furman at home with a nice blowout win W (81-0). All Army home games by default were played at Michie Stadium in West Point NY as was this season's opener. On Oct 1, Army beat #18 Penn State at home W (35–6). The next week on Oct 8, the Cadets lost the first of two in a row to Michigan at Michigan Stadium, Ann Arbor, MI L (2-26) On Oct 15, the Cadets were shut out by the Syracuse Orangemen at home L (0-13). Army got back on track on Oct 22 at home vs. Columbia winning in a big shutout W (45-0).

Then, on Oct 29, at home, Army defeated Colgate W (27–7). After this, on Nov 5 at the Yale Bowl in New Haven CT, Yale's #19 Bulldogs defeated the Cadets in a close match L (12-14). This was followed on Nov 12, at Franklin Field, Philadelphia PA, with a shutout win against the Penn Quakers W (40-0)

On Nov 26, with a 5-3 record, unranked Army played the #11 ranked Navy Midshipmen at Municipal Stadium Philadelphia, PA in the annual (Army–Navy Game). The game was close but it resulted in an Army win W (14–6).

1956 Coach Red Blaik

The Army Cadets football team represented the United States Military Academy in the 1956 college football season. It was Army's sixty-seventh season of intercollegiate football. They were led by Coach Earl "Red" Blaik in his sixteenth of eighteen seasons as head coach of the Cadets. As an independent football entity, the Army team had another fine season under coach Red Blaik 5-3-1.

The Cadets compiled a 5-3-1 record. Army shut out two opponents and outscored all opponents by a combined total of 223 to 153. In the annual Army–Navy Game, the Cadets tied the Midshipmen by a score of 7 to 7. The Cadets also lost to Michigan, Syracuse, and Pittsburgh. No Army players were honored on the 1955 College Football All-America Team.

The Cadets got the 1956 football season going on September 24 against VMI at home with a nice tough win W (32-12). All Army home games by default were played at Michie Stadium in West Point NY as was this season's opener. On Oct 6, at home against Penn State, the Cadets beat the Nittany Lions by one touchdown W (14-7). On Oct 13, at Michigan Stadium in Ann Arbor MI, the Cadets were beaten by the Wolverines L (14–48). On Oct 20, at Syracuse's Archbold Stadium in Syracuse, NY, Army took it on the chin from the Orangemen in a close shutout L (0–7). Oct 27 at Columbia in a game played at Baker Field in New York, NY, Army recovered well and whomped Columbia in a shut-out W (60-0).

On Nov 3, at home, the Cadets beat the Colgate Raiders W (55-46) in a shootout. On Nov 10, at home, Army defeated William & Mary W (34–6). Then on Nov 17 Pittsburgh got the best of Army at Pitt Stadium, Pittsburgh, PA L (7–20).

On Nov 26, with a 5-3 record, the unranked Army Cadets played the unranked Navy Midshipmen at Municipal Stadium Philadelphia, PA in the annual (Army–Navy Game). The game was as close as it could get and it ended in a tie T (7-7).

1957 Coach Red Blaik

The Army Cadets football team represented the United States Military Academy in the 1957 college football season. It was Army's sixty-eighth season of intercollegiate football. They were led by Coach Earl "Red" Blaik in his seventeenth of eighteen seasons as head coach of the Cadets. As an independent football entity, the Army team had another fine season under coach Red Blaik 7-2-1.

The Cadets compiled a 7-2-0 record; shut out one opponents and outscored all opponents by a combined total of 251 to 129. In the annual Army–Navy Game, the Cadets lost to the Midshipmen by a score of 14 to 0. The Cadets also lost to Notre Dame by a score of 23 to 21.

Army began the 1957 football season going on September 28 at home against Nebraska at home with a blowout shutout W (42-0). All Army home games by default were played at Michie Stadium in West Point NY as was this season's opener. On Oct 5 at #8 Penn State's New Beaver Field in University Park, PA, the Cadets beat the Nittany Lions in a close match W 27–13. On Oct 12, the # 12 Notre Dame Fighting Irish came to Municipal Stadium in Philadelphia, PA to play the #10 ranked Cadets. The Irish went home with the win L (L 21–23). The game was played before 95,000. On Oct 19 at home, the Cadets beat the Panthers of Pittsburgh W (29–13).

On Oct 26 October 26 at Scott Stadium in Charlottesville, VA, Army beat Virginia W (20–12). The following week, the Cadets beat the Raiders of Colgate at home in a shootout W (53-7). Next, on Nov 9, Utah came to Michie Stadium and in a close match were beaten by Army W (39-33) Then, on Nov 16, the Tulane Green Wave lost to the Cadets W (20-14).

On Nov 306, with a 7-1 record, the #10 ranked Army Cadets played the unranked Navy Midshipmen at Municipal Stadium Philadelphia, PA in the annual (Army–Navy Game). The game was close but Navy got the win in a shutout W (0-14).

1958 Coach Red Blaik

The Army Cadets football team represented the United States Military Academy in the 1958 college football season. It was Army's sixty-ninth season of intercollegiate football. They were led by Coach Earl "Red" Blaik in his eighteenth and last of eighteen seasons as head coach of the Cadets. As an independent football entity, the Army team had an undefeated season under coach Red Blaik 8-0-1.

Legendary Army coach Earl "Red" Blaik with talented halfback, Bob Anderson, in 1958.

The Cadets compiled an 8-0-1 record; shut out two opponents and outscored all opponents by a combined total of 264 to 49. In the annual Army–Navy Game, the Cadets beat the Midshipmen by a score of 22 to 6. The Cadets also tied Pittsburgh 14 to 14. At season's end, the team was third in the national rankings by both major polling organizations. Red Blaik had a phenomenal record at Army and is the premiere Army immortal coach with an overall record of 121-33-10. Just phenomenal!

On Sept 27, #8 ranked Army got its 1958 football season underway at home against South Carolina Nebraska at home with a major victory W (45-8). All Army home games by default were played at Michie Stadium in West Point NY as was this season's opener. Penn State was the next victim of this superior Army team on Oct 4 as #5 ranked Army pitched a shutout W (26-0). On Oct 11 at #4 Notre Dame, Army controlled the game and beat the big guns of ND at Notre Dame Stadium South Bend, IN for a very nice win W (14-2).

Next game was at home vs. Virginia as the #1 ranked Army squad laid it on for a fine W (35-6) victory.

Pete Dawkins was honored after this season with the Heisman Trophy.

On Oct 25, At Pittsburgh's Pitt Stadium in Pittsburgh, PA, Army suffered its only blemish of the year as the Panthers tied the Cadets T (14-14). It was enough to drop Army to #3 and the Cadets never got the top spot back. On Nov. 1, the #3 ranked Cadets defeated the Raiders of Colgate in a major shootout W (68-6). On Nov 8, still at #3, the Cadets defeated the Rice Owls at Rice Stadium Houston, TX, W (14–7). Next was a shutout against Villanova at home W (26-0)

This was a unique Army Navy game with two legends playing – one on each team. The game featured a matchup of two Heisman Trophy winners — Army's Pete Dawkins, the 1958 winner, and Navy's Joe Bellino, the 1960 winner. These two exceptional players were also exceptional men; Dawkins was ultimately a Rhodes Scholar, Brigadier General and candidate for Senate, while Bellino played for the AFL's Boston Patriots and served in the Navy and Naval Reserve for 28 years. Dawkins' Cadets finished the 1958 season unbeaten with a 22–6 win over the Midshipmen. Army had other fine years but this year would be Army's last unbeaten season and of course it was legendary coach Red Blaik's last at the helm.

Chapter 11 Coaches Hall & Dietzel 1959-1965

Hall   Coach # 24
Dietzel   Coach # 25

Year	Coach	Record	Conference	Record
1959	Dale Hall	4-4-1	Indep	4-4-1
1960	Dale Hall	6-3-1	Indep	6-3-1
1961	Dale Hall	6-4-0	Indep	6-4-0
1962	Paul Dietzel	6-4-0	Indep	6-4-0
1963	Paul Dietzel	7-3-0	Indep	7-3-0
1964	Paul Dietzel	4-6-0	Indep	4-6-0
1965	Paul Dietzel	4-5-1	Indep	4-5-1

Dale Hall replaces Red Blaik

Army Picks Dale Hall as Coach

DALE HALL
. . . unanimous choice.

West Point, N. Y., Jan. 31 [UPI]—Dale Hall, an unsung halfback on the outstanding Army football teams that included Doc Blanchard and Glenn Davis, Saturday was named head football coach at the United States military academy to succeed Earl [Red] Blaik.

The 34 year old Hall, who has been Blaik's No. 1 assistant for the past three seasons, thus becomes one of the youngest head coaches ever put in charge of the Cadets.

Hall, the unanimous choice of the five man athletic board at West Point, signed a three year contract at an undisclosed salary. The appointment was announced by Lt. Gen. Garrison H. [Gar] David-

Tulsa, and Johnny Green, who played guard on the same teams with Hall and who now is an assistant coach at Tulane.

Blaik, one of the nation's most successful coaches, announced on Jan. 13 that he

letics during his cadet career."

Hall served four years in the infantry and held the rank of 1st lieutenant at the time he was separated from the service in 1949. Then he launched his coaching career, serving as an assistant coach at Purdue, New Hampshire, and Florida before returning to the Point in 1956.

Hall was a member of Army's 1944 national championship team that went thru the season undefeated and untied. Altho Blanchard and Davis were on the same team, they did not play in the same backfield with Hall. The Cadets had such a wealth of talent that season, Blaik platooned two offensive backfields.

Dale Hall is like the guy who replaced Knute Rockne at Notre Dame – Hunk Anderson. Earl "Red" Blake who retired at 62-years of age was an immortal legacy at Army while he was still living. It is always a better deal to replace a bum coach or a poor manager and not typically a good deal to replace a legend who is loved by everybody.

Though nobody could have brought the big winning seasons of Red Blaik back to Army, Dale Hall did reasonably well following one of the best coaches of all time, Earl Blaik.

Ironically, Red Blaik had a fine assistant besides Dale Hall who might have done a bit better with the team. I am not second guessing here. The war years were over and high school graduates were not lining up for football at West point like they once did. Some might think that Army lost a big opportunity in hindsight when the Brass chose not to offer their own Vince Lombardi the job. Wanting the head coaching job at Army and yet also wanting a job, Lombardi is said to have asked for permission to call Green Bay. We all know the rest of that story.

Coach Dale Stanly Hall (June 21, 1924 – August 23, 1996) was an American football and basketball player and coach. He was good at sports, period and he was smart as a whip. He played football and basketball at the United States Military Academy, where he was a two-time All-American in basketball and was named the Sporting News Men's College Basketball Player of the Year in 1945. Hall served as the head football coach at West Point from 1959 to 1961, compiling a record of 16-11-2. He was also the head basketball coach at the University of New Hampshire during the 1951-52 season, tallying a mark of 11-9.

Dale Hall was an all-around athlete. At the U.S. Military Academy at West Point, N.Y., Hall was a Helms Foundation All-American basketball first-team selection in 1944 and 1945 and led Army to a 29-1 record, averaging 23 points a game.

He scored 23 touchdowns for the 1944 national champion football team and shared the backfield with a pair of Heisman Trophy winners, Doc Blanchard and Glenn Davis, who won the trophy the following two seasons. Hall graduated first in a West Point class of over 800. He had major athletic skills and had a vertical leap of 39 inches. He earned seven letters in three sports at Army and was a 4.0 student. Hall succeeded the legendary Earl "Red" Blaik as Army's football coach in 1959 and as noted, he led his team to a 17-11-2 record in three seasons.

He was always good. In high school, he is the only Parsons H.S. football player to have his number retired.

Hall retained Coach Blaik's staff when he took over in 1959. Hall was only the second civilian in the modern era to coach Army. After eighteen years with the same coach, one could expect a burp when a new guy took the rains. The burp was Hall's first season at 4-4-1 followed by two 6-win winning seasons.

1959 Coach Dale Hall

The Army Cadets football team represented the United States Military Academy in the 1959 college football season. It was Army's seventieth season of intercollegiate football. They were led by Coach Dale Hall in his first of three seasons as head coach of the Cadets. As an independent football entity, the Army team had a .500 season under coach Dale Hall 4-4-1.

The Cadets compiled a 4-4-1 record; shut out one opponent, and outscored all opponents by a combined total of 174 to 141. In the annual Army–Navy Game, the Cadets lost to the Midshipmen by a score of 43 to 12. The Cadets also lost to Illinois, Penn State, and Oklahoma.

<< Coach Dale Hall

On Sept 26, Army began its 1959 football season at home against Boston College at home with a major victory W (44-8). All Army home games by default were played at Michie Stadium in West Point NY as was this season's opener. On Oct 3, at Illinois Memorial Stadium Champaign, IL, Army lost to Illinois, L (14–20). Then, on Oct 10, Army lost at home to # 16 Penn State L (11-17). Next, the Cadets traveled to Duke Stadium in Durham, NC and beat the Blue Devils W (21–6). Then it was Colorado State on Oct 24 at home for the win, W (25-6.

Air Force came to Yankee Stadium for another battle of the Service Academies on Oct 31. They played the Army to a tie T (13-13). Then it was a shutout win against Villanova at home on Nov 7, W (14-0). Next in the schedule was a tough Oklahoma squad in a losing effort in a game played at Oklahoma Memorial Stadium Norman, OK L (20–28).

On November 28, like clockwork came the Army–Navy Game at Municipal Stadium in Philadelphia, PA, the Cadets lost to the Midshipmen L (12–43) The Army team was clearly missing Red Blaik after just one year.

1960 Coach Dale Hall

The Army Cadets football team represented the United States Military Academy in the 1960 college football season. It was Army's seventy-first season of intercollegiate football. They were led by Coach Dale Hall in his second of three seasons as head coach of the Cadets. As an independent football entity, the Army team had a fine season under coach Dale Hall 6-3-1.

The Cadets compiled a 6-3-1 record; shut out two opponents, and outscored all opponents by a combined total of 222 to 95. In the annual Army–Navy Game, the Cadets lost to the Midshipmen by a score of 17 to 12. The Cadets also lost to Penn State, and Nebraska.

Army began its 1960 football season at home very early on Sept 17, against Buffalo with a major shutout victory W (37-0). All Army home games by default were played at Michie Stadium in West Point NY as was this season's opener. On Sept 24, Boston College played Army at home and the Eagles were defeated by the Cadets W (20–7). On Oct 1, the Cadets got a big plane ride out to play California at California Memorial Stadium Berkeley, CA. For the Cadets, it was a nice trip and a fruitful trip as they beat California W (28–10). On October 8, at home, Penn State's Nittany Lions again beat the Army Cadets L (16–27).

On Oct 15 at Nebraska's Memorial Stadium in Lincoln, NE, the Cornhuskers had the Army's number in their close victory L (9–14).

On Oct 22 Villanova played Army at home and were whooped in a big shutout W (54–0). Then, on Oct 29, the Cadets defeated Miami of Ohio at home W (30-7). A tough Syracuse team was next on the schedule Nov 5 at Yankee Stadium Bronx, NY. The Cadets gained the big Win, in a close match W (9-6). The next game was right before Army-Navy. It was Nov 12, at Pitt Stadium in Pittsburgh, PA. The Cadets played the Panthers to a tie   T (7–7).

On November 26, undeniably, the Army-Navy game would be at Municipal Stadium in Philadelphia, PA. The Cadets lost again to the Midshipmen L (12–17) The Army team had yet to win one against Navy in the post Blaik years.

1961 Coach Dale Hall

The Army Cadets football team represented the United States Military Academy in the 1961 college football season. It was Army's seventy-second season of intercollegiate football. They were led by Coach Dale Hall in his third and last of three seasons as head coach of the Cadets. As an independent football entity, the Army team had a respectable season under coach Dale Hall 6-4-0.

The Cadets compiled a 6-4-0 record; shut out no opponents, and outscored all opponents by a combined total of 224 to 118. In the annual Army–Navy Game, the Cadets lost to the Midshipmen by a score of 13 to 7. The Cadets also lost to Michigan, West Virginia, and Oklahoma. No Army players were selected on the 1961 College Football All-America Team.

Army initiated its 1961 football season at home on Sept 23, against Richmond, with a major nice victory W (24-6). All Army home games by default were played at Michie Stadium in West Point NY as was this season's opener. On Sept 30[th, the] University in Boston, not the College came to West Point to play Army and were beaten W (31-7). Big Ten Teams are always tough as was Michigan on Oct 7 at Michigan Stadium in Ann Arbor, MI as the Wolverines dominated the Cadets L (8–38). Always tough to beat, Rip Engle's Penn State Nittany Lions invited Army to Beaver Stadium at University Park, PA, and Army paid for the invitation with a nice but close victory W (10–6).

Idaho showed up at Michie Stadium on Oct 21 and were beaten back big time W (51–7). West Virginia played tougher than Idaho and got the W on Oct 28 L (3-7). Detroit took its shot at Army at Michie Stadium but failed W (34-7). Next game was William & Mary on Nov 11 at home as the Cadets put on their steam-roller personality and crushed the opponent's W (48–13). A big game was next against Oklahoma on Nov 18 at Yankee Stadium Bronx, NY, and the Cadets got their third loss of the year to the Sooners

On December 2, the Army-Navy game went on as scheduled at Municipal Stadium in Philadelphia, PA the Cadets lost again to the Midshipmen L (7-13) The Army team had yet to win one against Navy in the post Blaik years. Yes, we are counting!

Paul Dietzel replaces Dale Hall at season-end

Coach Dietzel coached for seven seasons at LSU and produced a 46-24-3 record. His tenure included coaching Heisman Trophy winner Billy Cannon in 1959 and an SEC title in 1961.

He left after that season to be head coach at Army. Dietzel had served as a bomber pilot in the U.S. Army Air Corps in World War II and had two stints as an assistant coach there before becoming LSU's head coach.

Dietzel spent four seasons at West Point before moving on to coach at South Carolina. His nine seasons there included the 1969 Atlantic Coast Conference title.

His overall record as a college head coach was 109-95-5. He was inducted into the Louisiana Sports Hall of Fame in 1988.

Dietzel also spent several years as an athletics administrator, serving as AD at South Carolina from 1966-75, at Indiana from 1976-78 and at LSU from 1978-82. He also served a year as commissioner of the Ohio Valley Conference in 1975.

1962 Coach Paul Dietzel

The Army Cadets football team represented the United States Military Academy in the 1962 college football season. It was Army's seventy-third season of intercollegiate football. They were led by Coach Paul Dietzel in his first of four seasons as head coach of the Cadets. As an independent football entity, the Army team had another respectable season under coach Dietzel identical to the last year of Coach Dale Hall 6-4-0.

<< Coach Paul Dietzel

The Cadets compiled a 6-4-0 record; shut out two opponents, and outscored all opponents by a combined total of 152 to 104. In the annual Army–Navy Game, the Cadets lost to the Midshipmen by a score of 34 to 14. The Cadets also lost to Michigan, Oklahoma State, and Pittsburgh. No Army players were selected on the 1962 College Football All-America Team.

Army started its 1962 football season at home on Sept 22, against Wake Forest, with a major victory W (40-14). All Army home games by default were played at Michie Stadium in West Point NY as was this season's opener. On Sept 29 vs. Syracuse at the Polo Grounds in New York, NY, Army prevailed W (9–2). Then, on Oct 6 at Michigan Stadium in Ann Arbor, MI the Wolverines prevailed on the Cadets L (7–17). Moving through the schedule, on Oct 13 at home, Army barely got by Penn State W (9-6). This was followed by a win at home vs. VPI on Oct 27 W (20-12). Then, on Oct 27, the Cadets shut out George Washington in DC Stadium, Washington, DC W (14–0).

On Nov 3 at Boston University in a game played at Nickerson Field, Boston, MA, the Army won a nice one W (26–0). On Nov 10 Oklahoma State played Army at home and beat the Cadets in a close match L (7–12). On Nov 17, vs. Pittsburgh, the Cadets played and lost by one point in Yankee Stadium in The Bronx, NY, L (6–7).

In the annual Army-Navy game on December 1 at Municipal Stadium in Philadelphia, the Cadets lost again to the Midshipmen L (14-34) The Army team had yet to win one against Navy in the post Blaik years. Yes, we are counting!

1963 Coach Paul Dietzel

The Army Cadets football team represented the United States Military Academy in the 1963 college football season. It was Army's seventy-fourth season of intercollegiate football. They were led by Coach Paul Dietzel in his second of four seasons as head coach of the Cadets. As an independent football entity, the Army team had a fine season under coach Dietzel--7-3-0. This would be the last winning season for Army under Coach Dietzel.

The Cadets compiled a 7-3-0 record; shut out four opponents, and outscored all opponents by a combined total of 177 to 97. In the annual Army–Navy Game, the Cadets lost to the Midshipmen by a score of 21 to 15. The Cadets also lost to Minnesota and Pittsburgh.

Army started its 1963 football season at home on Sept 22, with a shutout against Boston University W (30-0). All Army home games by default were played at Michie Stadium in West Point NY as was this season's opener. On Sept 28, at home, the Cadets shut out the Cincinnati Bearcats W (22-0) Entering October with two wins and no losses, the Cadets met Minnesota at Memorial Stadium in Minneapolis, MN and were defeated by the Gophers L (8–24). The Cadets got back on the track on Oct 12 at Beaver Stadium in University Park, PA when they beat the Nittany Lions in a close match W (10-7). Next, at home, the Cadets blew-out the Wake Forest Demon Deacons W (47-0).

Army's third shutout of the season came on Oct 26 at home vs. Washington State W (23-0). On Nov 2, a tough Airforce team gave Army a tough time at Soldier Field in Chicago, IL, but lost in the end W (14-10). On Nov 9, Utah played the Cadets at home and Army prevailed by one point over the Utes W (8-7. Then, at Pittsburgh's

Pitt Stadium in Pittsburgh, PA on Nov 17, the Cadets were shut out by the Panthers L (0–28)

On Dec. 7 at Municipal Stadium in Philadelphia, PA, in the traditional Army–Navy Game, the Midshipmen again got the upper hand defeating the Cadets L (15–21). Losing had become the norm in this game for the Cadets and nobody was happy about it. The Army team had yet to win one against Navy in the post Blaik years.

1964 Coach Paul Dietzel

The Army Cadets football team represented the United States Military Academy in the 1964 college football season. It was Army's seventy-fifth season of intercollegiate football. They were led by Coach Paul Dietzel in his third of four seasons as head coach of the Cadets. As an independent football entity, the Army team had a losing season under coach Dietzel—4-6-0.

The Cadets compiled a 4-6-0 record; shut out one opponent, and were outscored by all opponents by a combined total of 118 to 147. In the annual Army–Navy Game, the Cadets defeated the Midshipmen by a score of 11 to 8. The Cadets also lost to #1 Texas, Penn State, Virginia, Duke, Syracuse, and Pittsburgh.

This year's home opener was on Sept 19 vs The Citadel., the Cadets shut out the Bulldogs W (34–0). On Sept 26, the Cadets defeated the Eagles of Boston College at home W (19-13). On Oct 3, at Texas Memorial Stadium in Austin, TX, the Cadets were defeated by the #1 Longhorns L (6–17). Penn State then added to the pain with a sliver close victory over Army L (2-6).

The third loss in a row came from Virginia on Oct 17 at Scott Stadium in Charlottesville, VA L (14–35). The fourth loss in a row came from Duke at home in a close shutout L (0-6). Army recovered in defeating Iowa State W (9-7) on Oct 31. Another loss for the Cadets came on Nov 7 at Yankee Stadium in the Bronx, NY. The Orangemen defeated the Cadets L (15-27). Then, on Nov 14, the Cadets suffered another loss. This time it was to the Panthers of Pittsburgh at home L (8-24).

On November 28, after losing five Army-Navy-Games in a row, the Cadets broke the streak and defeated the Midshipmen at JFK Stadium in Philadelphia, PA W (11-8).

1965 Coach Paul Dietzel

The Army Cadets football team represented the United States Military Academy in the 1965 college football season. It was Army's seventy-sixth season of intercollegiate football. They were led by Coach Paul Dietzel in his fourth and last of four seasons as head coach of the Cadets. As an independent football entity, the Army team had a losing season under coach Dietzel—4-5-1.

The Cadets compiled a 4-5-1 record; shut out one opponent, and were outscored by all opponents by a combined total of 132 to 119. In the annual Army–Navy Game, the Cadets tied the Midshipmen by a score of 7 to 7. The Cadets also lost to Tennessee, Notre Dame, Stanford, Colgate, and Air Force. No Army players were recognized on the 1965 College Football All-America Team.

This year's home opener was on Sept 18 vs The Tennessee Volunteers. The Cadets were shut out by the Volunteers L (0-21) in a rare opening season loss. On Sept 25, the Cadets defeated VMI at home W (21-7). On Oct 3, at home, the Cadets shut-out Boston College W (10-0). On Oct 9, at Shea Stadium in Flushing, the Fighting Irish of Notre Dame shut out the Army Cadets L (0-17).

On Oct 16 at home, Army defeated Rutgers W (23-6). Then the Cadets traveled to Stanford California and played in Stanford Stadium against the Stanford Cardinal and were defeated L (14-31). On Oct 30, Colgate's Raiders came to Michie Stadium and beat the Cadets by one-point L (28-29). Next, the Cadets were bean by the Air Force Fighting Falcons on Nov 6 at Soldier Field in Chicago, IL L (3-14. As a great prep for the Army-Navy Game, the Cadets shut out Wyoming at home W (13-0)

On November 27, the Army Cadets tied the Midshipmen of Navy in the annual Army-Navy-Game at JFK Stadium in Philadelphia, PA T (7-7).

Chapter 12 Coaches Tom Cahill & Homer Smith 1966-1978

Cahill   Coach # 26
Smith   Coach # 27

Year	Coach	Record	Conference	Record
1966	Thomas Cahill	8-2-0	Indep	8-2-0
1967	Thomas Cahill	8-2-0	Indep	8-2-0
1968	Thomas Cahill	7-3-0	Indep	7-3-0
1969	Thomas Cahill	4-5-1	Indep	4-5-1
1970	Thomas Cahill	1-9-1	Indep	1-9-1
1971	Thomas Cahill	6-4-0	Indep	6-4-0
1972	Thomas Cahill	6-4-0	Indep	6-4-0
1973	Thomas Cahill	0-10-0	Indep	0-10-0
1974	Homer Smith	3-8-0	Indep	3-8-0
1975	Homer Smith	2-9-0	Indep	2-9-0
1976	Homer Smith	5-6-0	Indep	5-6-0
1977	Homer Smith	7-4-0	Indep	7-4-0
1978	Homer Smith	4-6-1	Indep	4-6-1

Coach Cahill

Army Coach Tom Cahill, right, talks with four of his team stars on whom he'll depend in today's game against Navy in Philadelphia. From left Ken Johnson, captain; quarterback Steve Lindell, tight end Gary Steele and fullback Charlie Jarvis. (AP)

Thomas Cahill was hired in 1959 by Earl (Red) Blaik to coach freshman football and baseball at Army. He was then promoted to head coach in 1966 when Paul Dietzel resigned to take over at South Carolina.

Cahill exceeded the two losing seasons at the end of Dietzel's tenure immediately by finishing with an 8-2 record in his first season. This included an 11-0 victory over Penn State in Joe Paterno's first year there. Cahill was voted 1966 Coach of the Year by the American Football Coaches and the Football Writers and Touchdown Club of Washington, D.C.

"Life can change so quickly," Cahill said that first season. "For 20 years I put my shoes on the same way, then all of a sudden people want to know--'How does it look, Tom?'--people who never asked me anything before."

Army had another fine year in at 8-2 again in 1967 and then 7-3 in 1968. But Cahill's squads ran into some trouble winning games as they closed out the 1960s with a 4-5-1 mark. Then, his 1970 squad went 1-9-1. Army was 6-4 in each of the next two seasons, then in an unexplainable happening, went winless in 1973.

Before the 1973 finale against Navy, West Point administrators assured reporters that Cahill would return as coach, no matter the outcome. However, after Navy won by 51-0, the worst defeat in the history of the rivalry, Cahill was fired.

His coaching record at Army was 40-39-2 in eight years, including a 5-3 mark against Navy.

Coach Cahill later put in five seasons at Union College in Schenectady, going 12-27-1. In 1984, Cahill returned to West Point and became a fixture in the press box at Michie Stadium as an analyst on the Army radio network. He was scheduled to broadcast a game but died at 73-years of age on the Thursday before the Oct 31 Army v Eastern Michigan game. He would have enjoyed chirping about this game as the Cadets won big 57-17.

1966 Coach Thomas Cahill

The Army Cadets football team represented the United States Military Academy in the 1966 college football season. It was Army's seventy-seventh season of intercollegiate football. They were led by Coach Thomas Cahill in his first of eight seasons as head coach of the Cadets. As an independent football entity, the Army team had a fine record this season under coach Cahill—8-2-0.

The Cadets compiled an 8-2-0 record; shut out three opponents, and outscored all opponents by a combined total of 141 to 105. In the annual Army–Navy Game, the Cadets defeated the Midshipmen by a score of 20 to 7. The Cadets also lost to Notre Dame (35-0) and Tennessee (38-7).

This year's home opener was on Sept 17 vs Kansas State. The Cadets defeated the Wildcats W (21-6). Other than those games played in neutral fields, all Army home games are played on the West Point campus at Michie Stadium in West Point NY. On Sept 24 at home, Army shut-out Holy Cross W (14-0). On Oct 1, in a close game at Michie Stadium, the Cadets defeated W (11-0) It was joe Paterno's first year as head coach for the Nittany Lions. The next week, Army traveled to South Bend, Indiana to face the Fighting Irish of Notre Dame. The Irish shut out the Cadets L (0-35).

The following week, Oct 22, at home, the Cadets roughed up Pittsburgh in a shutout W (28-0). Just one week later, Oct 29, Army was playing Tennessee at Memphis Memorial Stadium in Memphis, TN, and as tough as they played, the Cadets were roughed up a bit by the Volunteers in a losing effort L (7-38). On Nov 5 at home, the Cadets beat George Washington W (20–7). After traveling across the country on Nov 12, the Cadets could only muster up six points but California only managed to get just three points v the tough Cadet defense. This game was played at California Memorial Stadium in Berkeley, CA, and the Cadets beat the Golden Bears W 6–3.

On November 26, the Army Cadets defeated the Midshipmen of Navy in the Annual Army-Navy-Game at JFK Stadium in Philadelphia, PA W (20-7).

1967 Coach Thomas Cahill

<< Coach Thomas Cahill

The Army Cadets football team represented the United States Military Academy in the 1967 college football season. It was Army's seventy-eighth season of intercollegiate football. They were led by Coach Thomas Cahill in his second of eight seasons as head coach of the Cadets. As an independent football entity, the Army team had a fine record this season under coach Cahill—8-2-0.

The Cadets compiled an 8-2-0 record; shut out one opponent, and outscored all opponents by a combined total of 183 to 94. In the annual Army–Navy Game, the Cadets lost to the Midshipmen by a score of 14 to 19. The Cadets also lost to Duke by a 7 to 10 score. No Army players received first-team honors on the 1967 College Football All-America Team

This year's home opener was on Sept 23 vs Virginia. The Cadets defeated the Wahoo's W (26-7). Other than those games played in neutral fields, all Army home games are played on the West Point campus at Michie Stadium in West Point NY. On Sept 30, the Cadets played at Boston College's Alumni Stadium in Chestnut Hill, MA and gained the win W (21–10). Duke's Blue Devils beat the Cadets at Michie Stadium on Oct 7 in a close match L (7-10). Then, at the Cotton Bowl in Dallas Texas, on Nov 13, the Cadets defeated SMU W (24–6)

One week later on Oct 21, Rutgers played tough in a Cadet home game but lost the match to the Cadets W (14-3). A rough and tough Stanford team played the Cadets at home on Oct 28 and went back to California with a loss W (24-20). The always-ready Air Force Squad played a tough match on Nov 4 at Falcon Stadium in Colorado Springs, CO but it was not enough to avoid being beaten by the Cadets W (10-7). The Cadets shut out Utah at home on Nov 11 W (22-0). The next week, at Pitt Stadium in Pittsburgh PA, the Cadets beat Pittsburgh W (21-12).

With an 8-1 record, yet unranked, on December 2, the Army Cadets were defeated by the Midshipmen of Navy in the Annual Army-Navy-Game at JFK Stadium in Philadelphia, PA L (14-9).

During the 1967 season, despite having a fine record for the second year in a row, the Army Cadets had not received the favor in any week of being in the top 20. I would suspect that it was because Army was an Independent team and many other collegiate programs were affiliated with conferences. After the drought of fine seasons after Red Blaik, it's like Army had been forgotten by the Sports press. This would be the best Army record for thirty years as the team spun into a period of darkness and Army was awakened in a 10-2 season until 1996. In 1996, with Coach Sutton, Army was not favored again by the press as they were ranked 24th in the country despite a nice 10-2 record.

1968 Coach Thomas Cahill

The Army Cadets football team represented the United States Military Academy in the 1968 college football season. It was Army's seventy-ninth season of intercollegiate football. They were led by Coach Thomas Cahill in his third of eight seasons as head coach of the Cadets. As an independent football entity, the Army team had a fine record this season under coach Cahill—7-3-0.

The Cadets compiled a 7-3-0 record; shut out two opponents, and outscored all opponents by a combined total of 270-137. In the annual Army–Navy Game, the Cadets defeated the Midshipmen by a score of 24 to 14. The Cadets lost to Vanderbilt by a 13 to 17 score, and to Missouri by a 3 to 7 score.

This year's home opener was on Sept 21 vs The Citadel. Attendance was 23,000. The Cadets defeated the Bulldogs W (34-14). Other than those games played in neutral fields, all Army home games were played on the West Point Campus at Michie Stadium in West Point NY. On Sept 28, at home, Vanderbilt defeated the Cadets L (13-17).

On Oct 5, at Missouri's Memorial Stadium in Columbia, MO, the Tigers got the best of the Cadets L (3-7) before 58,576. Then on Oct

12, the Cadets squeaked out a win against the visiting California Golden Bears W (10-7) before a sellout of 32,000.

On Oct 19, the Cadets shut out Rutgers W (24-0). A week later the Cadets went into high gear and pitched a blow-out against Duke W (57-25). On Nov 2, at Beaver Stadium in the Nittany Valley of Pennsylvania, before 49,122, Joe Paterno's Lions defeated the Cadets L (24-28). On Nov 9, the Cadets pounded Boston College at home to the tune of W (58-25). Then, on Nov 16 at Pittsburgh's Pitt Stadium in Pittsburgh, PA, the Cadets shut-out the Panthers W (26–0)

With a 6-3record, on November 30, the Army Cadets defeated the Midshipmen of Navy in the Annual Army-Navy-Game at JFK Stadium in Philadelphia, PA W (21-14). The game was available for viewing on ABC TV and it was seen by 102,000 at JFK. My dad and I were watching it at home that day.

1969 Coach Thomas Cahill

The Army Cadets football team represented the United States Military Academy in the 1969 college football season. It was Army's eightieth season of intercollegiate football. They were led by Coach Thomas Cahill in his fourth of eight seasons as head coach of the Cadets. As an independent football entity, the Army team had a losing record this season under coach Cahill—4-5-1.

The Cadets compiled an 4-5-1 record; shut out one opponent, and outscored all opponents by a combined total of 161 to 160. Despite the poor season, the Cadets came alive for Navy. In the annual Army–Navy Game, the Cadets shut-out the Midshipmen by a score of 27-0. The Cadets lost five games this year—one more than they had won. No Army players received first-team honors on the 1969 College Football All-America Team

This year's home opener was on Sept 20 vs New Mexico. The Cadets defeated the Lobos W (31-14). Other than those games played in neutral fields, all Army home games are played on the West Point campus at Michie Stadium in West Point NY. On Sept 27 at Vanderbilt's Dudley Field in Nashville, TN, the Cadets beat the Commodores W (16–6). Back at home on Oct 4, my wedding anniversary, Texas A&M got the best of the Cadets by a touchdown L (13–20). Ready for a rumble, Notre Dame shut out the Cadets at Yankee Stadium in the Bronx, NY by a big score L 0–45.

On Oct 18, taking on Utah State at home, the Cadets were beaten by the Aggies, L (7–23). Hosting Boston College on Oct 25, the Cadets prevailed with a nice win W (38-7). On Nov 1, the Fighting Falcons of Air Force never gave up the fight in this game and beat the Cadets by a touchdown L (6-13). After getting on a big plane on Nov 8 to Sutzen Stadium in Eugene Oregon, the Cadets had all they could do to tie the Ducks in a great football game T (17-17). Then, back from the jet lag, the Cadets were not ready for Pittsburgh at home and lost to the Panthers L (6-15).

On November 30, the Army Cadets recouped their whole season by this one victory over Navy. That's how big this service rivalry actually is. They shut out the Midshipmen of Navy in the Annual Army-Navy-Game at JFK Stadium in Philadelphia, PA W (27-0).

1970 Coach Thomas Cahill

The Army Cadets football team represented the United States Military Academy in the 1970 college football season. It was Army's eighty-first season of intercollegiate football. They were led by Coach Thomas Cahill in his fifth of eight seasons as head coach of the Cadets. As an independent football entity, the Army team had a terrible losing record this season under coach Cahill—1-9-1.

The Cadets compiled a 1-9-1 record; shut out one opponent, Holy Cross in their only win, and were outscored by all opponents by a combined total of 151 to 281. With their poor season, and Navy's equally one victory season, the Cadets did not come alive for Navy. In the annual Army–Navy Game, the Navy won by scoring four more points in a game that had no offense L (7-11)

This year's home opener was on Sept 12 vs Holy Cross. The Cadets shut out the Crusaders W (26-0) It was the first win of the season for the Cadets and the only win. Other than those games played in neutral fields, all Army home games were played on the West Point campus at Michie Stadium in West Point NY. The list of losses in this poor football year for Army are shown below. No amount of scribing can make this a better season:

September 19 Baylor, home L (7–10)
September 26 at Nebraska L (0–28)
October 3 at Tennessee L (3–48)
October 10 at Notre Dame L (10–51)
October 17 at Virginia L (20–21)
October 24 Penn State, home L (14–38)
October 31 at Boston College L (13–21)
November 7 Syracuse, home, L 29–31
November 14 Oregon, home, T (22–22)
November 28 Navy, site neutral @JFK L (7–11)

1971 Coach Thomas Cahill

The Army Cadets football team represented the United States Military Academy in the 1971 college football season. It was Army's eighty-second season of intercollegiate football. They were led by Coach Thomas Cahill in his sixth of eight seasons as head coach of the Cadets. As an independent football entity, the Army team had an OK record this season under coach Cahill—6-4-0.

The Cadets compiled a 6-4-0 record; shut out no opponents, and were outscored by all opponents by a combined total of 146 to 206. This was not a bad season for Army but Navy had a terrible 3-8 season. Navy's three victory season gave them little hope in the annual battle. The Cadets were ready for Navy. In the annual Army–Navy Game, the Cadets beat the Midshipmen by the skin of their teeth 24 to 23.

This year's home opener was on Sept 18 vs Stanford. The Cardinal kept up the pressure the whole game and defeated the Cadets in a rare opening game loss L (3-38). The Cadets then traveled to Grant Field in Atlanta GA to defeat the Georgia Tech Yellow Jackets W (16-13).

The next win was at home on Oct 2vs. Missouri W (22–6). Joe Paterno's Penn State Nittany Lions shut out the Cadets on Oct 9 in a lop-sided game at Beaver Stadium in University Park PA L (0-42).

Air Force's Fighting Falcons then got the best of the Cadets on Oct 16 at Falcon Stadium in Colorado Springs, CO L (7–20). On Oct 23, at home, the Cadets beat the Virginia Wahoo's in a close match W (14-9). This was followed by a one-point loss to the Miami Hurricanes that was played in the Miami Orange Bowl in Miami, FL L (13–24)

On Nov 6 at home, the Cadets solidly beat the Rutgers Scarlet Knights W (30-17) On Nov 13, the Cadets kept the win streak going by defeating Pittsburgh at home W (17-14).

In the Army-Navy-Game on November 27 at JFK Stadium in Philadelphia, the Cadets got by the Midshipmen by one point in a really exciting nail-biter W (24-23)

1972 Coach Thomas Cahill

The Army Cadets football team represented the United States Military Academy in the 1972 college football season. It was Army's eighty-third season of intercollegiate football. They were led by Coach Thomas Cahill in his seventh of eight seasons as head coach of the Cadets. As an independent football entity, the Army team had an OK record this season under coach Cahill—6-4-0.

The Cadets compiled a 6-4-0 record; shut out no opponents, and were outscored by all opponents by a combined total of 160 to 282. This was a bad season for Army but Navy had as terrible a season also at 4-7. Navy's six loss season before the game gave them little hope in the annual battle other than that Army was doing just as poorly. The Cadets, who had problems with their D all year, were ready for Navy. In the annual Army–Navy Game, the Cadets beat the Midshipmen by the skin of their teeth 23 to 15.No Army players were selected as first-team players on the 1972 College Football All-America Team.

This year's home opener was on Sept 23 vs Nebraska. The visitors were relentless in the Cornhuskers win against the Cadets L (7-77).

After this game, the Cadets beat Texas A&M on Sept 30 at KLE Field in College Station Texas. The Cadets did not give up but came back. This win put the Cadets on track for a winning season.

On Oct 7, the Cadets beat Lehigh at home W (26-21). The Cadets played another Pennsylvania team, # 15 ranked Penn State the following week and were not so fortunate, being shut-out L (0-45). On Oct 14, the Cadets beat the Scarlet Knights of Rutgers by a TD W (35-28). After this win came another loss on Oct 28, against Miami of Florida at home L (7-28). The next week, Army slipped by Air Force for the win in a close match at home W (17-14).

Then on Nov 11, the Cadets lost to Syracuse in Archbold Stadium • Syracuse, NY L (6–27). The following week, Army won the first of two in a row, defeating Holy Cross in a close match at home W (15-13).

In the Army-Navy-Game on December 2, at JFK Stadium in Philadelphia, the Cadets defeated the Midshipmen to win the Commander-in-Chief's Trophy in the Army-Navy game) W (23–15).

1973 Coach Thomas Cahill

The Army Cadets football team represented the United States Military Academy in the 1973 college football season. It was Army's eighty-fourth season of intercollegiate football. They were led by Coach Thomas Cahill in his eighth and last of eight seasons as head coach of the Cadets. As an independent football entity, the Army team had its worst record ever under any coach 0-10-0.

That means the Cadets compiled a 0-10-0 record; shut out no opponents, and were outscored by all opponents by a combined total of 382 to 67. This was a bad season for Army. Navy had a bad season but at least they had some wins at 4-7. Navy's six loss season before the big game gave them little hope in the annual battle other than that Army had not even won any games. The Cadets, who had problems with their game all year, were not ready for Navy or any other team this year.

In the annual Army–Navy Game, the Midshipmen clobbered the Cadets in a shutout W (53-0). They also lost to Notre Dame by a whopping 62 to 3. Nothing could explain such a poor season and Tom Cahill would not be around the following year to offer an explanation. No Army players were selected as first team players on the 1972 College Football All-America Team.

The season record for 1973 follows

The results of this dismal season follow:

22-Sep	Tennessee	Home	L 18–37
29-Sep	California	Home	L 6–51
6-Oct	at Georgia Tech	Atlanta, GA	L 10–14
13-Oct	at Penn State	Beaver Stadium	L 3–54
20-Oct	Notre Dame	Home	L 3–62
27-Oct	Holy Cross	Home	L 10–17
3-Nov	at Air Force	Falcon Stadium	L 10–43
10-Nov	Miami (FL)	Home	L 7–19
17-Nov	Pittsburgh	Home	L0–34
1-Dec	vs. Navy	JFK Stadium	L 0–51

It was just a bad day for Army as Cahill suffered his third loss to Navy against five victories since becoming the head coach of the Cadets in 1966.

Homer Smith replaces Tom Cahill

Homer Smith got an extra year after his 1977 winning season at Army. It was not a sure thing. Army's head football coach converted what many believed was a "mission impossible" into a successful Army football season by doing exactly as he was ordered to do—win seven games and beat Navy in 1977. So, Smith, whose original four-year contract at West Point expired at the end of the year got the word that he had satisfied the Army enough to be rewarded with a new contract.

Army brass initially refused to comment on Smith's future, although they had already met to determine just what to do and when to announce it. Meanwhile, Homer Smith was not about to be jobless. Princeton appeared to be waiting in the wings to possibly offer Smith the Princeton head-coaching job if Army did not sign him to a new contract.

Following Army's third straight losing season under Coach Smith in 1976, the Board of Athletic Control at the United States Military Academy called in Smith last January and told him he had to win or else. They quantified it that he had to win at least seven games in 1977, including the Navy game, in order to remain as Army's head coach. That was the meets minimum requirements number. Most fans and pundits felt Army would not be able to win that many games or beat Navy. That's why it appeared to be a "mission impossible" for Smith and his staff.

But the Army players and coaches turned experts into know-nothings as the Cadets concluded a 7-4 won-lost season with a gratifying 17-14 triumph over Navy, which was Army's first victory over Navy in Smith's four years as head coach. Luck would not be so kind in 1978.

1974 Coach Homer Smith

The Army Cadets football team represented the US Military Academy in the 1974 college football season. It was Army's eighty-fifth season of inter-collegiate football. They were led by Coach Homer Smith in his first of five seasons as head coach of the Cadets. As an independent football entity, the Army team had a poor record of 3-8-0.

Overall, the Cadets compiled a 3-8-0 record; shut out no opponents, and were outscored by all opponents by a combined total of 306 to 156. This was a bad season for Army. Navy also had a bad season but they out won army by one game-- 4-7. Both teams had three wins when they met. The Navy, who had a few problems with their game all year, were ready for Army this year. In the annual Army–Navy Game, the Midshipmen shut out the Cadets W (19-0). No Army players were selected as first-team players on the 1974 College Football All-America Team.

<< **Coach
Homer Smith**

This year's home opener was on Sept 14 vs Lafayette. The Cadets prevailed in a close match W (14-7) Other than those games played in neutral fields, all Army home games were played on the West Point campus at Michie Stadium in West Point NY. On Sept 21, the Cadets defeated the Green Wave of Tulane at home W (14-31). On Sept 28, the Cadets traveled to California to play the Golden Bears and lost the match L (14-27). The next game was against Joe Paterno's Nittany Lions on Oct 5. The Cadets could not keep up with Penn State but lost by just one TD L (14-21). e

On Oct 12, at Duke's Wallace Wade Stadium in Durham, NC the Cadets lost to the Blue Devils L (14–33). On Oct 19   at Notre Dame's Notre Dame Stadium, the House that Rick Built in South Bend, IN, the Cadets were shut out by the Fighting Irish L (0–48). On Oct 26, the Cadets beat Holy Cross in a close match at home W 13–10. Then, on Nov 2, at home, the Vanderbilt Commodores beat the Cadets L (14-38.

The next week on Nov 9, at home, Army squeaked out a victory over Air Force for the Commander-in-Chief's Trophy W (17–16). In the game before the Army-Navy Game, the Cadets lost a close match in a shootout against North Carolina at Kenan Memorial Stadium in Chapel Hill, NC L (42–56).

In the Army-Navy-Game on November 30, at JFK Stadium in Philadelphia, the Cadets were defeated in a shutout by the Midshipmen to win the Commander-in-Chief's Trophy (Army-Navy-Game) L (0-19).

1975 Coach Homer Smith

The Army Cadets football team represented the United States Military Academy in the 1975 college football season. It was Army's eighty-sixth season of intercollegiate football. They were led by Coach Homer Smith in his second of five seasons as head coach of the Cadets. As an independent football entity, the Army team had a poor record of 2-9-0.

Overall, the Cadets compiled a 2-9-0 record; shut out no opponents, and were outscored by all opponents by a combined total of 337 to 165. This was another bad season for Army. Navy had a fine season including a nice win against Army but they met. The Midshipmen beat the Cadets 6 to 30.No Army players were selected as first-team players on the 1974 College Football All-America Team.

This year's home opener was on Sept 13 vs Holy Cross. The Cadets won in a blowout W (44-7) Other than those games played in neutral fields, all Army home games were played on the West Point campus at Michie Stadium in West Point NY. On Sept 20, Army defeated Lehigh in a shootout W (54-32). This would be the last Army victory if the 1975 season.

The losses for the rest of the Cadets season follow in tabular form

27-Sep	Villanova	Home	L 0–10
4-Oct	at Stanford	Stanford CA	L 14–67
11-Oct	Duke	Home	L 10–21
18-Oct	Pittsburgh	Home	L 20–52
25-Oct	at Penn State	Beaver Stadium	L 0–31
1-Nov	at Air Force	Falcon Stadium	L 3–33
8-Nov	Boston College	Home	L 0–31
15-Nov	at Vanderbilt	Dudley Field	L 14–23
29-Nov	vs. Navy	JFK Stadium	L 6–30

1976 Coach Homer Smith

The Army Cadets football team represented the United States Military Academy in the 1976 college football season. It was Army's eighty-seventh season of intercollegiate football. They were led by Coach Homer Smith in his third of five seasons as head coach of the Cadets. As an independent football entity, the Army team had a poor record of 5-6-0.

Overall, the Cadets compiled a 5-6-0 record; shut out no opponents, and were outscored by all opponents by a combined total of 267 to 201. This was another poor record for Army, though they played well and lost a number of close games. Navy had a poor season also (4-7) but they were able to get a nice win against Army in the traditional rivalry game. The Midshipmen beat the Cadets 10 to 38.No Army players were selected as first-team players on the 1974 College Football All-America Team.

This year's home opener was on Sept 11 vs Lafayette The Cadets won in a close match W (16-6). Other than those games played in neutral fields, all Army home games were played on the West Point campus at Michie Stadium in West Point NY. On Sept 18, Army defeated Holy Cross in a very tight game W (26-24). On Sept 25, North Carolina defeated Army by just two points W (26-24). The Cadets won by even less (one point) vs Stanford the following week on Oct 2 W (21-20.

On Oct 9, Joe Paterno's Penn State squad beat the Cadets at beaver Stadium in University park, PA L (16-38) in the first of three losses in a row. The next loss was on Oct 16 against Tulane's Green Wave at The Louisiana Superdome in New Orleans, LA L (10–23). The third loss was on Oct 23 at home against Boston College   L (10–27). The Cadets recovered against the Fighting Falcons of Air Force on Oct 30 at home with a nice win W (24-7) competing for the Commander-in-Chief's Trophy.

On Nov at No. 2 Pittsburgh, the Panthers got the best of the Cadets L (7-37). The next game was Colgate at home. The Cadets played well and defeated the Raiders W (29-13)

In the Army-Navy-Game on November 27, at JFK Stadium in Philadelphia, the Cadets had a tough time scoring while Navy put 38-points on the board to defeat Army. The Midshipmen won this leg of the Commander-in-Chief's Trophy (Army-Navy-Game) L (10-38).

1977 Coach Homer Smith

The Army Cadets football team represented the United States Military Academy in the 1977 college football season. It was Army's eighty-eighth season of intercollegiate football. They were led by Coach Homer Smith in his fourth of five seasons as head coach of the Cadets. As an independent football entity, the Army team had a respectable record of 7-4.

Overall, the Cadets compiled a 7-4-0 record. They finished with their first winning season since 1972. Army's win over UMass was the 500th in school history. Leamon Hall threw five touchdown passes, including three to freshman Mike Fahnstock. Homer Smith– Eastern Coach of the Year (New York Football Writers Association). In the Army-Navy Game, the Cadets beat the Midshipmen 17 to 14 at JFK Stadium. Army won the Commander in Chief's Trophy.

This year's home opener was on Sept 10 vs UMass The Cadets won handily W (34-10) before 22,101. Other than those games played in neutral fields, all Army home games were played on the West Point campus at Michie Stadium in West Point NY. On Sept 17 at home vs VMI, the Cadets had what it takes to win the game and won W (27-14. On the road at 2-0, Army traveled to Alumni Stadium in Chestnut Hill, MA on Sept 24, where they found a tough and stubborn Boston College Eagles team that would not give up until they had pounded the Cadets defense for 49-points. BC won this match handily L (28-49).

Next on Oct 1 was a tough Colorado Buffaloes team that shut out the Cadets at home L (0-31). With two losses in a row, Army pulled out all the stops to beat a determined Villanova Squad W (34-32) in a nail-biter. The next week it was Dan Devine's Fighting Irish playing in Giants Stadium before 72, 594 fans. The Irish shut out the Cadets in a tough battle L 90-24). Lafayette was next at Michie Stadium and the Cadets made quick work of the Leopards W (42-6).

Holy Cross came next to battle the Cadets but the Cadets were too big, too powerful and too determined and so they beat the Crusaders in a shootout W (48-7) before a packed house of 41,376. The Cadets then traveled to Falcon Stadium in Colorado Springs CO on Nov 5 to face the Air Force for the Commander in Chief's Trophy. The Cadets earned the win W (31-6). On Nov 12, Pittsburgh beat the Cadets by two to one at Giants Stadium in East Rutherford, NJ L (26-52)

In the season finale, the Cadets played in the annual Army-Navy-Game, which this year was played on November 27 at JFK Stadium in Philadelphia. It was a low scoring game but the Cadets hung in there to defeat the Midshipmen by a field goal W (17-14). Since the Cadets also beat Air Force, they won the Commander-in-Chief's Trophy for 1977

1978 Coach Homer Smith

The Army Cadets football team represented the United States Military Academy in the 1978 college football season. It was Army's eighty-ninth season of intercollegiate football. They were led by Coach Homer Smith in his fifth of five seasons as head coach of the Cadets. As an independent football entity, the Army team had a respectable record of 4-6-1.

Overall, the Cadets compiled a 4-6-1 record. They finished with another losing season. Coach Smith would not get to coach the following year. Army pitched no shutouts against its opponents and they were outscored by their opponents by a combined total of 255 to 188. In the annual Army–Navy Game, the Cadets lost to the Midshipmen by a 28 to 0 score.at JFK Stadium. No Army players were selected as first-team players on the 1978 College Football All-America Team.

This year's home opener was on Sept 16 vs Lafayette. The Cadets won in a tough battle W (24-14). Other than those games played in neutral fields, all Army home games were played on the West Point campus at Michie Stadium in West Point NY. On Sept 23, Virginia busted into Michie Stadium ready to take a victory home with them.

In a very close game, the determined Wahoo's got their win L (17-21) and there were no happy Cadets. On Sept 30, a tough Washington State Squad played Army to a tie at Michie T (21-21).

On Oct 7, no team volunteered to lose but the Tennessee Volunteers played the best that day and they got the big W against the Cadets L (13-31). Then, on Oct 14, a team that once was a pushover for the Cadets decided to win and win big. Holy Cross whose days of fame were just in front of it, grabbed some fame in 1978 when they shut out the once vaunted Army Cadets big time L (0-31). As nice as it was for Holy Cross, nobody at Army was smiling.

On Oct 21, the up and coming Florida Gators whose dark days were way behind them turned their tricks on the Cadets at Florida Field • in Gainesville, FL, and they walked away with a nice win over Army L (7–31). Colgate was struggling sometimes in Division II and Army simply overpowered the Raiders on Oct 28, W (28-3). On Nov 4, the Air Force Fighting Falcons came to beat the Cadets but did not. It was just the opposite W (28-14).

On Nov 11, BC almost upset the Cadets at home but the Cadets scored a few more points than the Boston College Eagles, winning the game at home W (29-26) by three points. That's all it takes sometimes to win. On Nov 18, the Cadets lost by a 2 to 1 margin to Pittsburgh at Pitt Stadium in Pittsburgh, PA L (17–35).

In the season finale for Army, despite loving each other in real battles, on the gridiron, the Midshipmen were always looking to make the Army look bad. The Cadets again dutifully played in the annual Army-Navy-Game, planning to rip out a slice of the Navy squad. So, on December 2, at JFK Stadium in Philadelphia. It was a low (0) scoring game for Army but nobody told Navy to keep their guns silent. The Midshipmen walked out of JFK with a win W – a (28-0) shutout over the Cadets and they, not Army, won the Commander-in-Chief's Trophy for 1978

Chapter 13 Coaches Saban, Cavanaugh & Young 1979 - 1989

Saban   Coach # 28
Cavanaough   Coach # 29
Young   Coach # 30

Year	Coach	Record	Conference	Record
1979	Lou Saban	2-8-1	Indep	2-8-1
1980	Ed Cavanaugh	3-7-1	Indep	3-7-1
1980	Ed Cavanaugh	3-7-1	Indep	3-7-1
1982	Ed Cavanaugh	4-7-0	Indep	4-7-0
1983	Jim Young	2-9-0	Indep	2-9-0
1984	Jim Young	8-3-1	Indep	8-3-1
1985	Jim Young	9-3-0	Indep	9-3-0
1986	Jim Young	6-5-0	Indep	6-5-0
1987	Jim Young	5-6-0	Indep	5-6-0
1988	Jim Young	9-3-0	Indep	9-3-0
1989	Jim Young	6-5-0	Indep	6-5-0
1990	Jim Young	6-5-0	Indep	6-5-0

1979 Coach Lou Saban

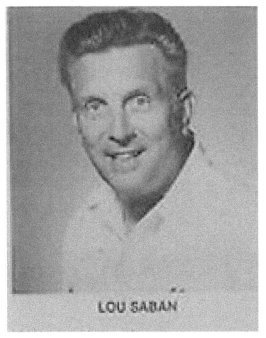

LOU SABAN

The Army Cadets football team represented the United States Military Academy in the 1979 college football season. It was Army's ninetieth season of intercollegiate football. They were led by Coach Lou Saban in his first and last of one season as head coach of the Cadets. As an independent football entity, the Army team had a terrible record of 2-8-1

Overall, the Cadets compiled a 2-8-1 record. They finished with another losing season. Coach Saban would choose not to coach the following year. Army pitched no shutouts against its opponents and they were not only outscored by their opponents but they had three shutouts thrown against them.

In the annual Army–Navy Game, the Cadets lost to the Midshipmen by a 31 to 7 score.at JFK Stadium. No Army players were selected as first-team players on the 1978 College Football All-America Team.

Coach Lou Saban could have brought victories to Army's flailing program at the time but his temperament did not blend in well with the Army Brass.

By the time Lou Saban joined the Army coaching "team," he had developed a reputation as an itinerant coach, a "notorious job-hopper" who was nevertheless respected for rebuilding teams in poor condition. Lou Saban needed to hold the steering wheel in his hand to steer the ship and he found others with a tight grip on the wheel that only a Superman and a super management negotiator could release. Saban was a coach and did not want that kind of job.

Saban said he wanted to stay at Army "until they put me out to pasture". I think he meant it but he needed to have the tools in his hand. Saban stayed at Army for only one season. He said he was unhappy with the academy's unwillingness to invest more in its football program. "This is a desperate situation", he said near the end of the 1979 season. "To fight alone as a football staff is impossible." He resigned in July 1980 after leading Army to a 2–8–1 record the previous season. Nobody missed him but they would have if he had control of the program. He was quite a coach with a 50-year career.

This year's home opener was on Sept 15 vs Connecticut. The Cadets won in a tough battle W (26-10). Other than those games played in neutral fields, all Army home games were played on the West Point campus at Michie Stadium in West Point NY. On Sept 22 at Stanford, in Stanford Stadium, Stanford, CA, the Cadets got the best of the Cardinal W (17–13). Then on Sept 29, at home, North Carolina came in tough and beat the Cadets L (3–41). Next up on Oct 6, was the Duke Blue Devils, who played the Cadets to a tie T (17-17).

Joe Paterno's Penn State squad played the Cadets at on Oct 13 at Beaver Stadium in University Park, PA and hung in for a games worth and got the win L (3–24). In the Army's first game against Baylor on Oct 20, that I can recall, things did not go well as the Bears decided to claw and pound the Cadets to the tune of a big loss L (0-55)

Once in a losing mode, the Cadets tried to recover but were defeated by Boston College at home on Oct 27 L (16-29). No games after the first two were wins so the losses came and came and came and did not go way for the whole season. At Air Force, the score was L (7-28). At Rutgers, the shutout score was L (0-20) and Pittsburgh at home was even worse L (0-40). The usual end of season Army-Navy-Game was also a stinker for Army with Navy whooping Army at the usual place and time (Dec 1) by the score of L (7-31)

1980 Coach Ed Cavanaugh

The Army Cadets football team represented the United States Military Academy in the 1980 college football season. It was Army's ninety-first season of intercollegiate football. They were led by Coach Ed Cavanaugh in his first of three seasons as head coach of the Cadets. As an independent football entity, the Army team had a terrible record of 3-7-1

Overall, the Cadets compiled a 3-7-1 record. They finished with another losing season. Army pitched no shutouts against its opponents and they were outscored by their opponents 295 to 204. Army had worst numbers with other coaches. They had no shutouts thrown against them. In the annual Army–Navy Game, the Cadets lost to Navy by a definitive 33 to 6 score. It was no fluke.

This year's home opener was on Sept 13 vs Holy Cross. The Cadets won W (28-7). Other than those games played in neutral fields, all Army home games were played on the West Point campus at Michie Stadium in West Point NY. On Sept 20, an always formidable foe, California's Golden Bars came to play at Michie and were held back by a determined Cadet Team W (26-19). There would be no transcontinental win for California this day. Heading out to the West Coast for the game the following week, the Cadets were defeated by Washington State L (18-31). Back on the schedule after many years, Harvard showed they were the team they always had been by defeating the Cadets at home L (10-15).

On Oct 11, Lehigh played Army to a tough earned tie T (24-24). On Oct 18, the Cadets traveled to play Notre Dame at Notre Dame Stadium in South Bend, IN, and were outscored by the Irish L (3–30). The following week, and always tough Boston College Squad met the Army at Alumni Stadium in Chestnut Hill, MA L (14–30). The Cadets lost this one. Then on Nov 1 Rutgers Scarlet Knights defeated the Cadets at home L 21–37. The next outing was Nov 8 at home against Air Force for the Commander-in-Chief's Trophy. The Cadets won the game W (47–24). On Nov 15, the Cadets lost big time to Pittsburgh at home L (7–45)

In the usual end of season Army-Navy-Game, the Cadets misfired for Army with Navy whooping Army at the usual place and time (Nov 29) by the score of L (6-33)

1981 Coach Ed Cavanaugh

The Army Cadets football team represented the United States Military Academy in the 1981 college football season. It was Army's ninety-second season of intercollegiate football. They were led by Coach Ed Cavanaugh in his second of three seasons as head coach of the Cadets. As an independent football entity, the Army team had a terrible record of 3-7-1

Overall, the Cadets compiled a 3-7-1 record. They finished with another losing season. Army pitched one shutout against Princeton and no others and they were outscored by their opponents 212 to 126. The team had two shutouts thrown against them – Rutgers & Pittsburgh. In the annual Army–Navy Game, the Cadets played the Midshipmen to a 3-3 tie.

This year's home opener was on Sept 12 vs Missouri. The Cadets lost L (10-24) to the Tigers. Other than those games played in neutral fields, all Army home games were played on the West Point campus

at Michie Stadium in West Point NY. On Sept 19 at home, the
Cadets were defeated by VMI by one TD L (7–14). Then, on Sept 26,
the Cadets beat Brown W (23-17) at home. On Oct 3, Army beat
Harvard W (27-13) in a game played at Harvard Stadium in Allston,
MA. Then on Oct 10, the Cadets were shut out by Rutgers at home L
(0-17).

On October 17, the Cadets got their only shutout of the year vs.
Princeton and they won this home game W (34-0). On Oct 24 at
home, Boston College pounded the Cadets L (6-41). In the
Commander in Chief game v Air Force on Oct 31, the Fighting
Falcons defeated the Cadets in a low-scoring close match L (3-7).
Holy Cross then got the best of Army on Nov 7 L (13-28). The next
week on Nov 14 at Pittsburgh's Pitt Stadium in Pittsburgh, PA, the
Panthers whomped the Cadets in a big shutout L (0-48).

On December 1, in the end of season Army-Navy-Game, the
Midshipmen tied the Cadets at Veterans Stadium in Philadelphia
Cadets T (3-3)

1982 Coach Ed Cavanaugh

The Army Cadets football team represented the United States
Military Academy in the 1982 college football season. It was Army's
ninety-third season of intercollegiate football. They were led by
Coach Ed Cavanaugh in his third and last of three seasons as head
coach of the Cadets. As an independent football entity, the Army
team had a terrible record of 3-7-1

Overall, the Cadets compiled a 3-7-1 record. They finished with
another losing season. Army pitched no shutouts and had no
shutouts thrown against them. They were outscored by their
opponents 271 to 164. In the annual Army–Navy Game, the Cadets
lost to the Midshipmen by a 24-7 score.

This year's season opener was on Sept 11 vs Missouri at Faurot
Field, Columbia, MO. The Cadets lost L (10-23) to the Tigers. Other
than those games played in neutral fields, all Army home games were
7played on the West Point campus at Michie Stadium in West Point
NY. On Sept 18 at home, the Cadets defeated Lafayette W (26–20).

Then, on Sept 25, the Cadets traveled to North Carolina's Kenan Memorial Stadium in Chapel Hill, NC, and they were pounded by the Tar Heels L (8–62). On Oct 2 at home, the Cadets defeated Harvard's Crimson W (17–13)

On Oct 9 at Giants Stadium in East Rutherford, NJ, the Cadets lost to Rutgers 3–24. Then on Oct 16 at Princeton's Palmer Stadium in Princeton, NJ, the Cadets came through with the win W (20–14). The following week at home, on Oct 23, Boston College defeated Army L (17–32). At the end of October, on the 30th, the Cadets beat the Columbia Raiders at home W (41–8). Next game on Nov 6, at home v Air Force, the Fighting Falcons defeated the Cadets L (9–27). Then it was Pitt at home on Nov 13. The Panthers defeated the Cadets L (6-24).

In the season finale on December 1, the Army-Navy-Game, the Midshipmen defeated the Cadets at Veterans Stadium in Philadelphia L (7-24)

Jim Young to replace Ed Cavanaugh as Army Head Coach

Football, even football at the college level service academies, is a tough business. Ed Cavanaugh was fired Monday, Dec. 6, 1982 after his third losing season. Ironically, it was Cavanaugh's best winning season of the three. As head football coach at Army, Cavanaugh sensed the inevitable after a loss to Navy on Saturday Dec. 4.

'I like to eat, but I'm realistic also,' Cavanaugh said after Saturday's defeat in the 83rd renewal of the classic rivalry.

'I'm very understanding about the situation and I know that coaching is judged by wins and losses.'

Cavanaugh succeeded Lou Saban after the 1979 season and registered a 10-21-2 record. The Cadets posted identical 3-7-1 records during the 1980 and '81 seasons. This year, they finished with a 4-7 mark.

'Cavanaugh worked very hard to improve the program according to the West Point Athletic Director, Carl Ulrich: "… we are grateful for his efforts. Though some progress has been made, we feel that it's time to make a change."

Ulrich planned to replace Cavanaugh by year end.

At a National Football Foundation and Hall of Fame lunch in New York City, Brig. General Bill Carpenter, Army's famed 'lonely end' of the late 1950's, said the Point's failure to recruit all-star high school and prep school talent contributes to the Academy's football failures. Some say overall leadership. One thing for sure, Army after Coach Blaik was a different program. Jim Young after his 2-9 start in 1983 was a breath of fresh air for the Army program.

On Nov. 10, 1984, the Pittsburgh Post-Gazette wrote an inspiring article that they make available today on their web site. Thank you for that. Jim Young in many ways brought back an Earl "Red" Blaik spirit to the Army Cadets.

WEST POINT, N Y. –

The kaleidoscope of colors swirling around Army's Michie Stadium fades with each passing frost; the scarlets and auburns and golds give way to shades of sepia along the palisades that plunge into the Hudson River. Yet the scene remains breathtaking and just a bit arrogant, like the brittle brown photographs of West Point graduates Robert E. Lee and Stonewall Jackson.

For the better part of the last decade, the autumn view was the only reason to climb Michie's bleachers on a Saturday afternoon. "I know Sports Illustrated came out and said this is the best place to watch a college football game," Army Athletic Director Carl Ullrich said. "I'm sick and tired of all that. I want to get to the point where they say it's a great place to watch a great college football team."

Army, now 5-2-1, isn't great. But by beating Air Force, 24-12, Saturday night at West Point, the Black Knights moved closer to a bowl trip -- their first ever. Scouts from the Hall of Fame, Liberty, Bluebonnet and Independence bowls watched Saturday's game.

"All four said before the game that they were as interested in us as they were in Air Force now 5-4," Ullrich said. "You're always looking for teams that have a good following, and the service academies will always bring people out," said Bill Oakley of the Hall of Fame Bowl committee. Said the Bluebonnet's Ted Nance: "Army and Virginia are two teams that have never been to a bowl; certainly, Army is a logical draw."

If Army loses at Boston College today and beats Montana (2-6-1) in Tokyo Nov. 17, it will be 6-3-1 going into its open weekend of Nov. 24, when the bowl committees announce their selections. Bowl scouts would be willing to take a chance on Army, banking that the Black Knights could beat Navy, Dec. 1 at Philadelphia.

Beat Navy. The plea is painted in letters, 20 feet tall, on the roof of Cullum Hall. You see it from anywhere at West Point, contrasting sharply with the staid gray granite walls of the nearby Cadet barracks and its adjacent parade ground, where the grass is clipped as close as a military buzz cut. Army last beat Navy in 1977; its record against the Midshipmen since 1973 stands at 1-9-1...

In 1973 the Black Knights went 0-10, losing to Navy 51-0. Homer Smith followed Cahill and introduced a passing offense that produced the only winning season in the last decade: 7-4 in 1977. The next year, however, Army went 4-6-1, losing to Navy 28-0. Smith was gone. He retreated to the Harvard School of Divinity and later resurfaced as offensive coordinator at UCLA. His dismissal was a bitter one "He didn't fit the image of Army football" - one Army official said, and Smith later took a list of alleged violations to the NCAA. The NCAA investigated and issued a warning, telling Army to clean up its record-keeping.

Meanwhile, Army hired Lou Saban. "That was one of our worst mistakes," said Col. Al Vanderbush, a deputy athletic director who played guard and linebacker on Army's last undefeated team: the 1958 squad that finished No. 3 in the nation with Heisman Trophy winner Pete Dawkins in the backfield.

"With Saban's track record and his age (57), why in the world did we hire him if we were trying to rebuild?" Vanderbush asked. "Then when he quit after one year he has a habit of doing that, we hired his assistant, Ed Cavanaugh. He (Ed) just didn't have the charisma; as far as I know, nobody here liked him."

From 1980 through 1982, Cavanaugh's teams went 10-21-2, continuing the trend that was set in motion after Blaik (121-33-10) retired. "In the 50's, we were comparable to the best teams in the country, but our program stagnated as other programs started getting better and better," Vanderbush said.

For a while, there was a Vietnam excuse, which sufficed. But then George Welsh arrived at Navy in 1973 and took the Midshipmen to three bowl games. Air Force took it from there, winning the 1982 Hall of Fame Bowl and the 1983 Independence Bowl. Ullrich spent 11 years at Navy, five as an assistant athletic director, before becoming the Army athletic director in 1980. "When I got here, we were 10 years behind the Naval Academy," said Ullrich, 56.

Army players were still required to go to class Saturday mornings before home games, getting out of Chemical Engineering 301 at 11 a.m. and running up the hillside to Michie in time for pregame warm-ups. They had no weight program; they waited in line with the rest of the Cadets at the academy's only weight room. They had no training table. Ullrich pushed for the new weight room and locker room complex. He adjusted players' schedules so they take fewer credit hours in the fall, ' more in the spring. He eliminated the Saturday morning classes.

Finally, he hired Jim Young. The road winds up the hill to Michie Stadium, passing the Cadet Chapel and taking a sharp right at Lusk Reservoir. There, at the bend, stands a statue as striking as Washington's Iwo Jima Memorial. Called "The American Soldier," it captures three GIs straining forward into battle. "Presented to the Corps of Cadets," the inscription reads. "The lives and destinies of valiant Americans are entrusted to your care and leadership."

All Cadets take classes in leadership, through the psychology department, the military science department, the philosophy department. Upon graduation, they are appointed second lieutenants in the regular U.S. Army.

"Military folks like to look to a confident leader," Vanderbush said. "People here at the academy, from the Cadets to the instructors to the career military men, became kind of cynical when they saw the lack of leadership in some of our recent football coaches." Jim Gentile is a senior linebacker who leads Army in tackles this season.

"You meet a lot of leaders here; you know what it takes. As soon as Coach Young got here, we knew it would be different." Karl Heineman, a senior offensive tackle, started all 11 games as a sophomore in Cavanaugh's first season. "In the last game, he called me No. 62," Heineman said.

"Coach Young knew all our name-; by the second day of practice." Some at the academy doubted Ullrich's judgment when he hired Young. They wanted someone with experience at a service academy preferably a West Point graduate. Ullrich, however, refused and looked to Young's credentials. He worked nine years as an assistant to Bo Schembechler. First at Miami of Ohio and then at Michigan.

In 1972, he left Michigan to become head coach at Arizona. He compiled a 31-13 record before becoming head coach at Purdue. Purdue had a great run with Young. Reaching three bowl games. Young, at 49, left coaching and took a year off as an associate athletic director at Purdue. Young hedged when asked why he gave up coaching and then one year later returned to the profession, at Army of all places.

"I thought I had quit coaching for good; I got rid of all my books." lie said. "But I missed the association with the players and coaches, and 1 missed the ups and downs of (-very Saturday ... I like it here. You never have to worry about the kids going to class, yet you play to win."

Last season, Young's first, his team went 2-9, so he scrapped the pro-style offense he installed at Purdue and reverted to the wishbone. "The Air Force Academy was having great success with it, and we had similar personnel," he said. Strapped by Army's entrance requirements, Young knew he'd have to make do with a slower offensive line more suited to run-blocking," Young generously commented.

The new Army coach started the grand experiment last spring. At the time. Nate Sassaman was a back-up defensive back, and Doug Black was trying to make the varsity after being cut as a freshman and spending his sophomore season in the Army intramural league. Both played the wishbone in high school, so Young made Sassaman his starting quarterback and Black his starting fullback.

When trying to explain Army's sudden success this year, Young flinches at the mention of the Army-Navy game, preferring to put it on hold until Thanksgiving weekend. But to understand football at West Point is to realize why this year's prospects for a bowl trip haven't sent the Army brass into frenzied celebration. "I don't want to sound too ho-hum; we are thrilled with how the season is going," Ullrich said after the victory over Air Force. "There was lots of hugging and cheering, but it wasn't boisterous because here, our season is not going to be complete unless we beat Navy."

No wonder Army's mascot is a mule. The stubborn streak inherent among the straight-backed officers at West Point greatly aided the decline and fall of Army football. They were Cadets in the halycon days when Doc Blanchard and Glenn Davis led coach Earl Blaik's troops to national championships in 1944 and 1945 - and they greeted Army's fall from grace with much wringing of hands. But they wouldn't change.

Tradition is everything at West Point, where the "Long Gray Line" of graduates includes Lee, Jackson, Douglass C. MacArthur, George S. Patton and Dwight D. Eisenhower. The place has a certain timeless grace, a sense of history as tangible as the musty smell of the Cadet Chapel's stone foundation. "It's a thrill for me to live here; 20 yards from my house are the ruins of a Revolutionary War fort," Young said. "It's like Camelot. A place that doesn't exist anymore." That's the romantic view. Those involved with Army football after Blaik retired in 1958 saw the program get trapped in a time warp it took decades to escape.

The latest bowl talk draws a cynical smile from Tom Cahill, who coached Army to a 40-39-2 record from 1966 to 1973. In his first season, the Black Knights went 8-2 and Cahill was proclaimed coach of the year. In 1967 Army beat Pitt to go 8-1 and earn an invitation to the Sugar Bowl. But the Secretary of the Army, the honorable Stanley R. Resor, declined the bid. "Because American troops were fighting in Vietnam, he decided it was inappropriate for Army to play in the carnival like atmosphere of New Orleans," said Cahill, who now does radio color commentary of all Army games for WNBR in Beacon, N.Y.

After the 2-9 season, Jim Young brought Army a lot of smiles going 8-3, then 9-3, then 8-5 before a losing season in 1987 5-6. He finished up as you will soon see with a great 9-3 season in 1988 followed by two 6-5 seasons before he turned the reins over to Bob Sutton in 1991. I can still smell the fresh air.

1983 Coach Jim Young

The Army Cadets football team represented the United States Military Academy in the 1983 college football season. It was Army's ninety-fourth season of intercollegiate football. They were led by Coach Jim Young in his first of eight seasons as head coach of the Cadets. As an independent football entity, the Army team had a terrible record of 2-9-0

Overall, the Cadets compiled a 2-9-0 record. They finished with another poor season. Army pitched no shutouts and had no shutouts thrown against them. They were outscored by their opponents 304 to 140. In the annual Army–Navy Game, the Cadets lost to the Midshipmen by a 42-13 score.

This year's opener was on Sept 10 vs Colgate at home. The Cadets lost to the Red Raiders in a close match L (13-15). Other than those games played in neutral fields, all Army home games were played on the West Point campus at Michie Stadium in West Point NY. On Sept 17 at Louisville's Cardinal Stadium in Louisville, KY, the Cardinals defeated the Cadets L (7–31).

With no victories yet in the season, Army determination helped the Cadets on Sept 24 to defeat the Dartmouth Big Green in a close, hard fought match W (13-12). On Oct 1, the Cadets lost to Harvard at Harvard Stadium in Allston, MA L (21–24). The Cadets second and last win of the season came on Oct 8 v Rutgers at home W (20-12).

On Oct 15, the Cadets took on Gerry Faust's Notre Dame Fighting Irish at Giants Stadium in East Rutherford, NJ and were defeated by the Irish L (0–42). Then, on Oct 22, at home, Lehigh's Mountain

Hawks defeated the Cadets in a one-point game L (12-13). On Oct 29 at Air Force's Falcon Stadium in Colorado Springs, CO in the Commander-in-Chief's Trophy) game, the Fighting Falcons beat the Cadets L (20–41). On Nov 5 at home, Boston College defeated Army handily L (14–34). Then in a precursor to the Army-Navy game, the Pitt game was always a tough one. This year was not different played at Pitt Stadium in Pittsburgh, PA, the Panthers defeated the Cadets L (7–38)

On November 25, in the season finale Army-Navy-Game, the Midshipmen beat the Cadets in Rose Bowl Stadium in Pasadena, CA in the Commander-in-Chief's Trophy game L (13–42).

1984 Coach Jim Young

The Army Cadets football team represented the United States Military Academy in the 1984 college football season. It was Army's ninety-fifth season of intercollegiate football. They were led by Coach Jim Young in his second of eight seasons as head coach of the Cadets. As an independent football entity, the Army team had a fine record of 8-3-1

Overall, the Cadets compiled an 8-3-1 record. They finished with a fine season record. Army pitched no shutouts and had no shutouts thrown against them. They outscored their opponents 320 to 218. In the annual Army–Navy Game, the Cadets defeated the Midshipmen by a 28-11 score. The Cadets also defeated Michigan State, 10–6, in the 1984 Cherry Bowl.

This year's home opener was on Sept 15 vs Colgate. The Cadets got the season off the right way with a convincing win against the Red Raiders W (41-15). Other than those games played in neutral fields, all Army home games were played on the West Point campus at Michie Stadium in West Point NY. On Sept 22, at Tennessee's Neyland Stadium in Knoxville, TN, the Volunteers played the Cadets to a tie T (24–24). On Sept 29 at home, the Cadets defeated the Duke Blue Devils W 13–9. With their best start in years at 3-0, on Oct 6, Army kept the streak going with their 4th win in a row v Harvard W (33-11).

Finally, the Cadets lost their first game of the season on Oct 13 to Rutgers L (7-14). On Oct 20, they got back on track by defeating Penn at home W (48–13). On Oct 27, after a trip to the Carrier Dome, Syracuse's new Stadium, the Cadets lost to the Orangemen L (16-27). Then, on Nov 3, Army defeated Air Force at home W (24-12). The following week in a tough game v Boston College on Nov 10, the Cadets lost to the Eagles L (31-45). On Nov 17 vs Montana in a game played in Tokyo Japan's Mirage Bowl, the Cadets won W (45-31)

On Dec 1 in the season finale, the Army-Navy-Game, the Cadets beat the Midshipmen at Veterans Stadium in Philadelphia, PA (Commander-in-Chief's Trophy) W (28–11)

In their first post-season Bowl game, the Cherry Bowl vs. Michigan State at the Pontiac Silverdome in Pontiac, MI, the Cadets prevailed W (10–6). Despite a fine year, Army was unranked by the major polling units.

1985 Coach Jim Young

The Army Cadets football team represented the United States Military Academy in the 1985 college football season – from 1890. It was Army's ninety-sixth season of intercollegiate football. They were led by Coach Jim Young in his third of eight seasons as head coach of the Cadets. As an independent football entity, the Army team had a fine record of 9-3-0

Overall, the Cadets compiled a 9-3-0 record. They finished with a fine season record. Army pitched no shutouts and had no shutouts thrown against them. They outscored their opponents 396 to 232. In the annual Army–Navy Game, the Cadets were defeated by the Midshipmen by a 7-17 score. The Cadets also defeated Illinois in the Peach Bowl, 31-29.

This year's opener was on Sept 14 vs Western Michigan at home. The Cadets got the season off the right way with a convincing win against the Broncos W (48-6). Other than those games played in neutral fields, all Army home games were played on the West Point campus at Michie Stadium in West Point NY. On September 21 at home, the Cadets defeated the Rutgers Scarlet Knights W (20–16). Then on Sept 28 at Penn in a game played at Franklin Field in Philadelphia, PA, the Cadets defeated the Quakers W (41–3). The following week on Oct 5, at home the Cadets defeated the Yale Bulldogs W (59-16)

Then, on Oct 12 Boston College came to Michie Stadium and were defeated by Army W 45–14. On Oct 19, Army had a close loss against Gerry Faust's Fighting Irish in a game played at Notre Dame Stadium in Notre Dame, IN L (10–24). On Oct 26, Colgate played a tough game against Army but the Red Raiders lost in a shootout by just two points to the Cadets W (45–43). Next on Nov 2, at home, the Cadets defeated the Holy Cross Crusaders W (34–12).

On Nov 9, the Cadets were beaten handily by the Air Force Fighting Falcons at Falcon Stadium in Colorado Springs, CO (Commander-in-Chief's Trophy). L (7–45). On Nov 16, Army defeated Memphis State at home in a blowout, W (49-7).

On Dec 7 in the season finale, the Army-Navy-Game, the Midshipmen beat the Cadets at Veterans Stadium in Philadelphia, PA (Commander-in-Chief's Trophy) L (7-17).

In their second post-season Bowl game in a row—The Peach Bowl vs. Illinois at Atlanta–Fulton County Stadium in Atlanta, GA, Army prevailed by a slim margin W (31–29)

1986 Coach Jim Young

The Army Cadets football team represented the United States Military Academy in the 1986 college football season. It was Army's ninety-seventh season of intercollegiate football. They were led by Coach Jim Young in his fourth of eight seasons as head coach of the Cadets. As an independent football entity, the Army team had a winning record of 6-5-0

Overall, the Cadets compiled a 6-5-0 record. They finished with a respectable season record. Army pitched no shutouts and had no shutouts thrown against them. They were outscored by their opponents 292 to 276. In the annual Army–Navy Game, the Cadets defeated the Midshipmen 27-7 score. There was no Bowl Game this year.

This year's opener was on Sept 13 vs Syracuse at home. The Cadets got the season off the right way with a win against the Orangemen W (33-28). Other than those games played in neutral fields, all Army home games were played on the West Point campus at Michie Stadium in West Point NY. On Sept 20 at Northwestern's Dyche Stadium in Evanston, IL, the Wildcats defeated the Cadets L (18–25). On Sept 27, at home, Wake Forest delivered another losing blow to the Cadets in a lopsided loss L (14–49). Next on Oct4, my Wedding Anniversary, at Yale's Yale Bowl in New Haven, CT, the Cadets defeated the Bulldogs, W (41–24).

Then on Oct 11 at Tennessee's Neyland Stadium in Knoxville, TN, the Cadets pulled out a close one W (25–21). Then a week later, the Cadets could not keep up with the crusaders of Holy Cross in a close loss L (14–17). Army suffered another loss on Oct 25 vs. Rutgers in Giants Stadium in East Rutherford, NJ L (7–35). The losses kept coming as Boston College defeated Army on Nov 1 at home L (20-27). Army recovered from the three-fall on Nov 8, defeating Air Force at home (Commander-in-Chief's Trophy)   W (21–11). On Nov 15, in a scoring shootout, the Cadets defeated the Lafayette Leopards at home W (56–48).

On Dec 4 in the annual season finale, the Army-Navy-Game, the Cadets defeated the Midshipmen at Veterans Stadium in Philadelphia, PA (Commander-in-Chief's Trophy) W (27-7).

1987 Coach Jim Young

The Army Cadets football team represented the United States Military Academy in the 1987 college football season. It was Army's ninety-eighth season of intercollegiate football. They were led by Coach Jim Young in his fifth of eight seasons as head coach of the Cadets. As an independent football entity, the Army team had a losing record of 5-6-0

Overall, the Cadets compiled a 5-6-0 record. They finished with a poor season record. Army pitched no shutouts and had no shutouts thrown against them. The Cadets were outscored by their opponents 277 to 223. In the annual Army–Navy Game, the Cadets defeated the Midshipmen by a 17-7 score. There was no Bowl Game this year.

This year's opener was on Sept 12 vs Holy Cross at home. The Cadets did not get the season off the right way and suffered a loss against the Crusaders L 24-34). Other than those games played in neutral fields, all Army home games were played on the West Point campus at Michie Stadium in West Point NY. On Sept 19 at Kansas State's KSU Stadium in Manhattan, KS, the Cadets beat the Wildcats W (41–14). Then on Sept 26 at home, Army defeated The Citadel W (48–6).

The next loss was Wake Forest in a close home match on Oct 3, L (13–17). The Eagles made it two losses in a row on Oct 10 at Boston College's Alumni Stadium in Chestnut Hill, MA, L (24–29) Three losses in a row came too quickly on Oct 17 as Colgate won in a nail-biter over the Army L (20–22)

Nobody wanted to be able to spell four losses in a row but had to do so on Oct 24 as a determined Rutgers squad beat the Cadets at home L (14–27). Temple helped the Cadets break the string of losses as Army beat the Owls at home W (17–7). Air Force put it together to beat the Army on Nov 7 at Falcon Stadium in Colorado Springs, CO (Commander-in-Chief's Trophy) L (10–27). That was it for 1987 losses. There would be two more wins. On Nov 14, in a shootout, the Cadets defeated the Leopards of Lafayette W (49–37).

On Dec 5 in The Army-Navy-Game, the Cadets defeated the Midshipmen at Veterans Stadium in Philadelphia, PA (Commander-in-Chief's Trophy) W (17-3).

1988 Coach Jim Young

The Army Cadets football team represented the United States Military Academy in the 1988 college football season. It was Army's ninety-ninth season of intercollegiate football. They were led by Coach Jim Young in his sixth of eight seasons as head coach of the Cadets. As an independent football entity, the Army team had a nice winning record of 9-3-0.

Overall, the Cadets compiled a 9-3-0 record. They finished with a great season record. Army pitched no shutouts and had no shutouts thrown against them. They Cadets outscored their opponents 336 to 226. In the annual Army–Navy Game, the Cadets defeated the Midshipmen by a 20-15 score. They also lost a very close game (one point) to Alabama by a score of 28 to 29 in the 1988 Sun Bowl.

This year's opener was on Sept 19 vs Holy Cross at home. The Cadets got the season off the right way with a nice win against the Crusaders W (23-3). Other than those games played in neutral fields, all Army home games were played on the West Point campus at Michie Stadium in West Point NY. Traveling to the West Coast on Sept 17, to Husky Stadium in Seattle, WA the Cadets were defeated by the Washington Huskies L (17-31) On Sept 24 at home. The Cadets defeated the Northwestern Wildcats W (23–7). Bucknell was next on Oct 1 as the Cadets smothered the Bisons in a blowout W (58-10).

On Oct 8 at Yale's Yale Bowl in New Haven, CT, the Cadets beat the Bulldogs W (33–18). Next up was Lafayette at home on Oct 15. The Cadets played tough in a close match and got the W by a score of W (24-17) On Oct 22 vs. Rutgers in Giants Stadium, East Rutherford, NJ, the Cadets hit their marks and came home with the victory W (34–24). On Nov 5, at home for (Commander-in-Chief's Trophy) vs Air Force, Army did better than the Fighting Falcons and the Cadets won the match W (28–15).

On Nov 12, The Vanderbilt Commodores tried to beat the Army Cadets at home but failed by a score of 24–19. Then, on Nov 19 at Boston College, playing in Lansdowne Road • Dublin, Ireland in the (Emerald Isle Classic), it was too much Irish all at once for the Cadets in a loss L (24–38).

December 24 vs. Alabama   Sun Bowl Stadium • El Paso, TX (Sun Bowl) L 28–29

On Dec 12, the Army-Navy-Game ended the football season for both Army and Navy. In this game, the Cadets defeated the Midshipmen at Veterans Stadium in Philadelphia, PA (Commander-in-Chief's Trophy) W (20-5).

Back in action again on December 24 in El Paso TX, the site of the 1988 Sun Bowl, in the post Bear Bryant years at Alabama, this Bill Curry coached Crimson Tide squad barely defeated our Army Cadets in the 1988 Sun Bowl L (28-29).

1989 Coach Jim Young

The Army Cadets football team represented the United States Military Academy in the 1989 college football season. It was Army's one hundredth season of intercollegiate football. They were led by Coach Jim Young in his seventh of eight seasons as head coach of the Cadets. As an independent football entity, the Army team had a winning record of 6-5-0.

Overall, the Cadets compiled a 6-5-0 record this season. They finished with a respectable season record but every Army fan of course was looking for more. Army pitched no shutouts and had no shutouts thrown against them. They Cadets outscored their opponents 316 to 212. In the annual Army–Navy Game, the Cadets were defeated by the Midshipmen by a 19-17 score.

This year's opener was on Sept 16 vs Syracuse at the fantastic Carrier Dome in Syracuse NY. As a football fan for many years, while at IBM for about twenty years, I ran a trip on behalf of the IBM Club and then after IBM I still ran the bus trip. There was nothing the kids on the bus liked better than parking our bus next to the Army bus and watching the Cadets in full regalia in the parking lot across from the stadium. No matter how cold the weather was later in the season, it was always 69 degrees in the Carrier Dome.

The Cadets began the season with a tough loss against the Orangemen L (7-10). Other than those games played in neutral fields, all Army home games were played on the West Point campus at Michie Stadium in West Point NY. Traveling On Sept 23, at home, the Cadets defeated Wake Forest in a close match W (14–10). Then, on Sept 30 at home, Harvard and Army kept pounding at each other but the Cadets pounded twice as hard to defeat the Harvard Crimson W (56-28).

On Sept 16 at Duke's Wallace Wade Stadium in Durham, NC, the Cadets lost a close match to the Blue Devils L (29–35). Gaining back their strength after the Duke loss, the Cadets found enough at home to pound the Holy Cross Crusaders W (45–9). Next up was the Lafayette Leopards on Oct 21 at home and the Cadets prevailed again W (34–20). Rutgers came in to Michie Stadium looking for a win but left with a kudo for a nice game played as the Cadets prevailed v the Scarlet Knights W (35-14).

On Nov 4, the flying academy got in the act for the (Commander-in-Chief's Trophy), at Air Force's Falcon Stadium in Colorado Springs, CO. The Air Force did not give an inch in this tough loss for the Cadets L (3–29). On Nov 11, Boston College took on the Cadets at home and the Eagles got the best of the game L (17–24). On Nov 18 at home, Colgate got a whooping from the Army W (59–14)

On Dec 9, always late in the season, the Army-Navy-Game ended the football season for both Army and Navy. In this game, the Cadets were defeated by the Midshipmen at Giants Stadium in East Rutherford, NJ (Commander-in-Chief's Trophy) L (17-19).

1990 Coach Jim Young

The Army Cadets football team represented the United States Military Academy in the 1988 college football season. It was Army's one-hundred-first season of intercollegiate football. They were led by Coach Jim Young in his eighth and last of seven seasons as head coach of the Cadets. As an independent football entity, the Army team had a winning record of 6-5.

Overall, the Cadets compiled a 9-3-0 record. They finished with an OK season record. Army pitched one shutout (Lafayette 56-0) and had no shutouts thrown against them. The Cadets outscored their opponents 295 to 264. In the annual Army–Navy Game, the Cadets defeated the Midshipmen by a 30-20 score. Knowing the importance of this game to Army, it was one of Young's great achievements in his final year as coach.

As an independent football entity, the Army team had a winning record of 6-5-0 in Jim Young's final season. Young had a masterful tenure while at Army and he is credited with having resurrected the program from where it had been.

Please enjoy this AP article which does a crisp summary of Jim Young's years at Army. After this we will pick up with the games of the season.

Army Coach Jim Young Will Retire

August 28, 1990|From Associated Press

WEST POINT, N.Y. — Jim Young, Army football coach for the last seven years, said today that he will retire after this season because of personal reasons.

Young, 55, will be replaced next year by Bob Sutton, 39, the associate head coach and defensive coordinator. Sutton, who came to Army in 1983, the same year as Young, has never been a head coach.

Young, who has resurrected the Army football program, has compiled a record of 45-34-1. Overall, including stints at Purdue and Arizona, his record is 114-66-2.

After this season, Young will remain at West Point as a member of the Performance Enhancement Program staff.

Since 1984, when Young installed the wishbone offense, the Cadets have ranked no lower than fifth in rushing offense in the nation. In the first year of the wishbone, they were No. 1 in rushing.

Big Bravo to a great coach – Jim Young!

This year's opener was on Sept 15 vs Holy Cross at home. The Cadets got the season off the right way with a nice win against the Crusaders W (24-7). Other than those games played in neutral fields, all Army home games were played on the West Point campus at Michie Stadium in West Point NY. On Sept 22 at home vs. VMI, the Cadets prevailed W (41–17). At 2-0 In the third game at Wake Forest played in Groves Stadium Winston-Salem, NC, the Cadets were beaten by the Demon Deacons L (14–52). Duke's Blue Devils beat the Cadets at home a week later on Oct 6 L (16-17). This was quickly followed by the third loss on Oct 13 at Boston College's Alumni Stadium Chestnut Hill, MA L (20–41).

On Oct 20, the Cadets got their oomph back by shutting out Lafayette in a blowout game W (56-0). It was the first shutout in years for the Cadets. On Oct 27, at home, the Cadets lost to the Orangemen of Syracuse L (14-26). Then, the Cadets found a W at Rutgers in a close match W (35-21). On Nov 10, at home, the Cadets lost to the Fighting Falcons of the Air Force. (Commander-in-Chief's Trophy) L (3-15). On Nov 17 at Vanderbilt's Vanderbilt Stadium • in Nashville, TN, the Cadets picked up their fifth win of the season W (42–38).

On December 8 in the annual (Army–Navy Game/Commander-in-Chief's Trophy), the Cadets defeated the Midshipmen, which put a smile on the faces a lot of Army supporters. The game was played at Veterans Stadium in Philadelphia, and the final score was W (30–20)

Chapter 14 Coaches Bob Sutton & Todd Berry 1991-2002

Sutton   Coach # 31
Berry   Coach # 32

Year	Coach	Record	Conference	Record
1991	Bob Sutton	4-7-0	Indep	4-7-0)
1992	Bob Sutton	5-6-0	Indep	5-6-0
1993	Bob Sutton	6-5-0	Indep	6-5-0
1994	Bob Sutton	4-7-0	Indep	4-7-0
1995	Bob Sutton	5-5-1	Indep	5-5-1
1996	Bob Sutton	10-2-0	Indep	10-2-0
1997	Bob Sutton	4-7-0	Indep	4-7-0
1998	Bob Sutton	3-8-0	C-USA	2-4-0
1999	Bob Sutton	3-8-0	C-USA	1-5-0
2000	Todd Berry	1-10-0	C-USA	1-6-0
2001	Todd Berry	3-8-0	C-USA	2-5-0
2002	Todd Berry	1-11-0	C-USA	1-7-0
2003	Todd Berry	0-7	C-USA	0-4-0

Coach Bob Sutton happy with the team

Bob Sutton is a great coach. Sutton served as the head football coach at the United States Military Academy from 1991 to 1999, compiling a record of 44–55–1. He had one phenomenally great year and the rest were medsa medsa. Before becoming head coach at Army in 1991, Sutton spent eight years as an assistant coach at Army.

His nine-year tenure as the head football coach at Army (1991 to 1999) is second in length only to Earl "Red" Blaik. His 44–55–1 record was not the best but he is well known for leading the 1996 Army squad to a 10–2 record, an appearance in the Independence Bowl, and a top 25 finish in both major polls. For his efforts that season, Sutton was awarded the Bobby Dodd Coach of the Year Award.

1991 Coach Bob Sutton

The Army Cadets football team represented the United States Military Academy in the 1991 college football season. It was Army's one hundred-second season of intercollegiate football. They were led by Coach Bob Sutton in his first of nine seasons as head coach of the Cadets. As an independent football entity, the Army team had a losing record of 4-7-0.

Coach Bob Sutton at Work

Overall, the Cadets compiled a 4-7-0 record. They finished with a poor season record. Army pitched one shutout (against Akron 19-0), and had one shutouts thrown against them (Air Force—0-25). The Cadets were outscored by their opponents 226 to 196. In the annual Army–Navy Game, the Cadets lost to the Midshipmen by a 3-24 score.

This year's opener was on Sept 14 vs Colgate at home. The Cadets got the season off the right way with a shootout win against the Red Raiders W (51-22). Other than those games played in neutral fields, all Army home games were played on the West Point campus at Michie Stadium in West Point NY. On Sept 21, at home. The Cadets were defeated by the Tar Heels of North Carolina L (12-20) Then on Sept 28 at home, the Cadets beat Harvard's Crimson W (21-20). On Oct 5, the Army lost to The State University of New Jersey (Rutgers Scarlet Knights) in a close battle L (12-14). This was followed one week later on Oct 12 by a tough loss against The Citadel L (14-20).

On Oct 19, at Louisville's Cardinal Stadium • in Louisville, KY, the Cadets picked up the win W (37–12). Next up was Boston College on Oct 26 at home and the Eagles defeated the Cadets L 17-28) On Nov 2 at home, the Cadets lost to Vanderbilt L (10–41). On Nov 9, the Army was shut out by Air Force at Falcon Stadium Colorado Springs, CO (Commander-in-Chief's Trophy) L (0–25). On Nov 16, Army, 4-6, shut out a Div. I-A opponent for the first time since a 27-0 victory over Navy in 1969. Akron, 4-6, had not won on the road this season. The final score was W (0-19).

November 16 Akron Michie Stadium • West Point, NY W 19–0
December 7   vs. Navy   Veterans Stadium • Philadelphia, PA
(Army-Navy game/Commander-in-Chief's Trophy)   L 3–24

On December 7 in the annual (Army–Navy Game/Commander-in-Chief's Trophy), the Midshipmen got the best of the Cadets L (3-24) The game was played at Veterans Stadium in Philadelphia.

1992 Coach Bob Sutton

The Army Cadets football team represented the United States Military Academy in the 1992 college football season. It was Army's one hundred-second season of intercollegiate football. They were led by Coach Bob Sutton in his second of nine seasons as head coach of the Cadets. As an independent football entity, the Army team had a losing record of 5-6-0.

Overall, the Cadets compiled a 5-6-0 record. They finished with a poor season record. Army pitched no shutouts, and had no shutouts thrown against them. The Cadets were outscored by their opponents 251 to 225. In the annual Army–Navy Game, the Cadets defeated the Midshipmen by a 25-24 score.

This year's opener was on Sept 12 vs Holy Cross at home. The Cadets got the season off the right way with a win against the Crusaders W (17-7). Other than those games played in neutral fields, all Army home games were played on the West Point campus at Michie Stadium in West Point NY. The next week on Sept 19, the Cadets lost to the Tar Heels at North Carolina's Kenan Memorial Stadium Chapel Hill, NC L (9–22). Then On Sept 26 at home, Army lost by one point to The Citadel L (14–15). In another nail biter, the two weeks later on Oct 10, Army beat Lafayette at home W (38-36).

On Oct 17, a tough Rutgers team pounded Army at Giants Stadium in East Rutherford, NJ, L (10–45). Another loss came on Oct 24 at Wake Forest's Groves Stadium in Winston-Salem, NC L (7–23). Then on Halloween, 1992, at home, Army trounced Eastern Michigan W (57–17). Next loss came against Air Force on Nov 7 at home (Commander-in-Chief's Trophy) L (3–7). The Cadets would win two of their last three games. First up was Northern Illinois on Nov 14 at home W (21–14). Next was Boston College at home on Nov 21 for a loss L (24–41).

And, so on December 5 in the Army Navy Game, the Cadets defeated the Midshipmen at Veterans Stadium Philadelphia, PA (Commander-in-Chief's Trophy Game) W (25–24).

1993 Coach Bob Sutton

The Army Cadets football team represented the United States Military Academy in the 1993 college football season. It was Army's one hundred-third season of intercollegiate football. They were led by Coach Bob Sutton in his third of nine seasons as head coach of the

Cadets. As an independent football entity, the Army team had a winning record of 6-5-0.

Overall, the Cadets compiled a 6-5-0 record. They finished with a respectable season record. Army pitched one shutout (Colgate 30-0), and had no shutouts thrown against them. The Cadets outscored their opponents 289 to 243. In the annual Army–Navy Game, the Cadets defeated the Midshipmen by a 16-14 score.

This year's opener was on Sept 11 vs Colgate at home. The Cadets got the season off the right way with a shutout win against the Red Raiders W (30-0). Other than those games played in neutral fields, all Army home games were played on the West Point campus at Michie Stadium in West Point NY. The next week (Sept 11) Army lost to Duke L (21-42). On Sept 25 at home, Army beat VMI W (31-9) The next week at home against Akron, the Cadets won again W (35-14). Three in a row came on Oct 9 at Temple in Veterans Stadium in Philadelphia, PA W (56—21)

Rutgers broke the Army win streak at three on Oct 16 at Michie Stadium L (38-45). Boston College piled on another loss the following week on Oct 23 at Alumni Stadium Chestnut Hill, MA L (14–41). Then on Oct 30, Western Michigan made it three losses in a row for the Cadets at home L (7-20). On Nov 6, Air Force made it four season losses in a row at Falcon Stadium Colorado Springs, CO (Commander-in-Chief's Trophy) L (6–25). Before the Army Navy game, the Cadets began a mini-two-game win streak to close out the season. The first up was Lafayette on Nov 13. The Cadets defeated the Leopards at home W (35-12).

On December 5 in the Army Navy Game, a nail biter again, the Cadets defeated the Midshipmen at Giants Stadium East Rutherford, NJ (Commander-in-Chief's Trophy Game) W (16-14).

1994 Coach Bob Sutton

The Army Cadets football team represented the United States Military Academy in the 1993 college football season. It was Army's one hundred-fifth season of intercollegiate football. They were led by

Coach Bob Sutton in his fourth of nine seasons as head coach of the Cadets. As an independent football entity, the Army team had a losing record of 4-7-0.

Overall, the Cadets compiled a 4-7-0 record. They finished with a poor season record. Army pitched no shutouts, and had no shutouts thrown against them. The Cadets were outscored by their opponents 252 to 215. In the annual Army–Navy Game, the Cadets defeated the Midshipmen by a 22-20 score.

This year's opener was on Sept 10 vs Holy Cross at home. The Cadets got the season off the right way with a blowout win against the Crusaders W (49-3). Other than those games played in neutral fields, all Army home games were played on the West Point campus at Michie Stadium in West Point NY. On Sept 15at Duke's Wallace Wade Stadium in Durham, NC, the Blue Devils defeated the Cadets L (7–43). Then on at home on Sept 24, Temple beat Army by a field goal L (20-23). On Oct 1, at Wake Forest's Groves Stadium Winston-Salem, NC, the Demon Deacons got the best pf the Cadets. In its fourth loss in a row on Oct 8, the Cadets fell to Rutgers L 14-16).

Then it was Louisville at Michie for a nail biter Cadet win W (30-29). On Oct 22, the Citadel came in tough and lost by just one point giving the Cadets the W (25-24). Struggling over the years with BC, 1994 was no different as the Eagles of Boston College made short work of the Cadets again L (3-30). Air Force kept on enjoying its victory streak at home in Michie and the Cadets endured another loss to the Fighting Falcons L (6-10). Boston University, the less talented cousin to Boston College came in and would not give the Cadets a home win before the Army-Navy Game L (12-21)

On December 3 in the Army-Navy-Game, a nail biter again, the Cadets defeated the Midshipmen at Veterans Stadium Philadelphia PA (Army-Navy-Game/Commander-in-Chief's Trophy) W 22–20

1995 Coach Bob Sutton

The Army Cadets football team represented the United States Military Academy in the 1995 college football season. It was Army's one hundred-sixth season of intercollegiate football. They were led by

Coach Bob Sutton in his fifth of nine seasons as head coach of the Cadets. As an independent football entity, the Army team had a break-even record of 5-5-1.

Overall, the Cadets compiled a 5-5-1 record. They finished with an OK season record. Army pitched no shutouts, and had no shutouts thrown against them. The Cadets were outscored by their opponents 325 to 211. In the annual Army–Navy Game, the Cadets defeated the Midshipmen by a 14-13 score.

This year's opener was on Sept 9 vs Lehigh at home. The Cadets got the season off the right way with a blowout win against the Mountain Hawks W (42-9). Other than those games played in neutral fields, all Army home games were played on the West Point campus at Michie Stadium in West Point NY. On Sept 16, the Duke Blue Devils defeated the Cadets L (21-23). On Sept 23, the Cadets lost again at Washington L (13-21).

Next was the Rice Owls, who played the Cadets to a tie, on Sept 30 T (21-21). Next up was Lou Holtz's Notre Dame Fighting Irish who played the Cadets to an almost tie but the Irish got the win L (27-28)

This year, the Cadets were able to put away the other Irish guys from Boston, Boston College without all the work it took to lost to Notre Dame. On Oct 21, the Cadets beat BC's Eagles in a blowout W (49-7). Go Cadets! The Cadets had begun a powerful win streak that began with BC and continued through this Colgate encounter.

In another unprecedented blowout, the Cadets destroyed the Red Raiders of Colgate. It was short lived as East Carolina mounted an attack that was enough to defeat the Army team on Nov 4, L (25-31). Next up was the new nemesis of the Service Academies, Air Force, and the Fighting Falcons kept their win streak against the Cadets going in this latest L (20-38) win. Army got their moxie back on Nov 18 when they would not stop against Bucknell in a nice victory W (37-6).

The Bucknell win got the Army ready to keep winning and with the next game being long-time nemesis Navy, the practice game helped the Cadets focus.

On December 2 in the Army-Navy-Game, an even closer nail biter, the Cadets defeated the Midshipmen at Veterans Stadium Philadelphia PA (Army-Navy-Game/Commander-in-Chief's Trophy) W 14-13).

1996 Coach Bob Sutton

The Army Cadets football team represented the United States Military Academy in the 1996 college football season. It was Army's one hundred-seventh season of intercollegiate football. They were led by Coach Bob Sutton in his sixth of nine seasons as head coach of the Cadets. As an independent football entity, the Army team had a fine regular season record of 10-1-0. With the Bowl Game, it was a 10-2-0 record

Overall, the Cadets compiled a 10-2-0 record. They finished with an excellent season record – the best in thirty years. Yet, with such a great record, Army pitched no shutouts, and had no shutouts thrown against them. The Cadets outscored their opponents 379 to 224. In the annual Army–Navy Game, the Cadets defeated the Midshipmen again, by a larger margin yet it was just four points. Navy and Army always played best against each other. In such a season with a few losses, somebody plays better than your team. In this case, after losing to Syracuse near the end of the season, 17-42, Army lost to Auburn, 32–29, in the 1996 Independence Bowl.[2]

This year's opener was on Sept 14 vs Ohio at home. The Cadets got the season off the right way with a win W (27-20) (30,500 fans). Other than those games played in neutral fields, all Army home games were played on the West Point campus at Michie Stadium in West Point NY. On Sept 21, the Cadets knocked off the Duke Blue Devils W (35-17). On Sept 28, at North Texas's Texas Stadium • in Irving, TX, the Cadets prevailed W (27–10). Then, on Oct 5, Yale came back to Michie Stadium to be defeated by the Cadets W (39–13). On Oct 12, at home, the Cadets finished off another opponent that had been a nemesis in the prior years, W (42-21) Rutgers lost big at Giants Stadium in East Rutherford, NJ before a small crowd of 19,101.

On Oct 19, the Cadets whipped Tulane at home W (34-10). On Oct 26, at Miami (OH)'s Yager Stadium   Oxford, OH, Army was the victor W 27–7 before 16,543. On Nov 2, Lafayette came with guns a blazing but in this 10-1 regular season year Army was enjoying, the Cadets snuffed out their guns and turned in a double your bet win W (42-21) at home before 39,269. On Nov 9, Air Force finally could not withstand the constant pressure from Army and the Fighting Falcons had to give up a loss to the Cadets at home in the (Commander-in-Chief's Trophy) W (23–7) before a max crowd of 41,251 at Michie.

On Nov 16, at 6:00 p.m., Syracuse was in the top twenty and they were gunning for Army to get to the championship consideration area. Army was # 22 and undefeated and ready to block #19 Syracuse no matter how many men it took. The game was played at the Carrier Dome in Winter weather but in 69-degree comfort in Syracuse, NY. Army could not keep up and lost the game L (17–42) before 49,257. It was an exciting game because of the stakes.

On December 7 in the Army-Navy-Game, in a close game as usual, the #23 ranked Cadets defeated the Midshipmen at Veterans Stadium Philadelphia PA (Army-Navy-Game/Commander-in-Chief's Trophy) W 28-24) before 69,238.

Because Army qualified for a Bowl Game, the season was not over.

On December 31, New Years' Eve at 3:30 p.m. vs unranked Auburn, the #24 ranked Cadets lost this game— (The Independence Bowl)— played at Independence Stadium in Shreveport, LA. The final score was L (29–32). Army had played a fine game yet had lost. It would be a long time for another coach to take Army so far.

1997 Coach Bob Sutton

The Army Cadets football team represented the United States Military Academy in the 1997 college football season. It was Army's one hundred-eighth season of intercollegiate football. They were led by Coach Bob Sutton in his seventh of nine seasons as head coach of the Cadets. As an independent football entity, the Army team had a losing season record of 4-7-0.

Overall, the Cadets compiled a 4-7-0 record. They finished with a poor season record after one of the best in the prior year. In 1997, Army pitched no shutouts, and had two shutouts thrown against them (Tulane 0-41) and (Air Force 0-24). The Cadets were outscored by their opponents 311 to 221. In the annual Army–Navy Game, after many years on top, the Midshipmen defeated the Cadets big time. Army might well have not showed up for the game. Navy and Army always played best against each other but not this year.

This year's opener was on Sept 6 vs Marshall at home. The Cadets got the season off the wrong way with a loss L (25-35) Other than those games played in neutral fields, all Army home games were played on the West Point campus at Michie Stadium in West Point NY. On Sept13, the Cadets beat Lafayette's Leopards W (41-14). Then, on Sept 20, the Cadets took it on the chin from Duke's Blue Devils at Durham NC L (17-20) Then Miami of Ohio tried to put on the hurt to the Cadets and they succeeded L (14-38> On Oct 4, my wedding anniversary, the Cadets were shut out by Tulane in a big loss L (0-41)

On Oct 18, the Cadets beat Rutgers at home W (37-35). In another close win, the victim was Colgate a team that went down by a small margin to Army W (35-27). On Nov 8, Air Force pounded the Cadets in a shutout L (0-24) North Texas was ready to win on Nov 15 but lost nonetheless as the Cadets would not permit it W (25-14). Boston College felt the same way in the game, played in Chestnut Hill, Mass. The Eagles picked up a big win against the Cadets L (0-24)

On December 6 in the Army-Navy-Game, in an unusual runaway game, the Midshipmen whooped the Cadets L (7-39) in a big loss at Giants Stadium in East Rutherford NJ . (Army-Navy-Game/Commander-in-Chief's Trophy)

1998 Coach Bob Sutton

The Army Cadets football team represented the United States Military Academy in the 1998 college football season. It was Army's one hundred-ninth season of intercollegiate football. They were led by Coach Bob Sutton in his eighth of nine seasons as head coach of the Cadets. As a new member of Conference USA, the Army team had a losing season record of 3-8-0.

Overall, the Cadets compiled a 3-8-0 record. The Cadets were 2-4 in the C-USA Conference. They finished with a very poor season record after one of the best just two years prior. In 1998, Army pitched no shutouts, and had no shutouts thrown against them. The Cadets were outscored by their opponents 325 to 257. In the annual Army–Navy Game, the Cadets defeated the Midshipmen in a close match W (34-30).

This year's opener was on Sept 12 vs Miami of Ohio at home. The Cadets got the season off the wrong way with a loss L (13-14) Other than those games played in neutral fields, all Army home games were played on the West Point campus at Michie Stadium in West Point NY. On Sept 19, at home, the Cadets defeated the Cincinnati Bearcats W (37-20). The second loss of the season came on Sept 26 when Rutgers from the Big East defeated Army in New Jersey L (15-27). Next up was a game at East Carolina on Oct 3 which resulted in another Army loss L (25-30). On Oct 10, at Houston the Army squad snapped back and gained the victory W (38-28).

On Oct 17, at home, Army lost to Southern Mississippi L (13-37). Defeated. The next week at Notre Dame, in a close match, the Fighting Irish defeated the Cadets L (17-20). On Nov 7 Air Force continued its dominance over Army at home L (7-35). This was followed at home on Nov 14 in the Army's fourth loss in a row. This time Tulane's green wave triumphed in a shootout L (35-49). At Louisville on Nov 21, the Army lost its fifth in a row L (25-35).

On December 5 in the Army-Navy-Game, the Cadets defeated the Midshipmen W (34-30) in a big win at Veterans Stadium in Philadelphia--(Army-Navy-Game/Commander-in-Chief's Trophy)

1999 Coach Bob Sutton

The Army Cadets / Black Knights football team represented the United States Military Academy in the 1998 college football season.

It was Army's one hundred-tenth season of intercollegiate football. They were led by Coach Bob Sutton in his ninth and last of nine seasons as head coach of the Cadets / Black Knights. As a new member of Conference USA, the Army team had a losing season record of 3-8-0.

Overall, the Black Knights compiled a 3-8-0 record. The Cadets were 1–5 in the C-USA Conference. They finished with a very poor season record after one of the best two years prior. In 1998, Army pitched no shutouts, and had two shutouts (Southern Miss – 0-24 and Air Force – 0-28) thrown against them. The Black Knights were outscored by their opponents 317 to 225. In the annual Army–Navy Game, the Cadets lost to the Midshipmen in a close match L (9-19)

Throughout the years from 1890 onward, Army teams were known as the "Cadets." In the 1940s, several papers called the football team "the Black Knights of the Hudson." From then on, "Cadets" and "Black Knights" were used interchangeably until this season (1999), when the team was officially nicknamed the Black Knights. Some pundits continue to call the team either Army or the Cadets and though not official, those names are most acceptable

Another change happened during this time. Between the 1998 and 2004 seasons, Army's football program was a member of Conference USA, but starting with the 2005 season Army reverted to its former independent status. Army competes with Navy and Air Force for the Commander-in-Chief's Trophy. When there is a tie, all are winners but the trophy stays in the last clean winner's locale.

This year's opener was on Sept 11 vs Wake Forest at home. The Cadets got the season off the wrong way again with a loss against the Demon Deacons L (15-34) Other than those games played in neutral fields, all Army home games were played on the West Point campus at Michie Stadium in West Point NY. On Sept 18, at Tulane, the Green Wave prevailed in a shootout L (28-48). On Sept 25, Army defeated Ball State W (41-21). Then on Oct 2, Army lost to East Carolina at home L (14-33). On Oct 7, at home in a rare Thursday game, Army defeated Louisville in a wild shootout W (59-52).

Then, on Oct 16 @ Southern Mississippi, the Golden Eagles shut out the Cadets L 0-24). On Oct 23, Army defeated New Mexico State at home W (35-18). On Nov 6, Army was shut out by the Air Force L (0-28) On Nov 13, at Memphis, the Cadets lost to the Tigers L (10-14). On Nov 20, at home, Houston defeated Army L (14-26).

On December 4 in the Army-Navy-Game, the Midshipmen defeated the Cadets L (9-19) at Veterans Stadium in Philadelphia--(Army-Navy-Game/Commander-in-Chief's Trophy)

Despite being the winningest coach against Navy in the modern era and despite Navy victories being so important, the Army Brass forgot how hard it was always to defeat the Midshipmen and they fired Bob Sutton because he did not bring in his last Navy opportunity.

As I look at all the coaches at Army, I find it tough to fault them. In 2000, as Bob Sutton passed the keys to Todd Berry, nobody expected Todd Berry, another qualified coach to fail. Todd Berry had rebuilt Illinois State football and had led the school to the Division I-AA playoffs the past two seasons. Army brought him into the bigger leagues but he was already a fine coach.

Berry of course replaced Bob Sutton, who had a rough go of it for three years after his 10-2 season. Many think Sutton should have been retained but who knows what was going on behind the scenes. Bob Sutton was fired two days after Army lost to Navy on Dec. 4 in the 100th meeting between the teams. The accolades coming in for the new coach Todd Berry were deafening. Nobody anticipates failure with any new coach or they don't hire them.

"Coach Todd Berry is an inspiring coach," Army superintendent Lt. Gen. Daniel Christman said in announcing Berry's hiring today. "Anyone who comes into contact with him cannot help but be impressed with his commitment to this institution."

Berry has a history with players and coaches across College Football. He reunited in this hiring with athletic director Rick Greenspan, Illinois State's athletic director for six years and the man who hired Berry in 1995. Greenspan took the Army AD job in April and chose to fire Sutton after the 19-9 loss to Navy.

"I have never been as inspired by a place until I got here," Berry said. "I expect that in the near future we'll be 11-0. Anything else would be an injustice to this institution." Considering Berry's actual record at Army, he might have easily predicted that Army would be winning the football Championships on both the Moon and Mars in the near future.

Greenspan said the 39-year-old coach had all the attributes West Point was looking for. He said Berry has "passion, recruiting skills, he's a teacher of the game, a tireless worker, and someone who appreciates the values of Army." Berry however, never had to deal with the Army Leadership to be successful in life before taking the job.

It is true that he had rebuilt Illinois State football, leading the Redbirds to the Gateway Conference title this season and an 11-3 record. Illinois State lost to Georgia Southern 28-17 in last week's I-AA semifinals.

Berry was voted the league's coach of the year. His overall record at the school is 24-24 in four seasons.

"He's been just incredible for our program," Illinois State assistant athletic director Kenny Mossman said. I wonder if Army would be happy with 24-24?

He was an assistant coach for 13 years before taking the job at Illinois State, including four years as offensive coordinator at East Carolina. He also was an assistant at Southeast Missouri State, Mississippi State and Tennessee-Martin.

Sutton, Army's coach for nine years, was fired just three seasons after guiding Army to a school-record 10 wins. His record against Navy was 6-3, and he left with a 44-55-1 record. Some would say that 24-24 is a better percentage than Sutton achieved. The verdict came in quick when Coach Todd Berry put the Black Knights on the field against opponents.

2000 Coach Todd Berry

The Army West Point Black Knights football team represented the United States Military Academy in the 2000 college football season.

It was Army's one hundred-eleventh season of intercollegiate football. They were led by Coach Todd Berry in his first of four seasons as head coach of the Black Knights. As a new member of Conference USA, the Army team had a losing season record of 1-10-0.

Overall, the Black Knights compiled a 1-10-0 record. They were 1–6 in the C-USA Conference. They finished with a very poor season record. In 1998, Army pitched no shutouts, and had no shutouts thrown against them. The Cadets were outscored by their opponents 372 to 224. In the annual Army–Navy Game, the Cadets lost to the Midshipmen in a close match L (28-30)

<< Coach Todd Berry

This year's opener was on Sept 4 at Cincinnati. The Black Knights got the season off the wrong way again with a loss against the Bearcats L (17-23) Other than those games played in neutral fields, all Army home games were played on the West Point campus at Michie Stadium in West Point NY. The only game the Black Knights won this year was against Tulane W (21-17) on Oct 21. All other games as listed below were losses:

Sept 9	Boston College	L17-55
Sept 16	at Houstom	L 30-31
Sept 23	at memphis	L 16-26

Oct 7	at New Mexico State	L 23-42
Oct 14	at East Carolina	L 21-42
Oct 21	Tulane	W 21-17
Nov 4	Air Force	L 27-41
Nov 11	Louisville	L 17 – 38
Nov 18	UAB	L 7 – 27

On December 2 in the classic Army-Navy-Game, the Midshipmen defeated the Cadets L (28-30) at Baltimore (Army-Navy-Game/Commander-in-Chief's Trophy)

2001 Coach Todd Berry

The Army West Point Black Knights football team represented the United States Military Academy in the 2001 college football season. It was Army's one hundred-eleventh season of intercollegiate football. They were led by Coach Todd Berry in his second of three seasons as head coach of the Black Knights. The Army team had a losing season record of 3-8-0.

Overall, the Black Knights compiled a 3-8-0 record. They were 2-5 in the C-USA Conference. They finished with another very poor season record. In 1998, Army pitched no shutouts, and had no shutouts thrown against them. The Black Knights were outscored by their opponents 365 to 229. In the annual Army–Navy Game, the Midshipmen defeated the Black Knights W (12-58). Army changed its nickname from the Cadets to the Black Knights.

This year's opener was on Sept 8 at home vs Cincinnati. The Cadets got the season off the wrong way again with a loss against the Bearcats L (21-24) Other than those games played in neutral fields, all Army home games were played on the West Point campus at Michie Stadium in West Point, NY. On Sept 22, at the University of Alabama Birmingham (UAB), the Blazers bombed the Army West Point Black Knights in a blowout L (3-55).

Boston College at Alumni Stadium in Massachusetts added to the pain, sticking the Army with their third straight loss without a win this season L (10-31) Finally in game four the Black Knights got a win against Houston at home W (28-14). Then, along came two more losses with the first against East Carolina at home on Oct 13, L (26-49) and on Oct 20, it was L (20-38) at Texas Christian (TCU).

Army came up for air on Oct 20 to defeat Tulane at home W (42-35). This was followed by another loss at Air Force on Nov 3 L (24-34). Then at home on Nov 10, Army lost to Buffalo L (19-26). On Nov 17, at Memphis, the Tigers defeated Army L (10-42).

On December 1 in the classic Army-Navy-Game, the Black Knights defeated the Midshipmen W (17-3) at Veterans Stadium in Philadelphia, PA (Army-Navy-Game/Commander-in-Chief's Trophy). This gave the Black Knights their third victory of the season and to many Army fans a win over Navy is a successful season.

2002 Coach Todd Berry

The Army West Point Black Knights football team represented the United States Military Academy in the 2002 college football season. It was Army's one hundred-thirteenth season of intercollegiate football. They were led by Coach Todd Berry in his third and last of three seasons as head coach of the Black Knights.

Overall, the Black Knights compiled a 1-11-0 record. They were 1-7 in the C-USA Conference. They finished with another very poor season record. In 1998, Army pitched no shutouts, and had one shutout thrown against them (Rutgers 0-44). The Cadets were outscored by their opponents 365 to 229. In the annual Army–Navy Game, the Cadets were pounded by the Midshipmen W (12-58). Army changed its nickname in 1999 from the Cadets to the Black Knights.

This year's opener was on Sept 7 at home vs Holy Cross. In another poor record year, the Black Knights got the season off the wrong way again with a loss against the Crusaders L (21-30) Other than those games played in neutral fields, all Army home games were played on the West Point campus at Michie Stadium in West Point NY. On Sept 14, at Rutgers, the Scarlet Knights shut out the Black Knights of Army L (0-44). The Black Knights won just one game the whole season and lost 11. The win came on Nov 16 at Tulane W (14-10). Since the rest of the year were all losses, rather than prolong the misery, I provided the rest of the season for your edification in tabular form below:

Sept 21	Louisville	L (14-45)
Sept 28	Southern Mississippi	L (6-27
Oct 5	at East Carolina	L (24-59)
Oct 12	TCU	L (27-46
Oct 19	Houston	L (42-56)
Oct 26	UAB	L (26-29)
Nov 9	Air Force	L (30-49)
Nov 23	Memphis	L (10-38)
Dec7	Navy	L (12-58)

On December 7 in the classic Army-Navy-Game, the Black Knights were blown-out by the Midshipmen L (12-58) at Giants Stadium in East Rutherford, NJ (Army-Navy-Game/Commander-in-Chief's Trophy). This gave the Black Knights their eleventh loss of the season and to many Army fans this loss was the worst of the year.

2003 Coach Todd Berry

Todd Berry Lasted six games in 2003 before he was fired. The season record was 0-6 before he was replaced mid-season The losses in 2003 for Todd Berry are as follows:

Sept 6	Connecticut	L (21-48)
Sept 13	Rutgers	L (21-36
Sept 20	Tulane	L 33-50)
Sept 27	South Florida	L (0-28)
Oct 4	at TCU	L (0-27)
Oct 11	at Louisville	L 10-34
Oct 18	East Carolina	L (32-38) * **Mumford here and below**
Oct 25	at Cincinnati	L (29-33
Nov 1	UAB	L (9-24)
Nov 8	at Air Force	L (3-31)
Nov 15	Houston	L (14-34)
Nov 22	at Hawaii	L (28-59)
Dec 6	Navy	L (6-34)

The other games were by Coach Mumford – Chapter 17—

Army became the first team to finish 0-13 in major college history. The Arizona Sun published this short story of what happened to Coach Berry

WEST POINT, N.Y. (AP) — Army coach Todd Berry was fired Monday with the team 5-35 in his four seasons and mired in an eight-game losing streak.

"The Corps of Cadets and the fans of Army football deserve a competitive program that is representative of this great institution," said Lt. Gen. William Lennox Jr., superintendent of the U.S. Military Academy.

Army (0-6) has just one win in its last 17 games. The Black Knights are averaging 63.8 yards rushing to rank last in the nation and are the only team averaging under 2 yards per carry.

South Florida, playing its inaugural Conference USA game last month, shut out Army 28-0 at Michie Stadium, marking the first time the Black Knights had been blanked at home since 1981.

Here is one of my favorite quotes from me:

"Nothing in life worth having, is easy"

Here is another quote of mine that I just came up with from having read about Coach Berry's Black Knights.

"11-0 has the same numbers as does 0-11 but the meaning is a lot different!"

Chapter 15 Coaches Mumford, Ross, Brock, & Ellerson 2003 – 2013

Mumford   Coach # 33
Ross   Coach # 34
Brock   Coach # 35
Ellerson   Coach # 36

Year	Coach	Record	Conference	Record
**2003	John Mumford	0-13	C-USA	0-8
2004	Bobby Ross	2-9	C-USA	2-6
2005	Bobby Ross	4-7	Indep	4-7
2006	Bobby Ross	3-9	Indep	3-9
2007	Stan Brock	3-9	Indep	3-9
2008	Stan Brock	3-9	Indep	3-9
2009	Rich Ellerson	5-7	Indep	5-7
2010	Rich Ellerson	7-6	Indep	7-6
2011	Rich Ellerson	3-9	Indep	3-9
2012	Rich Ellerson	2-10	Indep	2-10
2013	Rich Ellerson	3-9	Indep	3-9

** Todd Berry coached six losses listed under Mumford in 2003

Coach John Mumford checking things out

2003 Coaches Todd Berry / John Mumford

The Army West Point Black Knights football team represented the
United States Military Academy in the 2003 college football season.

It was Army's one hundred-fourteenth season of intercollegiate football. They were led by Coach Todd Berry, in his fourth and last season. Berry was fired after six games in. John Mumford coached the last seven games. Things were not going well for Army and Coach Mumford did not provide a fix.

Overall, the Black Knights compiled a 1-11-0 record. They were 0-8 in the C-USA Conference. They finished with another very poor season record. In 1998, Army pitched no shutouts, and had two shutouts thrown against them (TCU & Louisville – Berry's last two games). The Cadets were outscored by their opponents 476 to 206. In the annual Army–Navy Game, the Cadets defeated the Midshipmen W (6-34).

This year's opener was on Sept 6 at home vs Connecticut. In another poor record year, the Black Knights got the season off the wrong way again with a loss against the Huskies L (21-48). Other than those games played in neutral fields, all Army home games were played on the West Point campus at Michie Stadium in West Point NY. On Sept 13, the Black Knights lost its second of thirteen games this season.

The full 2003 season's games are listed as follows. All Games on the list are losses. It was Army's worst record ever.

Sept 6	Connecticut	L (21-48)
Sept 13	Rutgers	L (21-36
Sept 20	Tulane	L 33-50)
Sept 27	South Florida	L (0-28)
Oct 4	at TCU	L (0-27)
Oct 11	at Louisville	L 10-34
Oct 18	East Carolina	L (32-38)
Oct 25	at Cincinnati	L (29-330
Nov 1	UAB	L (9-24)
Nov 8	at Air Force	L (3-31)
Nov 15	Houston	L (14-34)
Nov 22	at Hawaii	L (28-59)
Dec 6	Navy	L(6-34)

On December 7 in the classic Army-Navy-Game, the Black Knights were blown-out by the Midshipmen L (12-58) at Lincoln Financial

Field in Philadelphia PA (Army-Navy-Game/Commander-in-Chief's Trophy). This gave the Black Knights their thirteenth loss of the season.

Bobby Ross

Bobby Ross was the next Army coach in the pipeline. When you look at Ross's record, 9-25, with three losing seasons, you can see a similarity with Bob Sutton, except for one thing. Sutton showed that if he got the players, he could bring out their talents as in his 10-2 season.

2004 Coach Bobby Ross

The Army West Point Black Knights football team represented the United States Military Academy in the 2004 college football season. It was Army's one hundred-fifteenth season of intercollegiate football. They were led by Coach Bobby Ross in his first of three seasons. As an independent football entity, the Army team had a very poor season record of 2-9.

Overall, the Black Knights compiled a 2-9 record. They were 2-6 in the C-USA Conference (their last year). They finished with another very poor season record. In 1998, Army pitched no shutouts, and had no shutouts thrown against them. In the annual Army–Navy Game, the Midshipmen defeated the Black Knights W (13-42).

This year's opener was on Sept 11at home vs Louisville. In another poor record year, the Black Knights got the season off the wrong way again with a loss against the Cardinals L (21-52). Other than those games played in neutral fields, all Army home games were played on the West Point campus at Michie Stadium in West Point NY. On Sept 18, the Black Knights lost its second of nine games this season and # 2 of four in a row at Houston L (21-35) It would be two more losses to get to the first win of 2004. Loss #3 on Sept 25, was at Connecticut L (3-40). The next loss of the four was against Texas Christian L (17-21).

Coach Bobby Ross at work

The Black Knights then defeated the Bearcats of Cincinnati on Oct 9 W (48-29 at Cincinnati The second win in a row and last win of the year came a week later on Oct 16 at South Florida W (42-35. The rest of the season was one loss after another for five in a row. The first was at East Carolina on Oct 30, L (28-38). The next loss of five was against Air Force on Nov 6, L (22-31). Next was at Tulane on Nov 13, L (31-45) Then it was UAB on Nov 20 L (14-20). All those came before # 5, the big one against Navy.

On December 4 in the classic Army-Navy-Game, the Black Knights were well-handled by the Midshipmen L (13-42) at Lincoln Financial Field in Philadelphia PA (Army-Navy-Game/Commander-in-Chief's Trophy). This gave the Black Knights their ninth loss of the season.

2005 Coach Bobby Ross

The Army West Point Black Knights football team represented the United States Military Academy in the 2005 college football season.

It was Army's one hundred-sixteenth season of intercollegiate football. They were led by Coach Bobby Ross in his second of three seasons. Out of conference play for good, as an independent football entity, the Army team had another very poor season record of 4-7.

Overall, the Black Knights compiled a 4-7 record. They had exited the C-USA Conference in 2004. They finished with another very poor season record. Army pitched one shutout 20-0 v Akron) and had no shutouts thrown against them. In the annual Army–Navy Game, the Midshipmen defeated the Black Knights W (23-42).

This year's opener was on Sept 10at home at Boston College In another 4-win, poor record year, the Black Knights got the season off the wrong way again with a loss against the Eagles L (7-44). The game was played at Alumni Stadium Chestnut Hill MA. Other than those games played in neutral fields, all Army home games were played on the West Point campus at Michie Stadium in West Point NY. On Sept 17, at home, the Black Knights were defeated by the Baylor Bears L 10-20). There would be four more losses before the first win.

On Sept 23 at home, #22 Iowa State defeated the Black Knights L (21-28) before 25,007 fans. On Oct 1, Connecticut got its licks in the defeat of Army in a high scoring win L (13-47), Before a max Michie Stadium crowd of 38, 482. On Oct 8, at home, Central Michigan beat Army L 10-14). The final loss before the first win was at # 25 TCU's Amon G. Carter Stadium Fort Worth, TX L 17-38). The Black Knights got sick of losing and won the next four games. The first was at Akron W (20-0) before 12,203 fans. The next win was against Air Force at Falcon Stadium Colorado Springs, CO (Commander-in-Chief's Trophy) W (27–24)

On Nov 12, it was #5 UMass at home. The Black Knights won in a close match W (34–27). The final win of a four-win season came on Nov 19 at home when the Black Knights took Arkansas State for a losing ride W (38-10). The last game was the Army Navy Game.

On December 3 in the classic Army-Navy-Game, the Black Knights were again pushed back by the Midshipmen L (23-42) at Lincoln Financial Field in Philadelphia PA (Army-Navy-

Game/Commander-in-Chief's Trophy). This gave the Black Knights their seventh loss of the season.

2006 Coach Bobby Ross

The Army West Point Black Knights football team represented the United States Military Academy in the 2006 college football season. It was Army's one hundred-seventeenth season of intercollegiate football. They were led by Coach Bobby Ross in his third and final season of three seasons. The Army team had another very poor season record of 3-9.

Overall, the Black Knights compiled a 3-9 record. They finished with another very poor season record. Army pitched no shutouts and had no shutouts thrown against them. In the annual Army–Navy Game, the Midshipmen defeated the Black Knights L (23-42).

This year's opener was on Sept 2 at Arkansas State's ASU Stadium in Jonesboro, AR. In a 3-win, poor record year, the Black Knights got the season off the wrong way again with a loss against the Red Wolves L (6-14). Other than those games played in neutral fields, all Army home games were played on the West Point campus at Michie Stadium in West Point NY. On Sept 9, at home, Army defeated Kent State W (17-14). On Sept 16, at Texas A &M, in the Alamodome, in San Antonio, TX, the Black Knights did not have enough juice and gave up the ghost L (24-28). On Sept 23, at Baylor's Floyd Casey Stadium in Waco, TX, the Black Knights prevailed W (27–20).

Moving through the season, on Sept 30, the Rice Owls came to Michie Stadium and defeated the Army Black Knights in a shootout L (14–48). Then, on Oct 7 at home, Army defeated VMI in a rout W 62–7 before 31,069. On Oct 14, at Connecticut's Rentschler Field in East Hartford, CT, the Huskies beat the Black Knights L 7–21. On Oct 21 at home, Army lost to TCU L 17–31 before 33,614.

On Oct 28, at the Louisiana Superdome in NO LA, Tulane got the better of the Army L (28–42) before 21,053. Air Force came back after last year's loss to torment Army again at home in a big win L (7-43). On Nov 18, the Big Guns from Notre Dame invited Army to

Notre Dame Stadium in South Bend, IN (Army-Notre Dame football rivalry). The Irish stole the win L (9–41) before 80,795.

On December 2 in the classic Army-Navy-Game, the Black Knights were again defeated by the Midshipmen L (14-26) at Lincoln Financial Field in Philadelphia PA (Army-Navy-Game /Commander-in-Chief's Trophy). This gave the Black Knights their ninth loss of the season.

There are a lot of great coaches who took their turns at Army. Some are great people and some are simply great coaches. Army was always looking for great coaches but sometimes stumbled on great people who could not coach as well as they might have. Bobby Ross got three years at Army and in a tough scenario, he did not perform up to expectations So, he retired. As the good man that he is, he expressed profound gratitude for the opportunity to coach the storied Black Knights of Army West Point.

Ross Retires After Three Years At Army; Brock Is New Coach

By Adam Kilgore
Washington Post Staff Writer
Tuesday, January 30, 2007; E04

Bobby Ross retired as head coach of Army yesterday, ending a three-year stint in which his teams finished 9-25 and did not beat Navy. Ross, 70, who coached Maryland for five seasons in the 1980s and took the San Diego Chargers to the Super Bowl in 1994, will be succeeded by offensive line coach Stan Brock, 48.

"I think there's a point in time when you feel like it's your time to retire, and I think I've reached that time," Ross said at a news conference at West Point. "I think there is an issue of having a certain degree of energy, which I feel is very important for anyone leading a college football program. I feel that I was lacking in that area as well."

As head coach of Maryland from 1982 to '86, Ross became known for high-scoring, quick-strike offenses and compiled a 39-19-1 record while grooming Boomer Esiason, and Frank Reich to become NFL quarterbacks. He won ACC titles from 1983 to '85, going undefeated in the league each season. He was the last Terrapins coach to win the ACC before Ralph Friedgen did so in 2001.

Friedgen spent 14 seasons as an assistant to Ross, a union that began when Friedgen was a graduate assistant at Maryland from 1969 to '72 while Ross was an assistant coach. Friedgen served as an assistant at The Citadel in 1973, when Ross accepted his first head coaching job. Friedgen also worked under Ross as offensive coordinator and offensive line coach at Maryland in 1982 and then became an assistant to Ross at Georgia Tech, where they won a national championship in 1990, and the Chargers.

Ross was a head coach for 28 seasons, 18 in college and 10 in the NFL with San Diego and the Detroit Lions.

At the news conference yesterday, Army Athletic Director Kevin Anderson gave the names of several coaches he's worked with, including Bill Walsh of the San Francisco 49ers, and said, "Coach Ross ranks on top of that list, both as a coach and a man."

Army went 3-9 last season and lost its last six games, including a 26-14 defeat against Navy.

Brock played for Ross in the NFL.

"I am not going to replace Bobby Ross. No way," Brock said. "He is the best coach I ever played for."

Upon his hiring at Army, Ross spoke about how his military background shaped his decision to accept the position. Ross graduated from the Virginia Military Institute and served in the U.S. Army from 1960 to '62 as a lieutenant. He sent one son to the Air Force Academy and another to the Naval Academy.

"My desire to always coach at West Point was a great one," Ross said in a statement. "I will be indebted to our administration forever for providing me the opportunity to do that."

2007 Coach Stan Brock

The Army West Point Black Knights football team represented the United States Military Academy in the 2007 college football season. It was Army's one hundred-eighteenth season of intercollegiate football. They were led by Coach Stan Brock in his first of two seasons. The Army team had another very poor season record of 3-9. It was the second 3-9 season of three in a row.

Stan Brock before the Tulane game

Overall, the Black Knights compiled a 3-9 record. They finished with another very poor season record. Army pitched no shutouts and had no shutouts thrown against them. In the very important annual Army–Navy Game, the Midshipmen defeated the Black Knights L (3-38).

This year's opener was on Sept 1 at Akron in the Cleveland Browns Stadium Cleveland In another 3-win, poor record year, the Black Knights got the season off the wrong way again with this loss against the Zips L (14-22). Other than those games played in neutral fields, all Army home games were played on the West Point campus at Michie Stadium in West Point NY. On Sept 8, Army defeated Rhode Island at home in OT W (14-7). On Sept 15 at Wake Forest's BB&T

Field Winston-Salem, NC, army lost by L (10-21). On Sept 22, at #14 Boston College's Alumni Stadium Chestnut Hill, MA, the Eagles defeated the Black Knights L (17–37) before 40,329.

On Sept 29 at home, Army defeated Temple W (37–21) before 34,176. Then on Oct 6, Army grabbed another win, two in a row, at home from Tulane W (20–17) in OT. The Black Knights then lost to Central Michigan on Oct 13 at Central Michigan's Kelly/Shorts Stadium Mount Pleasant, MI L (23–47) before 21,013. On Oct 20 at Georgia Tech's Bobby Dodd Stadium Atlanta, GA, the Yellow Jackets got the best of the Black Knights L (10–34) before 50,242 fans.

On Nov 3 at Air Force's Falcon Stadium Colorado Springs, CO, the Army was beaten by the Air Force, L (10–30) before a packed crowd of 46,144. On Nov at home, Rutgers put a lick on Army at home L (6-41). On Nov 17, at home, Tulsa defeated Army L (39-49).

On December 1 in the classic Army-Navy-Game, the Black Knights were again defeated handily by the Midshipmen L (3-38) at Lincoln Financial Field in Philadelphia PA (Army-Navy-Game /Commander-in-Chief's Trophy). The attendance was overflowing the field for this game at 71,610. This again gave the Black Knights their ninth loss of the season.

2008 Coach Stan Brock

The Army West Point Black Knights football team represented the United States Military Academy in the 2008 college football season. It was Army's one hundred-nineteenth season of intercollegiate football. They were led by Coach Stan Brock in his second and last of two seasons. The Army team had another very poor season record of 3-9. It was the third 3-9 season of three in a row.

Overall, the Black Knights compiled a 3-9 record. They finished with another very poor season record. Army pitched no shutouts and had one shutout thrown against them in the Army-Navy-Game. In the very important annual Army–Navy Game, the Midshipmen defeated the Black Knights L (0-34).

This year's opener was on August 29 at home against Temple. This was the first time that an Army opener was played in August. It was part of another 3-win, poor record year. The Black Knights got the season off the wrong way again with this loss against the Owls L (7-35) before 1`,822. Other than those games played in neutral fields, all Army home games were played on the West Point campus at Michie Stadium in West Point NY. On Sept 6, in a home encounter at 1:00 PM for good TV viewing on a Saturday afternoon, New Hampshire took Army for a losing spin L (10-28).

Then, on Sept 20 at home, Akron beat Army L (3-22) before 27,040. On Sept 27, at Texas A&M's Kyle Field College Station, TX, Army went down L 21–17 before 84,090 fans, then on Oct 4, my wedding Anniversary, at Tulane's Tad Gormley Stadium New Orleans, LA, Army whooped the Green Wave W 44–13. On Oct 11, at home, Eastern Michigan could not keep up with Army at home W (17–13) before 27,096.

On Oct 18 at Buffalo's UB Stadium Buffalo, NY, the Bulls beat the Black Knights L (27–24) in OT. Then on Oct 25 at home, Army beat Louisiana Tech W (14–7) before a crowd of 27,383.

On Nov 1, at home, Air Force, fighting for the (Commander-in-Chief's Trophy) beat Army L (16–7) before a packed house of 37,409. Then, on Nov 8 at Rice in Rice Stadium Houston, TX, Army lost the match L 31-38) before 19,243. On Nov 22 at Rutgers' Rutgers Stadium in Piscataway, NJ, Army lost another game L (3-30) before 42,212 Rutgers fans.

On December 6 in the classic Army-Navy-Game, the Black Knights were again defeated in a shutout by the Midshipmen L (0-34) at Lincoln Financial Field in Philadelphia PA (Army-Navy-Game /Commander-in-Chief's Trophy). The attendance was huge again for this meeting at 69,144.

This again gave the Black Knights their ninth loss of the season. Navy had always been the lesser player but in the recent years, the Midshipmen had begun to play better football than Army all season long and this trend affected the Army-Navy Game.

Since Navy was doing well, and since Air Force was doing well during this period, what is clear is that Army West Point, a fine service academy had not yet figured out how to win in the modern age. Out of nowhere, Navy is now ten games ahead in the win-loss coulmn.

We have been walking through some of the years in which this happened. However, this occurred, a team of generals ought to be able to figure out how to help their Cadets win football games in the same fashion as they always win wars. There should be no excuses. That's what I think.

Stan Brock took a lot of heat in 2008 from critics after changing from the pro-style offense to a triple option-like offensive scheme after the previous season. Some pundits dubbed it the "Brock Bone" or "quadruple" option, due to an added passing element. The team as noted above finished the season with a disappointing 3–9 record, with the biggest disappointment being the 34–0 rout by archrival Navy.

Brock was subsequently fired and replaced this year by former Cal Poly head coach, Rich Ellerson. The 2008 Army–Navy Game was the first shut-out of Army by Navy since 1978. One consolation was that in the game's final play, Army fullback Collin Mooney, in the last play of his college football career, broke the school record for single-season rushing by a single yard.

Brock Out; Ellerson In at Army from NY Daily News

WEST POINT, N.Y. - Army filled its football coaching vacancy by heeding a core West Point value: History matters.

Rich Ellerson grew up around Black Knights football and is leaving his coaching job at Cal Poly to come to a place he knows well. His father and two brothers graduated from the U.S. Military Academy, where brother John led the 1962 team to a 6-4 record. And he's worked before with former Army coaches known for running successful schemes on both sides of the ball.

Ellerson replaces Stan Brock, who was fired Dec. 12 after a pair of 3-9 seasons. This season ended with a 34-0 loss to Navy. Brock, a former New Orleans Saints offensive lineman, was Army's offensive line coach for three years before replacing Bobby Ross in early 2007.

Academy officials, who announced the selection Friday, said Ellerson expressed interest in the position when it was open in the past. They were impressed by his familiarity with a program in need of a quick turnaround.

"I will never receive, nor have I ever received a finer compliment professionally or personally than to be entrusted with the Army football program at this point in its history," said Ellerson, who turns 55 on Jan. 1.

Before his eight years as Cal Poly's coach, Ellerson worked with former Army coach Jim Young at Arizona, where Ellerson was an assistant. Young, who ran a successful option attack at Army, had retired from the Black Knights after the 1990 season and assumed a volunteer role on the Arizona coaching staff.

Ellerson also assisted Army coach Bob Sutton when he installed his "Desert Swarm" defense at West Point, which helped carry the Black Knights to a 10-2 record and a berth in the Independence Bowl in 1996.

Cal Poly made it to the Football Championship Subdivision playoffs four times under Ellerson and was ranked as high as No. 3 this season. He was 56-34 in his eight years at Cal Poly.

Athletic director Kevin Anderson said he's long admired Ellerson's work with the triple option at Cal Poly.

"One of our primary goals of the search was to find someone capable of turning around our program immediately, and we are confident Rich is the perfect individual to accomplish that," he said.

Despite all the confidence like many before him, Rich Ellerson was unable to deliver more than just one slightly winning season out of five. Most of the squad's seasons with Coach Ellerson were well underplayed. Four losing seasons out of five says a lot.

2009 Coach Rich Ellerson

The Army West Point Black Knights football team represented the United States Military Academy in the 2009 college football season. It was Army's one hundred-twentieth season of intercollegiate football. They were led by Coach Rich Ellerson in his first of five seasons. The Army team had a losing season record of 5-7. They won two games more than the prior year.

Overall, the Black Knights compiled a 5-7 record. They finished with another relatively poor season record. Army pitched no shutouts and had no shutouts thrown against them. In the very important annual Army–Navy Game, the Midshipmen defeated the Black Knights L (3-17).

Rich Ellerson coaching for Army Black Knights

This year's opener was on Sept. 5 at Rynearson Stadium Ypsilanti, MI against Eastern Michigan. The Black Knights began the season with a win against the Eagles W (27-14) before 14,449. Other than those games played in neutral fields, all Army home games were played on the West Point campus at Michie Stadium in West Point NY. On Sept 12, at home Army picked up its first loss of the season under Coach Ellerson against Duke L (19-35) On Sept 19, Army recovered from the loss to Duke and came back to win against Ball State W (24-17).

The Black Knights were defeated on Sept 26 at Iowa State's Jack Trice Stadium, Ames, IA L 10–31 before 50,532. Then on Oct 3, the Army Homecoming, Tulane spoiled the day by sneaking in a one-point win against the Black Knights L (16-17). On Oct 10 at home, the Black Knights defeated the Commodores in OT W (16–13). Temple then beat Army L (13-27) on Oct 17 at Temple in a game played at the Lincoln Financial Field in Philadelphia, PA. Attendance was 14,275. On Oct 23, Army lost to Rutgers at home L (10-27).

On Nov 7, the Black Knights were defeated at Air Force's Falcon Stadium Colorado Springs, CO (Commander-in-Chief's Trophy), by the Fighting Falcons L (7–35) before 46,212. On Nov 14 at home the Black Knights defeated VMI W (22-17). Army picked up its 2nd win in a row against North Texas on Nov 21 at Fouts Field Denton, TX W 17-13 before 23,647.

On December 12 in the classic Army-Navy-Game, the Black Knights were again defeated by the Midshipmen L (3-17) at Lincoln Financial Field in Philadelphia PA (Army-Navy-Game / Commander-in-Chief's Trophy). The attendance was high again for this meeting 69,541. This game was the seventh loss for the Black Knights this season.

2010 Coach Rich Ellerson

The Army West Point Black Knights football team represented the United States Military Academy in the 2010 college football season. It was Army's one hundred-twenty-first season of intercollegiate football. They were led by Coach Rich Ellerson in his second of five seasons. The Army team had a winning season record of 7-5, their first season above 500 since 1996. They won two games more than the prior year.

Overall, the Black Knights compiled a 7-5 record. They finished with an OK season record. Army pitched a shutout against North Texas –

24-0, and had no shutouts thrown against them. In the very important annual Army–Navy Game, the Midshipmen defeated the Black Knights L (17-31).

By winning 6 regular season games, Army became bowl-eligible for the first time since the 1996 season. They were invited to the Armed Forces Bowl against SMU, in University Park, Texas replacing a team from the Mountain West Conference. They defeated SMU 16–14 in the bowl to finish the season 7–6, their first winning season since 1996.

This year's opener was on Sept. 4 at Rynearson Stadium Ypsilanti, MI against Eastern Michigan. The Black Knights began the season with a win against the Eagles W (31-27) before 11,318. Other than those games played in neutral fields, all Army home games were played on the West Point campus at Michie Stadium in West Point NY. On Sept 11, Army lost to Hawaii at home L (28-31). Next up was North Texas on Sept 18. The Black Knights picked up a shutout win W (24-0). On Sept 25, the Black Knights defeated the Duke Blue Devils W (35-21). Then on Oct 2, Temple won a close game (one TD) from Army L (35-42).

At Tulane on Oct9, playing in the Louisiana Superdome, the Black Knights defeated the Green Wave W (41-23). Rutgers was next at New Meadowlands Stadium in East Rutherford, NJ on Oct 16. Army got the loss L (20-23) in a close match. On Oct 30, at home vs VMI, Army won handily W (29-7). On Nov 6, first weekend in November, Air Force defeated Army L 922-42). On Nov 13, at Kent State's Dix Stadium in Kent, OH, Army won another W (45–28). In the game before THE GAME, Notre Dame defeated Army in Yankee Stadium Bronx, NY L (3-27).

On December 11 in the classic Army-Navy-Game, the Black Knights were again defeated by the Midshipmen L (17-31) at Lincoln Financial Field in Philadelphia PA (Army-Navy-Game /Commander-in-Chief's Trophy). The attendance was high again for this meeting 69,541. This game was the sixth of six losses for the Black Knights this season.

On December 30, 12:00 p.m. at SMU in the Armed Serviced Bowl played at Gerald J. Ford Stadium University Park, TX, the Black Knights defeated the Mustangs W 16–14 before a crowd of 36,742.

2011 Coach Rich Ellerson

The Army West Point Black Knights football team represented the United States Military Academy in the 2011 college football season. It was Army's one hundred-twenty-second season of intercollegiate football. They were led by Coach Rich Ellerson in his third of five seasons. The Army team had a losing season record of 3-9. They lost four more games than the prior year.

Overall, the Black Knights compiled a 3-9 record. They finished with a poor season record. Army pitched a shutout against Fordham 55-0, and had no shutouts thrown against them. In the very important annual Army–Navy Game, the Midshipmen defeated the Black Knights 21-27.

This year's opener was on Sept. 4 at Northern Illinois' Huskie Stadium against Northern Illinois. The Black Knights began the season with a loss to the Huskies L (26-49) before 17,003. Other than those games played in neutral fields, all Army home games were played on the West Point campus at Michie Stadium in West Point NY. On Sept 10, Army lost to San Diego State at home L (20-23).

Next up was Northwestern on Sept 17. The black Knights picked up their first win of the season W (21-14). On Sept 24, the Black Knights were defeated L (21-48) by Ball State at Scheumann Stadium • Muncie, IN. Then on Oct 1, at home Army pounded Tulane W (45-6).

On Oct 8 at Miami (OH)'s Yager Stadium Oxford, OH, the Black Knights were defeated by the Red Hawks. L (28–35). Next was Vanderbilt at Vanderbilt Stadium Nashville, on Oct 22 L (21–44). Then on Oct 29, the Black Knights walloped Fordham's Rams W 55-0 before 39,481 fans at Michie.

On Nov 5 at Falcon Stadium • Colorado Springs, CO, the Air Force's Fighting Tigers defeated the Army Black Knights   L 14–24 before an attendance of 46,709. On Nov 2, at Yankee Stadium Bronx, NY, Rutgers defeated Army L (12-27) before 30,028. On Nov 19, at Temple in a game played at Lincoln Financial Field in Philadelphia, PA, the Army lost the match L (14-42) by a wide margin.

On December 10 in the classic Army-Navy-Game, the Black Knights were again defeated by the Midshipmen L (21-27) at FedEx Field in Landover MD (112th Army-Navy-Game / Commander-in-Chief's Trophy). The attendance was high 80,789. This game was the ninth loss for the Black Knights this season.

2012 Coach Rich Ellerson

The Army West Point Black Knights football team represented the United States Military Academy in the 2012 college football season. It was Army's one hundred-twenty-third season of intercollegiate football. They were led by Coach Rich Ellerson in his fourth of five seasons. The Army team had a losing season record of 2-10. They lost one more game than the prior year.

Overall, the Black Knights compiled a 2-10 record. They finished with a poor season record. Army pitched no shutouts, and had no shutouts thrown against them. In the very important annual Army–Navy Game, the Midshipmen defeated the Black Knights again 13-17. Things were not looking good for Coach Ellerson or the Army program.

This year's opener was on Sept 8 at San Diego State's Qualcomm Stadium San Diego, CA. The Black Knights began the season with a loss to the Aztecs L (7-42) before 30,799. Other than those games played in neutral fields, all Army home games were played on the West Point campus at Michie Stadium in West Point NY.

On Sept 15, Army lost a one-pointer to Northern Illinois at home L (40-41). On Sept 22, at Wake Forest's BB&T Field Winston-Salem, NC, the Black Knights were defeated by the demon Deacons L (37-

49). On Sept 29, at home Army was defeated by Stony Brook L (3-23)

On Oct 6 at home vs Boston College, Army prevailed by a close margin W (34-31). Next was Kent State on Oct 13 at home in a losing effort L (17-31) Eastern Michigan was next to defeat Army on Oct 20 at Rynearson Stadium Ypsilanti, MI L (38-48).

Then on Oct 27, the Black Knights lost to the Ball State Cardinals L (22-30). Air Force was ready as always on Nov 3 for Army but not ready enough as the Black Knights defeated the Fighting Falcons W (41-21) at home before 37,707. On Nov 10 at Rutgers in High Point Solutions Stadium Piscataway, NJ, the Scarlet Knights defeated the Black Knights L (7-28) On Nov 17, at home, Temple pounded Army L (32-63) in a shootout win.

On December 8 in the classic Army-Navy-Game, the Black Knights were again defeated by the Midshipmen L (13-17) at Lincoln Financial Field in Philadelphia PA (113th Army-Navy-Game /Commander-in-Chief's Trophy). This game was the tenth loss for the Black Knights this season. Rich Ellerson's team brought in just two wins.

2013 Coach Rich Ellerson

The Army West Point Black Knights football team represented the United States Military Academy in the 2013 college football season. It was Army's one hundred-twenty-fourth season of intercollegiate football. They were led by Coach Rich Ellerson in his fifth and last of five seasons. The Army team had a losing season record of 3-9. They won just one more game than the prior year.

Overall, the Black Knights compiled a 3-9 record. They finished with a poor season record. Army pitched no shutouts, and had no shutouts thrown against them. In the very important annual Army–Navy Game, the Midshipmen smothered the Black Knights 7-34. Following the loss to Navy on December 14 and finishing the season 3-9, head coach Rich Ellerson was fired.

This year's opener was on Aug 30 at Morgan State at home. The Black Knights began the season with a nice win against the Bears W (28-12) before 24245. Other than those games played in neutral fields, all Army home games were played on the West Point campus at Michie Stadium in West Point NY. On Sept 7, Army lost to Ball State at Scheumann Stadium Muncie, IN L (14-40). On Sept 14, against Stanford at home, the Black Knights lost to the Cardinal L (20-34). Before 39, 644. On Sept 21, Wake Forest defeated Army at home L (11-25). Then, on Sept 28, against Louisiana Tech, playing in Cotton Bowl Stadium Dallas, TX (Heart of Dallas Classic), Army picked up the win W (35–16).

On Oct 5 at Boston College's Alumni Stadium at Chestnut Hill, MA, the Eagles defeated the Black Knights L (27-48). Then on Oct 12 at home, Army defeated Eastern Michigan in a shootout W (50-25). On Oct 19 at Temple, played at Lincoln Financial Field Philadelphia, PA, the Owls defeated the Black Knights L (14–33). On Nov 2, at Air Force's Falcon Stadium Colorado Springs, CO (Commander-in-Chief's Trophy), the Fighting Falcons defeated the Army Black Knights L (28–42) before 36,512.

On Nov 9 at home against Western Kentucky (WKU), the Hilltoppers defeated the Black Knights L 17–212. On Nov 30, 11:00 p.m.   at Hawaii's Aloha Stadium in Honolulu, Hawaii, the Black Knights were defeated by the Rainbow Warriors L 42–49 before 32,690.

On December 14 in the classic Army-Navy-Game, the Black Knights were again defeated by the Midshipmen L (7-34) at Lincoln Financial Field in Philadelphia PA (114th Army-Navy-Game /Commander-in-Chief's Trophy). This game was the ninth loss for the Black Knights this season. 65,612 fans were in attendance.

Our acknowledgment to ESPN for this article about Rich Ellerson.

Army fires coach Rich Ellerson

Dec 16, 2013

Army has fired Rich Ellerson after five seasons, the school confirmed Sunday.

Ellerson was 20-41 at Army, including 0-5 against Navy.
The firing comes one day after Army lost 34-7 to Navy, the Black

Knights' 12th straight loss in the lopsided series.

Rich Ellerson's 34-7 loss to Navy on Saturday turned out to be his last game on Army's sideline.

"I love that football team,'" Ellerson said after the game. "I want desperately for them to have a better feeling today. That's what is killing me."

Army finished 3-9 this season.

"Obviously, in the body of work, we've made some progress," Ellerson said Saturday. "But I wasn't brought in to make progress. I was brought in to win some football games and beat Navy. I've lost to our rival five times."

The Midshipmen haven't lost to Army since 2001 and lead the series 58-49-7. Navy's 12-game run is the longest in the history of the rivalry that began in 1890.

"I thought we closed the gap the last two years, but that gap opened back up," Ellerson said.

In 2010, Ellerson led Army to its first bowl win since 1985 by beating SMU in the Armed Forces Bowl. But the last three years, Army went 8-28.

The triple-option wasn't the problem. Ellerson's offense averaged more than 300 yards rushing the past three seasons, but the rest of the team never developed. He had two years left on his contract.

"Rich Ellerson has represented West Point and the Army football program extremely well since taking over as our head coach five years ago," Army athletic director Boo Corrigan said in a statement. "Unfortunately, our team has not experienced the level of success on the football field that we expect, and we feel it is necessary to make a change in the leadership at this time."

Corrigan said deputy athletic director Col. Joe DeAntona will assume day-to-day operations of the football program until a new coach is hired.

Ellerson, 60, came to Army after eight seasons in charge of Cal Poly, where he went 56-34 with two NCAA playoff appearances. Information from The Associated Press was used in this report

Chapter 16 Coach Jeff Monken 2014-17+

Monken   Coach # 37

Year	Coach	Record	Conference	Record
2014	Jeff Monken	4-8	Indep	4-8
2015	Jeff Monken	2-10	Indep	2-10
2016	Jeff Monken	8-5	Indep	8-5
2017	Jeff Monken			

Coach Jeff Monken with the Army Team

Who is Coach Jeff Monken?

Jeff Monken is the new Sherriff in town. Others who came before him could not turn this seemingly lawless team around. Nobody has been blaming the Sherriff per se but every few years, the Army gets rid of the Sherriff and brings in a "better" lawman to bring justice to the people of Dodge City. But, the same old things happen. The bad guys come into Michie Stadium and face the ravage the townspeople.

Will this happen again? It was a good question in 2014 for sure as the new Sheriff, Jeff Monken had not even checked out his posse.

When 2014 was said and done, there was a lot of devastation (4-8 record) and the townspeople had been hurt like the olden days. But, they figured that Sherriff Monken was still getting his posse together so the Town Council kept him on.

Then came 2015, and the posse was getting formed and they looked stronger. But, the bad guys played harder than the prior year (2-10). While this was going on, Sherriff Monken was culling his posse into the best there ever was. Despite a 2-10 bad guy record, twice as bad statistically as the prior year, the townspeople also looked at the posse and they figured protection and victories over adversaries would come in 2016.

It did!

Jeff Monken, who was named Army's 37th individual head coach on Dec. 24, 2013, is now ready to begin his fourth season as head football coach. The Sherriff now has a fine posse.

Monken shows a 50-39 career record as a head coach and a 6-18 mark at Army.

Last year, 2016, was a breakout season for the Black Knights under Monken. He led them to their first win over Navy since 2001 and they won a bowl game for the first time in six seasons. The last time the Black Knights accomplished both feats in the same season was in 1984.

In 2016, Army was second in the nation in rushing offense and ran for an Army single-season record of 46 touchdowns, which eclipsed the 1945 national championship team. On the defense side, Army was consistently in the top 10 in total defense and finished the year fourth in the nation. They handled the bad guys on both sides of the ball.

In 2015, Sherriff Monken led Army to a pair of wins over Bucknell and Eastern Michigan. Under coach Monken, the Black Knights had five players reach 100 yards rushing in a game in 2015 and had three different quarterbacks throw for 100 yards. Signal callers Ahmad Bradshaw and Chris Carter ran and threw for 100 yards each in their career debuts. Army won on the road for the first time since 2010 with a 58-36 win over Eastern Michigan. The townspeople, the fans, and the Academy were beginning to believe.

Army finished the season ranked 12th in the country in rushing offense at 244.3 yards per game. Linebacker Andrew King was the top player in the national rankings. He was 21st in tackles for loss with an average of 2.1 per game and 26th in fumbles recovered with two.

In Monken's first season at Army, he guided the Black Knights to home victories over Buffalo, Ball State and Fordham, in addition to a dramatic win against Connecticut at Yankee Stadium.

Under his guidance, running back Larry Dixon, linebacker Jeremy Timpf, defensive back Josh Jenkins and offensive lineman Matt Hugenberg earned 11 citations on postseason all-star teams and two players, Joe Drummond and Dixon competed in The Medal of Honor Bowl Game and East-West Shrine Game, respectively.

Army was fifth in the country in rushing offense at 296.5 yards per game in Monken's first season and sixth in fewest penalties per game with just 4.08 infractions per contest.

Monken tutored a host of players who listed in the national rankings. Timpf was seventh in the nation in solo tackles per game and 23rd in tackles per game. Jenkins was eighth in the country in blocked kicks and 33rd in interceptions per game and both Lamar Johnson-Harris and Xavier Moss ranked 11th in punt return touchdowns. Dixon listed nationally in rushing yards per carry (30th), rushing yards (39th) and rushing yards per game (41st).

With a 47-39 win against Buffalo, Monken became the first head coach to win his first game since Bob Sutton did so in 1991 with a victory over Colgate. Prior to Monken, the last Army coach to win his first game against a Football Bowl Subdivision opponent was Ed Cavanaugh in 1980.

Monken came to the banks of the Hudson River following a successful stint as a head coach at Georgia Southern.

He spent four seasons as head coach at Georgia Southern after learning the triple-option offense under one of the nation's premier option proponents, Paul Johnson, during assistant coaching stints at Navy and Georgia Tech.

During his four seasons at Georgia Southern, Monken authored a 38-16 mark and spearheaded the programs transition to the elite Football Bowl Subdivision level from the Football Championship Subdivision (FCS) ranks.

Georgia Southern, which joined the Sun Belt Conference following Monken's tenure, was a member of the FCS and qualified for the NCAA playoffs in all three eligible seasons under Monken, advancing to the national semifinals each year while posting double-digit victory totals.

Monken guided tradition-rich Georgia Southern to some of the biggest wins in school history, with the most memorable arguably a 26-20 victory at Florida in November at the vaunted "Swamp." Despite that headline-grabbing victory, Georgia Southern was not eligible for the FCS playoffs this season due to its transitional status.

"I am thrilled to accept the head coaching position at West Point," said Monken at the time of his hiring. "Not only is the United States Military Academy one of the most prestigious academic institutions in the world, it boasts one of the nation's richest, most historic traditions in all of college football.

"There are so many people I would like to thank for this tremendous opportunity, starting with Director of Athletics Boo Corrigan and our Superintendent, Gen. Bob Caslen. I am honored and humbled by their trust in me to lead the West Point football program. I have had the privilege of serving as a coach for several outstanding institutions and am thankful to all of the student-athletes, coaches, and administrators with whom I have worked. Because of their commitment, dedication, and loyalty, this opportunity to serve at West Point has been afforded to me. More than anyone else, I want to thank the men and women who have served and continue to serve our nation in the United States Army. I am proud to be your head football coach."

Monken and Johnson are the only coaches in Georgia Southern school history to win at least 10 games in each of their first three seasons.

"Jeff Monken is an outstanding football coach. He is a tireless worker who will do the right things to build a program and he will be a great leader," said Johnson.

A finalist for the 2012 Liberty Mutual Coach of the Year award, Monken guided Georgia Southern to 10 wins his first season, 11 his second and 10 in his third. His 2013 squad posted a 7-4 mark, including the stunning, season-ending upset of Florida in Gainesville.

Under Monken's guidance, Georgia Southern was one of the top rushing teams at the FCS level, claiming the NCAA rushing title in 2012 at 399.36 yards per contest. Walter Payton Award candidate Jerick McKinnon and running back Dominique Swope established the NCAA record for rushing yards by teammates with 3,063.

Monken coached a lengthy list of all-stars, including the school's highest-ever National Football League draft choice, safety J.J. Wilcox, a third-round selection of the Dallas Cowboys in 2013.

In 2011, Georgia Southern was ranked No. 1 in both FCS polls for seven weeks and stopped Wofford, 31-10, to win its ninth Southern Conference championship. Five players were named All-America, Brent Russell was selected Southern Conference Defensive Player of the Year, Monken earned conference Coach of the Year plaudits and Swope was named Southern Conference Freshman of the Year. Home playoff wins against Old Dominion and Maine were part of the Eagles' memorable 11-3 campaign.

Monken got off to a great start in his first year as Georgia Southern's head coach, knocking off top-ranked and previously unbeaten Appalachian State as part of a 10-5 season. Georgia Southern ended the season with three straight wins to qualify for the postseason and registered three playoff victories to advance to the national semifinals.

In addition to the success on the field, Monken helped Georgia Southern reemerge academically with the team's cumulative grade point average ranking as the highest in school history in each of his first two seasons. Not only was Georgia Southern successful in the classroom and on the football field under Monken, but the players and staffs were part of several community service programs and local events.

Monken was named Georgia Southern's head coach in November of 2009, continuing a family history of football coaches. Jeff's father, Mike, and a dozen family members have coached at the high school, collegiate or professional levels.

Monken's first head coaching job came after accumulating 20 years of experience as an assistant, 13 of them with his mentor Johnson. Monken coached slotbacks at Georgia Southern from 1997 to 2001 before joining Johnson first at Navy and then Georgia Tech.

As an assistant coach at Georgia Southern, Monken was part of two NCAA FCS National Championship squads (1999 and 2000) and five straight playoff teams. Georgia Southern was among the top-five rushing teams in all five seasons and twice led the nation in rushing. Four out of five seasons, the Eagles ranked in the top-15 in scoring as well.

After serving as an assistant at Georgia Southern, Monken accepted a position on Johnson's coaching staff at Navy. Monken not only mentored slotbacks, he later added special team's coordinator duties.

In Annapolis, Monken helped the Midshipmen to five straight Commander in Chief trophies and five consecutive bowl appearances, including a 10-win season in 2004. Following his time at Navy, Monken moved to Georgia Tech where for two seasons he served as slotbacks coach and special teams coordinator. The Yellow Jackets posted double-digit wins in 2009 and captured the Atlantic Coast Conference championship, although that title was later vacated.

Monken began his coaching career in 1989 as a graduate assistant at the University Hawaii and later spent one season at Arizona State

University. Monken moved to University of Buffalo as the wide receivers and tight ends coach and also handled recruiting. He served on the staffs at Morton (Ill.) High School as head coach and at Concordia University in Illinois as the offensive line coach as well.

A native of Joliet, Ill, Monken played wide receiver for four years and earned two varsity letters in track and field while earning his bachelor's degree from Millikin University in 1989. He was inducted into the school's Athletic Hall of Fame in October and collected his master's degree from Hawaii in 1991.

Monken and his wife Beth now reside at West Point with their three daughters, Isabelle, Amelia and Evangeline. We of the Army Football Community know Jeff Monken can produce great teams. We are sure wishing and hoping and praying that his energy holds out and that he gets the support of the institution for the long haul.

When the fan base and the pundits begin to put the word "Red" in between Jeff and Monken, I think we (Army) will have more than arrived.

2014 Coach Jeff Monken

The Army West Point Black Knights football team represented the United States Military Academy in the 2014 college football season. It was Army's one hundred-twenty-fifth season of intercollegiate football. They were led by Coach Jeff Monken in his first of three seasons. Monken is also the current coach and he had a good year in 2016 so we hope he is around for a while. The Army team had a losing season record of 4-8. They won one more game than the prior year.

Overall, the Black Knights compiled a 4-8 record. They finished with a poor season record, losing twice as many games as they won. Army pitched no shutouts, and were shut out by Stanford 0-35. In the very important annual Army–Navy Game, the Midshipmen smothered the Black Knights 10-17. Assistant Coach Danny Verpaele brought back the tight end position to Army

This year's opener was on Sept 6 at home against Buffalo. The Black Knights began the season with a shootout win against the Bulls (47-39) before 28643. Other than those games played in neutral fields, all Army home games were played on the West Point campus at Michie Stadium in West Point NY. On Sept 13, Army was shut out L (0-35) by #15 Stanford in Stanford Stadium—Stanford, CA, Wake Forest played army at BB&T Field Winston-Salem, NC for the win L (21-24), On Sept 27 at Yale's Yale Bowl New Haven, CT, the Bulldogs defeated the Black Knights in OT L (43–49) before 34,142

On Oct 4, my wedding anniversary to my beautiful Bride, Pat, Army defeated Ball State at home W (33–24) before a fairly packed house of 31,384. On Oct 11, at home, Rice defeated Army L (21-41) in an even more packed house of 37,011. Then, on Oct 18   3:30 p.m. at Kent State's Dix Stadium Kent, OH, the Army lost another away game L (17–39). Air Force was always ready for Army and again this year, at home, the Fighting Falcons defeated the Black Knights (Commander-in-Chief's Trophy) L 6–23 before an overflow crowd of 40,479. On Nov 8, at Yankee Stadium in the Bronx, NY, Army defeated Connecticut W 35–21 before 27,453.

Then on Nov 15 at Houchens Industries–L. T. Smith Stadium Bowling, KY, Army was defeated by WKU in a shootout L (24–52) before 16,819 On Nov 22 at home, the Black Knights defeated the Fordham Rams at home W (42–31) before 33,793.

On December 13 in the classic Army-Navy-Game, the Black Knights were once again defeated by the Midshipmen L (10-17) M & T Bank Stadium Baltimore MD (115th Army–Navy Game/Commander-in-Chief's Trophy) This game was the eighth loss for the Black Knights this season. 70, 935 fans were in attendance.

2015 Coach Jeff Monken

The Army West Point Black Knights football team represented the United States Military Academy in the 2015 college football season. It was Army's one hundred-twenty-sixth season of intercollegiate football. They were led by Coach Jeff Monken in his second of three seasons. Monken is also the current coach and he had a good year in 2016 so we hope he is around for a while. The Army team had a losing season record of 2-10. They won two less games than the prior year.

Overall, the Black Knights compiled a 2-10 record. They finished with a very poor season record, losing five times as many games as they won. Army pitched no shutouts, and were not shut out by any opponent. In the very important annual Army–Navy Game, the Midshipmen smothered the Black Knights 17-21. This game was close but no cigar. Would Coach Jeff Monken get to light up a cigar in 2016? We'll see soon!

This year's opener was on Sept 4 at home against Fordham. The Black Knights began the season with a poor showing against a second-tier team with this loss against the Rams L (35-37) before 22523. Other than those games played in neutral fields, all Army home games were played on the West Point campus at Michie Stadium in West Point NY. On Sept 12, Army lost in a close match L (17-22) at Connecticut's Connecticut Rentschler Field East Hartford, CT before 28,301.

Wake Forest played Army at home on Sept 19, and the Demon Deacons defeated the Black Nights by no more than a hair L (14-17). On Sept 26 at Eastern Michigan's Rynearson Stadium Ypsilanti, MI, Army got the win in a shootout W (58–36). On Oct 3 with Coach Franklin leading PSU at Penn State's Beaver Stadium University Park, PA, Army played to a one touchdown differential but lost L (14–20) before a massive crowd of 107,387.

On Oct 10, at home, the Duke Blue Devils overpowered the Army Black Knights in a rout L 3–44 before 39,712. On Oct 17, Army beat a willing Bucknell team W (21–14) before 33,257. The Black Knights went on the road the next week to play Rice's Owls at Rice Stadium Houston, TX and Army almost came home with the bacon but missed out by a TD L (31–38) before 24,409. On Nov 7 at Air Force's Falcon Stadium Colorado Springs, CO (Commander-in-Chief's Trophy), Army could not match the Air Power and succumbed L (3–20) before 37,716.

Next against a team from New Orleans, the non-gambling Fun Capitol of America, on Nov 14, in a homecoming game played at West Point, the Black Knights almost gave the home team a big victory against Tulane but it was a field goal off L (31-34). Wrapping up the non-Navy part of the season. The Black Knights faced the Scarlet Knights of Rutgers on Nov 21. Rutgers got the best of Army that day L (21-31) before 31,217 at home. The people are counting on Jeff Monken to deliver lots less seasons like this one.

On December 12, before 69,277 fans in the classic Army-Navy-Game, the Black Knights were once again defeated by the Midshipmen L (17-21). Now the difference to overcome is just four points and we all think Jeff Monken is the modern coach to get the job done. This game was played a Lincoln Financial Field Philadelphia PA (116th Army–Navy Game/Commander-in-Chief's Trophy) This game was the tenth loss for the Black Knights this season.

2016 Coach Jeff Monken

The Army West Point Black Knights football team represented the United States Military Academy in the 2016 college football season. It was Army's one hundred-twenty-seventh season of intercollegiate football. They were led by Coach Jeff Monken in his third if XXXX seasons. Monken is the current coach and he had a good year this year in 2016 so we all hope he is around for a while. The Army team had a winning record of 8-5. They won six more games than the prior year. Looks like Monken is what the doctor ordered!

Overall, the Black Knights compiled an 8-5 record. They finished with the best season since air was invented or so it seemed. Army pitched no shutouts, but the Black Knights were not shut out by any opponent. In the very important annual Army–Navy Game, the Midshipmen were finally defeated by the neve-say-die Black Knights 38-31. This game gained the Army Black Knights a big Cigar. It was close but the Cigar was achieved. Coach Jeff Monken got to light up a big cigar in 2016? We'll see about 2017 soon! Army fans are confident in making sure their cigar lighting lighters are available for the 2017 season.

This year's opener was on Sept 2 at home against Temple in a game played at Lincoln Financial Field • Philadelphia, PA. The Black Knights began the season with a fine showing against a first-tier team with this win against the Owls W (28-13) before 34005. Other than those games played in neutral fields, all Army home games were played on the West Point campus at Michie Stadium in West Point NY. On Sept 10, at home, Army defeated Rice W (31-14). It had been so long ago that the Black Knights won its two opening games that Army was filled with confidence. Army won its third game in a row against UTEP in a major shootout on Sept 17 in the Sun Bowl Stadium El Paso, TX W (66-16).

On Sept 24 at Buffalo's UB Stadium in Amherst, NY, the Bulls got enough steam going to defeat the Black Knights L (20–23) in OT. On Oct 8, at Duke's Wallace Wade Stadium Durham, NC. Duke's Blue Devils triumphed over the Black Knights L (6–13) in a close match. On Oct 15, at home, Lafayette lost in a shootout to the Army Team in a big win W (62–7) before 38,394.

Then on Oct 22 at noon, Army took on North Texas at home and were saddled with a defeat from the Mean Green L (18–35) before 31,127. Then on Oct 29, Army beat Wake Forest W (21-13) at Wake Forest in BB&T Field Winston–Salem, NC. On Nov 5 at home, Air Force chose to win and did (Commander-in-Chief's Trophy) L (12–31) before 38,443 at Michie.

Even in a good year, Army had trouble with Air Force and other great teams such as Notre Dame which they played the next week at the Alamodome in San Antonio, TX. ND defeated a very game Army Team L 6–44 before a stadium fan set of 45,762 On Nov 19, at home, Army beat Morgan State W 60–3 in front of 28,290 fans.

On December 10, before 71,600 fans in the classic Army-Navy-Game, the Black Knights, coached by Jeff Monken played to win the game. They were not only not defeated by the Midshipmen by any score, they kept with Navy through the whole game, and hung in and won. This is our father's Army team. Last year's L (17-21) four-point differential was reversed and though the score was the same Army had beaten Navy W (21-17) this time. Bravo!

This game was played at M&T Bank Stadium • Baltimore, MD (117th Army–Navy Game/Commander-in-Chief's Trophy) This game was the seventh win for the Black Knights this season. Win # 8 came in the heart of Dallas Bowl game.

Army Navy Game 2016

On December 27 at 11:00 a.m. when the NY revelers were ready to celebrate early, Army gave lots of reasons why. Army played North Texas in the Cotton Bowl Stadium in Dallas, TX celebrating the (Heart of Dallas Bowl). The Black Knights prevailed in OT W (38–31) before 39,117

The article immediately below is courtesy of USA today. It offers a look at the status of Army Football right before the Army-Navy Game of 2016. The next article is a writeup of the game by the sports press:

Army building winning culture behind coach Jeff Monken

Ted Berg, USA TODAY Sports Published 6:02 p.m. ET Dec. 8, 2016 Updated 12:02 a.m. ET Dec. 10, 2016

Previewing the annual Army-Navy game

The 117th edition of the game will kick off on Saturday.
USA TODAY Sports

(Photo: Matt Cashore, USA TODAY Sports)

WEST POINT, N.Y. — Army's first bowl game in six seasons seems likely to serve more as a coda to a successful season than a climax, given the gravity of its annual matchup against Navy on Saturday.

But the berth nonetheless stands as Army's first since 2010 and only its second since 1996, and a step forward for a program that has finished with a losing record in 18 of the past 20 seasons.

The Dec. 27 matchup with North Texas in the Heart of Dallas Bowl also represents a rematch of a regular-season contest that North Texas won at Michie Stadium in October.
"Playing in a bowl game is a measure of success for everybody that plays at this level," coach Jeff Monken told USA TODAY Sports. "So, to say we're going to play in a bowl game is certainly an accomplishment. I'm proud of our kids and I'm proud of our

coaches, and I'm proud for West Point to be able to represent our academy in that fashion."

Army dominates on both sides in 60-3 win over Morgan State

In his third season as Army's head coach, Monken endeavors the huge challenge of restoring to respectability a program that was one of college football's most successful in the early days of the sport but which last saw back-to-back winning seasons in 1989-90. An assistant coach at Navy from 2002-2007, Monken took over as Army's head coach already familiar with the particulars of recruiting top-flight high school players to a military academy, a prospect that comes with both rigorous academic standards and, for most, a five-year service commitment following graduation. It means Monken must draw on a different group of recruits than most other Division I head coaches.

"The pool's smaller — or gets smaller in a hurry — because of the military commitment," he said. "And it's a challenge. No matter how much they understand that this is a world-class degree and an opportunity to play a very high level of football, there's still the fact that we're a military school.

Navy looks beyond injuries as it readies for Army

"It is an environment — a university or college environment — that's not traditional. Our guys don't go out and drink beer until 4 in the morning on a Tuesday night. You can do that other places. (At other schools), they can sleep in and miss math class if they want — hey, they might get in trouble. But you can't do that here.
"That's the challenge in recruiting here: You've got to find the right guy. It doesn't have to be a guy that necessarily has dreamed of being in the Army his whole life; it has just got to be the right kind of guy."

College football bowl schedule, results for 2016-17

Cadets at West Point pay no tuition, so the program need not consider NCAA scholarship limitations. For some, the service commitment seemed an inevitability.

Jeremy Timpf, a senior linebacker and team captain prepping for an assignment in field artillery next year, always intended to enroll at a military academy. Another senior linebacker, Andrew King, said the opportunities associated with attending West Point made it "a perfect fit" as he was "not really a party-goer."

But for others, the commitment gave some pause.

"You hear about the service commitment, and it kind of shakes you a little bit," said Christian Poe, a sophomore receiver who followed his older brother, Edgar, to Army. "It's just something you've got to do. You're getting paid when you serve; it's not like you're serving for free. You're doing something for millions of people and you're getting paid to do it. It's a beautiful thing: You get a job coming straight out of here. It's more exciting than anything, once you get the hang of it."

Focus of coaching carousel lands on American Athletic Conference

Until the spring of 2016, committing to Army — or any of the military academies — meant postponing any NFL dreams, as prospective pro players were expected to fulfill at least two years' worth of active duty before applying to the department of defense for a special waiver allowing for a transfer to selective reserve service so they could pursue pro careers. But after the Baltimore Ravens drafted Navy quarterback Keenan Reynolds in the sixth round of the NFL draft in April, Defense Secretary Ashton Carter announced that Reynolds and teammate Chris Swain would be allowed to defer their commitments to immediately join NFL teams.

"If they're good enough to play in the NFL, they can do that from here, too," Monken said. "That's absolutely a possibility."

Though Monken and defensive coordinator Jay Bateman contended coaching Cadets differed little from coaching Division I athletes at other schools, Bateman pointed out the type of player drawn to the Army program could help the team secure a strategic advantage: A playbook hardly seems daunting to minds tasked with the school's arduous academics and officer training.

"The kids that come here, the biggest thing is how bright they are," Bateman said. "Schematically, you have a lot of different options because they understand it; they're able to process things — if/then equations, calls. They're not always compliant — they're Division I football players, so they're tough dudes. But the kid that comes here, certainly, is a bright kid that's willing to commit to something bigger than himself, so I think the brotherhood, the team, is a big part of our success here."

Follow Berg on Twitter @OGTedBerg

Army beats Navy 21-17 to end 14-year losing streak in series

Published December 10, 2016   Associated Press

Army running back Andy Davidson (40) celebrates his touchdown with teammates in the first half of the Army-Navy NCAA college football game in Baltimore, Saturday, Dec. 10, 2016. (AP Photo/Patrick Semansky)

Army ended a 14-year run of frustration against Navy, using an overpowering running game and opportunistic defense to carve out a long overdue 21-17 victory Saturday.

With future commander in chief Donald Trump looking on, the Black Knights blew a 14-point lead before quarterback Ahmad

Bradshaw scored on a 9-yard run with 6:42 left to give Army the win it had been waiting for since 2001.

The Black Knights' 14-game losing streak was the longest by either academy in a series that began in 1890. Army (7-5) now trails 60-50-7 in one of the nation's historic rivalries.

Navy (9-4) was coming off a physical 34-10 loss to Temple in the American Athletic Conference title game and had only one week to prepare for Army with a new quarterback, sophomore Zach Abey, who was making his first college start. Abey took over Will Worth, who broke his foot against Temple.

Abey ran for two touchdowns but passed for only 89 yards and was intercepted twice. Navy had four turnovers, three in the first half.

By halftime, Army led 14-0 and owned a 14-1 advantage in first downs.

After watching from the Navy side of the field before halftime, Trump visited the TV booth on the Army side in the third quarter. The interview with the president-elect coincided with a big shift in momentum.

Andy Davidson lost a fumble on the Black Knights' first possession of the second half and the Midshipmen recovered at the Army 32. A screen pass for 16 yards set up a 1-yard touchdown run by Abey to get Navy to 14-7.

Minutes later, the Midshipmen got a field goal after a replay overturned a lost fumble by Abey at the Army 11.

A 41-yard touchdown run by Abey gave Navy the lead with 12:42 remaining. But Army wasn't done.

The Black Knights put together a 12-play, 80-yard drive that lasted nearly seven minutes and ended with Bradshaw's TD with 6:42 remaining.

Bradshaw went 2 for 4 for 35 yards and an interception in Army's first win in Baltimore since 1944.

Davidson ran for 87 yards and two first-half scores, and Kell Walker carried

2017 Commentary

Army's Black Knights have had a lot of devastating near misses over the years, and these classic Army-Navy Game from December 2016 nearly went down among the worst. But, it did not! Now, Army is set for 2017.

As we know, Army dominated the first half and staked themselves to a two-touchdown lead at the break. Jeff Monken's team was clearly intent on not leaving another tight finish to chance. In the end, however, as the game rolled on, the Black Knights had to sweat it out again. To Monken and the team's credit, they managed to do it, and maybe with the closeness of the game, it is all sweeter in the end.

Navy had some personnel issues but nobody was making excuses. Sophomore Zach Abey made his first career start for Navy, in relief of the injured Will Worth. It was a tough situation for an inexperienced player to get tossed into. Army was able to get Abey off balance. At the half, the substitute QB completed more passes (two) to Army players than Navy players (one), and the Midshipmen had run 13 first-half total plays to the Knights' 14 first downs. Things just were not clicking at all for Navy—at least not at first.

Of course, Navy's opportunity was coming and they were ready to take it. The Middies cut the lead to 14-10 by the start of the third quarter. Abey found the end zone for Navy's first touchdown. Then the newbie QB ripped off a 41-yard scoring run to give Navy its first lead with 12:42 left.

The Black Knights were taken back but were not laying down. Army answered the call. After Abey's score, the Knights mounted a 12-play, 80-yard drive that ended with Bradshaw's critical score. It was a game-turning response, right as Army was in trouble. The Black Knights then forced a punt after that, and they drained the clock along with Navy's spirit upon getting the ball back.

That was the game.

Like all Army-Navy Games, this game mattered a ton. It always does.

Navy lost more than just this game. The Midshipmen fell short of an American Athletic Conference title and a potential Cotton Bowl bid this year. Their chance to make it 15 in a row against arch rival Army meant everything to them and it did not happen. The Black Knights entered with their best record since 2010 and their best shot in years at ending the streak. The Black Knights ended the streak.

Navy entered as a 5-point favorite with a scoring total over/under around 47, meaning Vegas forecasted a final score in the area of Navy 26, Army 21.

With fourteen wins in a row and having a fine season, Navy began the day with the country's No. 25 offense, despite being down to their third-string QB Abey. Army hadn't been nearly as lethal on offense this year, but the Black Knights had been much better than Navy on defense. Wait 'til we all see how well Army does in 2017.

Coach Monken brought the Black Knights back to the party; now we get to find out if they can stay there this time. Signs point to yes.

There is no question this past 2016 season was a great one. The Army-Navy-Game was at its best again. Of course, Army plans to get through the whole season successfully and not just make its season by winning the Navy Game. Jeff Monken is aware that Navy overcame injuries to finish 9-5 in its past season that surpassed expectations.

However, when it came to one of the game's most historic rivalries with Army (8-5), the Black Knights ended the 14-year drought with a 21-17 win. Now, with both programs coming off impressive seasons, the 2017 edition of the rivalry is expected to be another classic.

I would suggest that we all circle our calendars for Dec. 9, when the two armed-forces face off again at Lincoln Financial Field at 3 p.m. ET. I sure plan to be there. Bring your copy of the book and I would be happy to sign it for you. The best.

That's All Folks!

We hope to bring out another version of Great Moments in Army Football in about five years. It will have a nice section on Army West Point Football that offers a commentary on what's new Thank you for choosing this book among the many that are in your options list. I sincerely appreciate it! We plan to offer two new Army titles over the next six months highlighting great players and great coaches of the Black Knights from over the years.

The best to you all – Go Army West Point Black Knights!

LETS GO PUBLISH! Books by Brian Kelly
(Sold at www.bookhawkers.com; Amazon.com, and Kindle.).

Great Moments in Army Football Army Football at its best.

Great Moments in Florida Gators Football Gators Football from the start. This is the book.

Great Moments in Clemson Football CU Football at its best. This is the book.

Great Moments in Florida Gators Football Gators Football from the start. This is the book.

The Constitution Companion. A Guide to Reading and Comprehending the Constitution

The Constitution by Hamilton, Jefferson, & Madison – Big type and in English

PATERNO: The Dark Days After Win # 409. Sky began to fall within days of win # 409 .

JoePa 409 Victories: Say No More!: Winningest Division I-A football coach ever

American College Football: The Beginning From before day one football was played.

Great Coaches in Alabama Football Challenging the coaches of every other program!

Great Coaches in Penn State Football the Best Coaches in PSU's football program

Great Players in Penn State Football The best players in PSU's football program

Great Players in Notre Dame Football The best players in ND's football program

Great Coaches in Notre Dame Football The best coaches in any football program

President Donald J. Trump, Master Builder: Solving the Student Debt Crisis!

President Donald J. Trump, Master Builder: It's Time for Seniors to Get a Break!

President Donald J. Trump, Master Builder: Healthcare & Welfare Accountability

President Donald J. Trump, Master Builder: "Make America Great Again"

President Donald J. Trump, Master Builder: The Annual Guest Plan

Great Players in Alabama Football from Quarterbacks to offensive Linemen Greats!

Great Moments in Alabama Football AU Football from the start. This is the book.

Great Moments in Penn State Football PSU Football, start--games, coaches, players,

Great Moments in Notre Dame Football ND Football, start, games, coaches, players

Four Dollars & Sixty-Two Cents—A Christmas Story That Will Warm Your Heart!

My Red Hat Keeps Me on The Ground. Darraggh's Red Hat is magical

Seniors, Social Security & the Minimum Wage. Things seniors need to know.

How to Write Your First Book and Publish It with CreateSpace

The US Immigration Fix--It's all in here. Finally, an answer.

I had a Dream IBM Could be #1 Again _The title is self-explanatory

WineDiets.Com Presents The Wine Diet Learn how to lose weight while having fun.

Wilkes-Barre, PA; Return to Glory Wilkes-Barre City's return to glory

Geoffrey Parsons' Epoch... The Land of Fair Play Better than the original.

The Bill of Rights 4 Dummmies! This is the best book to learn about your rights.

Sol Bloom's Epoch ...Story of the Constitution The best book to learn the Constitution

America 4 Dummmies! All Americans should read to learn about this great country.

The Electoral College 4 Dummmies! How does it really work?

The All-Everything Machine Story about IBM's finest computer server.

Brian has written 124 books. Others can be found at amazon.com/author/brianwkelly

CPSIA information can be obtained
at www.ICGtesting.com
Printed in the USA
FSHW020621201218
54593FS